Olympic politics

second edition

Christopher R. Hill

Manchester University Press

Manchester and New York

Distributed exclusively in the USA and Canada by St Martin's Press

Copyright © Christopher R. Hill 1996

Published by Manchester University Press
Oxford Road, Manchester M13 9NR, UK
and Room 400, 175 Fifth Avenue, New York, NY 10010, USA

Distributed exclusively in the USA and Canada
by St Martin's Press, Inc., 175 Fifth Avenue, New York, NY 10010, USA

British Library Cataloguing-in-Publication Data
A catalogue record for this book is available from the British Library

Library of Congress Cataloging-in-Publication Data
  Hill, Christopher R.
    Olympic politics / Christopher R. Hill. — 2nd ed.
      p.   cm.
    Includes bibliographical references (p.   ) and index.
    ISBN 0–7190–4450–2. — ISBN 0–7190–4451–0 (pbk. : alk. paper)
    1. Olympics—Political aspects.   I. Title.
  GV721.5.H54   1996
  796.48—dc20   95–36982
                                                             CIP

ISBN 0 7190 4450 2 *hardback*
      0 7190 4451 0 *paperback*

First published 1992

00 99 98 97 96   10 9 8 7 6 5 4 3 2 1

Typeset in Great Britain
by Northern Phototypesetting Co Ltd, Bolton
Printed in Great Britain
by Bell & Bain Ltd, Glasgow

Contents

Acknowledgements

I have a great many people to thank for allowing me to interview them and for helpful advice. I conducted my interviews on the basis that the information obtained would not be attributed, but in most cases I was permitted to include my informants' names in these acknowledgements. I apologise to any whom I may have overlooked.

I am especially grateful to Her Royal Highness The Princess Royal (who is a member of the International Olympic Committee) for receiving me.

His Excellency Juan Antonio Samaranch, President of the International Olympic Committee, was also kind enough to allow me to interview him.

The staff at the headquarters of the International Olympic Committee at Lausanne gave me unstinting help during a number of visits. I am particularly grateful to Maître François Carrard, Dr Karel Wendl and Madame Michèle Veillard.

I am very much indebted to the staff of the Organising Committee of the 1992 Games at Barcelona; the Manchester Olympic Committee, especially Bob (later Sir Robert) Scott and Richard Parry, who were generous with their time and allowed me to consult documents at their offices; the International Amateur Athletic Federation, especially its General Secretary, John Holt; and to the late Victor Deacon, Honorary Archivist at Much Wenlock, Shropshire and his successor, Glyn McDonald, both of whom received me most courteously and guided me through the archives in their charge.

Others to whom I wish to record my thanks are: Albert Augusti, Shahbaz Behnam, Miss Anne Beddow, Alfred Bosch, Guillermo Brugarolas, Joàn Brunet, Daniel Carbonell, Xavier Casadó, Miss Evie Dennis, Gunnar Ericsson, Bill Eadington, Carlos Ferrer, Raymond

Gafner, Mrs (later Dame) Mary Glen Haig, Sir Arthur Gold, John
Goodbody, Mademoiselle Miriam Gross, The Rt Hon Denis Howell,
MP (later Lord Howell), Patrick Jourdain, Lord Killanin, David
Miller, Josep Muñoz, Dr Primo Nebiolo, George Nicholson, Pedro
Palacios, Charles Palmer, Richard Palmer, Michael Payne, Charles
Randriamanantenasoa, Mrs Jennifer Rushworth, Mark Ridley, Dr
Harvey Schiller, Bernard Schneider, Sir David Scott, Alexandru
Siperco, David Spanier, Howard Stupp, Leonard Steinberg, Andreu
Mercé Varela, Mademoiselle Michèle Verdier, Josep Maria Vilaseca,
George Walker, Madame Françoise Zweifel.

I am grateful to the Trustees of the Nuffield Foundation for their
generosity in making me a grant in the early stages of the project and
to Miss Pat Thomas, Deputy Director of the Foundation, for her wise
advice.

Finally, it is a pleasure to thank Hugo Watson Brown, who read the
whole typescript and suggested numerous improvements, and Dawn
Newbery, who was a patient and calming research assistant, and has
an invaluable gift for organising material.

Additional acknowledgements for the second edition

Many of the individuals who helped me with the first edition were
kind enough to continue with their good offices, and I am extremely
grateful to them.

In addition, it is a pleasure to thank a number of people who have
given me help of one kind or another in connection with this new
edition. They include: Don Anthony, Ngconde Balfour, Alison
Burchell, John Coates, Lamartine Da Costa, John Donald, Kevan
Gosper, David Jefferies, Kevin Kevany, Dominic Mahony, Andre
Odendaal, Richard Pound, Craig Reedie.

During 1994 I had the pleasure of taking part in a number of
Olympic activities. I taught at the International Olympic Academy,
took part in an academic seminar at Lausanne, whose members had
been called together by the organisers of the Paris Congress for an
advance discussion of the themes of the Congress, and finally took
part in the Congress itself. For all these opportunities I am most
grateful, and shall mention in particular Fernandos Serpieris, the
President of the International Olympic Academy, and Kostas
Georgiadis, its Dean.

Finally, I am glad to be able to acknowledge that I have made use of some material which has appeared in *Parliamentary Affairs* and in a compendium assembled for its M.Sc. students by the Centre for Research into Sport and Sociology at the University of Leicester.

Acronyms

AAA	Amateur Athletic Association (UK)
AAU	Amateur Athletic Union (USA)
ABC	American Broadcasting Corporation
ACOG	Atlanta Committee for the Olympic Games
AIWF	Association of International Winter Sports Federations
ANC	African National Congress
ANOC	Association of National Olympic Committees
ANOCA	Association of National Olympic Committees of Africa
ARISF	Association of IOC-Recognised International Sports Federations
ASOIF	Association des Fédérations Internationales Olympiques d'Eté
BOA	British Olympic Association
CBS	Columbia Broadcasting System
CCPR	Central Council of Physical Recreation
COE	Comité Olímpico Español
COOB 92	Comité Olímpico Organisador Barcelona, 1992
COSAS	Confederation of South African Sport
DJP	Democratic Justice Party
EBU	European Broadcasting Union
ETA	Euskadi ta Askatsuna (Basque terrorist organisation)
FEI	Fédération Equestre Internationale
FIFA	Fédération Internationale de Football Association
FINA	Fédération Internationale de Natation Amateur
FISA	Fédération Internationale des Sociétés d'Aviron
GAISF	General Association of International Sports Federations
GANEFO	Games of the New Emerging Forces
IAAF	International Amateur Athletic Federation

IF	International Federation
INOCSA	Interim National Olympic Committee of South Africa
IOC	International Olympic Committee
ISL	International Sports and Leisure
ISOH	International Society of Olympic Historians
KASA	Korean Amateur Sports Association
KOC	Korean Olympic Committee
LAOOC	Los Angeles Olympic Organising Committee
NBC	National Broadcasting Corporation
NOA	National Olympian Association
NOC	National Olympic Committee
NOCSA	National Olympic Committee of South Africa
NOSC	National Olympic and Sports Congress
OAU	Organisation of African Unity
PAC	Pan-Africanist Congress
PRC	People's Republic of China
SACOS	South African Council of Sport
SANOC	South African National Olympic Committee
SANROC	South African Non-Racial Olympic Committee
SAONGA	South African Olympic and National Games Association
SASA	South African Sports Association
SCSA	Supreme Council on Sport in Africa
SLOOC	Seoul Olympic Organising Committee
TOP	The Olympic Programme
UNESCO	United Nations Educational, Social and Cultural Organisation
USFSA	Union des Sociétés Françaises de Sports Athlétiques
USOC	United States Olympic Committee
USSR	Union of Soviet Socialist Republics

Chronology

Summer Olympic Games	Winter
1896 Athens	
1900 Paris	
1904 St Louis	
1908 London	
1912 Stockholm	
1916 Cancelled (Berlin)	
1920 Antwerp	
1924 Paris	Chamonix
1928 Amsterdam	Saint-Moritz
1932 Los Angeles	Lake Placid
1936 Berlin	Garmisch-Partenkirchen
1940 Cancelled (Tokyo/Helsinki)	
1944 Cancelled (London)	
1948 London	Saint-Moritz
1952 Helsinki	Oslo
1956 Melbourne	Cortina d'Ampezzo
1960 Rome	Squaw Valley
1964 Tokyo	Innsbruck
1968 Mexico City	Grenoble
1972 Munich	Sapporo
1976 Montreal	Innsbruck
1980 Moscow	Lake Placid
1984 Los Angeles	Sarajevo
1988 Seoul	Calgary
1992 Barcelona	Albertville
1994	Lillehammer

1996 Atlanta
1998   Nagano
2000 Sydney

Presidents of the International Olympic Committee

1894–1896   Demetrius Vikelas (Greece)
1896–1925   Baron Pierre de Coubertin 1925–1942 (France)
1925–1942   Count Henri de Baillet-Latour (Belgium)
1946–1952   J. Sigfrid Edstrom (Sweden)
1952–1972   Avery Brundage (USA)
1972–1980   Lord Killanin (Ireland)
1980–   Juan Antonio Samaranch (Spain)

Selected dates mentioned in the text

776 B.C.   first ancient Games
A.D. 261 or 363   end of the ancient Games
1850   first Olympian Games at Much Wenlock, Shropshire, England
1859   first Greek Olympic Games
1863   birth of Baron Pierre de Coubertin
1865   foundation of National Olympian Association, Liverpool, England
1870   second Greek Olympic Games
1875   third Greek Olympic Games
1883   Coubertin's first visit to England
1889   fourth Greek Olympic Games
1890   Coubertin visits Much Wenlock
1894   International Athletic Congress, Paris
       International Olympic Committee founded with Demetrius Vikelas as President
1895   death of Dr William Penny Brookes
1896   Coubertin becomes President of the IOC
1906   'intermediate' Olympic Games, Athens
1922   IOC recognises Chinese National Olympic Committee
1937   death of Coubertin
1945   division of Korea
1948   establishment of North and South Korea
1950   IOC grants provisional recognition to West German National Olympic Committee

1950–3   Korean War

1951   full recognition of West German National Olympic Committee
National Olympic Committee of the USSR recognised

1952   USSR and West Germany participate in Helsinki Games
People's Republic of China permitted to compete at Helsinki,
although its NOC has not yet been recognised. Taiwan withdraws in protest
Avery Brundage elected President of the IOC

1954   National Olympic Committee of People's Republic of China
recognised as 'Olympic Committee of the Chinese Republic'.
Taiwan's NOC still recognised as Chinese Olympic Committee

1955   full recognition of National Olympic Committee of 'geographical area' of East Germany

1956/60/64   joint East and West German teams compete at
Melbourne, Rome and Tokyo Games

1956   People's Republic of China withdraws from Melbourne Games
in protest at continuing recognition of separate NOC in
Taiwan

1957   designation of National Olympic Committee of People's
Republic of China changed to 'Olympic Committee of People's
Democratic Republic of China'

1958   People's Republic of China withdraws from Olympic movement and from all International Federations

1959   IOC decides that National Olympic Committee of Taiwan may
not continue as 'Chinese Olympic Committee'

1960   Taiwan competes as 'Formosa' at Rome Games
first Olympic television rights sold
South Africa's last participation in the Games until 1992

1962   IOC grants provisional recognition to National Olympic Committee of North Korea

1963   full recognition of North Korean National Olympic Committee

1964   North Korea competes at Tokyo Games

1965   IOC grants provisional recognition to East German National
Olympic Committee

1968   East German National Olympic Committee recognised as
NOC of German Democratic Republic and competes
separately at Mexico City Games
confirmation of designation of Taiwan Olympic Committee as

'Olympic Committee of the Republic of China'

1970   IOC withdraws recognition of South African National Olympic Committee

1971   expulsion of Taiwan from United Nations Organisation; admission of People's Republic of China

      IOC resolves to reinstate People's Republic of China

1972   President Richard Nixon visits People's Republic of China

      Avery Brundage retires as President of the IOC, Lord Killanin elected President

1973   Congress of the Olympic movement, Varna

1974   Games of 1980 awarded to Moscow

1976   Canadian Government refuses to admit Taiwanese team if 'China' appears in its title

1978   Juan Antonio Samaranch appointed Spanish Ambassador to USSR

      Games of 1984 awarded to Los Angeles

1979   Soviet invasion of Afghanistan

1980   Juan Antonio Samaranch elected President of IOC in succession to Lord Killanin

      IOC recognises National Olympic Committees of People's Republic of China and of Taiwan as 'Chinese Olympic Committee' and 'Chinese Taipeh Olympic Committee'

      (February) President Jimmy Carter launches boycott of Moscow Games

      IOC announces that Seoul is a candidate to host the Games of 1988

1981   Barcelona announces bid for Games of 1992

      Congress of the Olympic movement, Baden-Baden

      Games of 1988 awarded to Korea

1983   (August) Soviets shoot down Korean aircraft

1984   (May) USSR announces boycott of Los Angeles Games

1985   ISL takes over Olympic marketing on behalf of IOC

      Madame Monique Berlioux 'resigns' as Executive Director of IOC

      Birmingham adopted as British candidate for Games of 1992

1986   Games of 1992 awarded to Barcelona

1987   death of Horst Dassler, Chairman of ISL and of Adidas

      North Koreans blow up South Korean aircraft in flight

1988   Manchester adopted as British candidate for Games of 1996

1990   Games of 1996 awarded to Atlanta

Introduction

Few enthusiasts of élite sport nowadays believe that it can be separated from politics, though there must be many who wish that it could. In fact they interlock at a number of different levels, the international, the national and, within sports organisations, the purely domestic. At the level of international politics it is impossible for sport to distance itself from the political questions which beset the world, especially questions relating to the recognition of states. This applies to all kinds of international sports organisations, but the necessary engagement with politics is especially obvious and important within the Olympic movement because of the extraordinary interest generated worldwide by the Olympic Games, the great amounts of money involved and the movement's aspirations to universality.[1] The fact that it has outposts throughout the world renders it peculiarly vulnerable to the demands of international politics.

It might be thought that for the International Olympic Committee (IOC), the ruling body of the Olympic movement, to give recognition to a new National Olympic Committee (NOC), or to withhold it, would be no more important than any other decision by keen sports people about whether or not to compete with one another. However, the decision to recognise or not to recognise an NOC contributes to the far more important decision as to whether a territory with aspirations to recognition as a state (like East Germany after the Second World War) is to achieve it, or whether a country like South Africa, whose internal policies have been widely reviled, should continue to enjoy normal relations with other states. In such cases governments use sport as a weapon in the struggle, and sports people are bound to react.

At the second level, that of individual countries, sport and politics also interlock. Governments do not merely use sport as a means of projecting a national image abroad, but in order to achieve social and political objectives at home: these may include promoting racial harmony; improving conditions in the inner cities; keeping young people off the streets, or simply seeking to maintain a reasonable level of health among the general population. A common grievance among sports people in Britain is that not nearly enough is spent by central government on sport, and among educationalists its failure, until recently, to give prominence to physical education in the curriculum of state schools has been a cause of something approaching despair. (Exactly what type of physical education is another matter; from the point of view of exercise, disco dancing must be at least as beneficial as hockey.)[2]

At the domestic level, within sports bodies, that is to say, the same processes may be seen at work as in national or international politics. When one studies the rise to power of Juan Antonio Samaranch, President of the IOC, or of Primo Nebiolo, President of the International Amateur Athletic Association, one could be examining the ascent of a conventional politician.[3] Of course, a diagnosis of this kind is not unique to sport. Much the same could be said of the rise to eminence of any prominent man or woman, whether it be in the Church, journalism, business, the academic world or the armed forces. Similar processes of bargaining, alliance forming, luck, and idealism mixed with the desire for power are at work.

This, then, is a study in politics. Most of it concerns the events of very recent years, starting with the award to Moscow of the Games of 1980, but more remote events are briefly covered. The opening chapter gives an account of the ancient Games and of their revival in the 1890s by Baron de Coubertin. He too was no mean operator and without his political skills the modern Games might never have existed. The second chapter reminds the reader of some of the great issues of international politics which have necessarily affected the Olympic movement since Coubertin's day. It would never have been possible for the International Olympic Committee to ignore apartheid in South Africa, the Rhodesian rebellion of 1965, or, going further back in time, such questions as those posed by two territories, mainland China and Taiwan, each claiming to be the true China, the division of the Korean peninsula, or the problem of the two Germanies.

Chapters III and IV address the internal organisation of the movement, how power is exercised within it and how it is financed. Although these are internal matters they cannot be divorced from more obviously public concerns: men and women may rise within sport on merit, but their careers cannot be understood in isolation from the broader political background. For example, the USSR's late involvement in the movement, starting as recently as the Helsinki Games of 1952, inevitably politicised elections to the IOC's Executive Board, a trend which could not be resisted, given the movement's overriding interest in promoting its own universality and therefore in pleasing the states of the Soviet bloc. To discuss the financing of the Games necessarily provokes thoughts about whether they should now be seen more as a successful example of international capitalist entrepreneurship than as a festival of sport.

Chapter V discusses how and why cities vie with one another for the privilege of playing host to the Games, with particular reference to the unsuccessful attempts made by Birmingham and Manchester. It will be clear from this and later chapters that to understand why a city bids for the Games it is necessary to know something about the internal political situation in that country and about its international position.

Detailed studies of the politics of a series of modern Games are presented against this background analysis of the movement's power structure and finance. Moscow 1980 and Los Angeles 1984 are chiefly remembered for the boycotts organised by the United States and the Soviet Union respectively, and Chapters VI and VII examine those events in detail. The Seoul Games of 1988 (Chapter VIII) provide a prime example of a government which saw the advantages of the Olympics as a means of projecting itself worldwide and which masterminded the bid to host the Games for reasons unconnected with sport. The Barcelona Games of 1992, which form the subject of Chapter IX, provide a study of peculiar interest because of the complicated politics of Spain, and because Barcelona's bidding campaign was conducted with enormous skill and confidence. The 1992 Games were universally pronounced an outstanding success and provided a television spectacular of unexampled splendour and audience appeal.

There follows a completely new chapter on South Africa's involvement with the Olympic Movement, concentrating on its expulsion and its reacceptance after many years in the wilderness. This is the most obvious recent example of the Olympics being caught up in great political issues: there are many others, such as that of the former Yugoslavia, for which there has been no space in this volume.

After a short note on the forthcoming Games at Atlanta, the final chapter examines some of the problems facing the Olympic movement and speculates about its future. The problem of which the movement is most conscious is, as it has been for many years, that of 'gigantism' – the Games' tendency to become ever bigger and more unwieldy, which is in part a consequence of its aspiration to universality. The powers and composition of the IOC are also under constant scrutiny within the movement, as became apparent at its centenary Congress in Paris in 1994, and to this preoccupation must be linked the debate about the distribution of power between the IOC, the NOCs and the International Federations (IFs) of the various sports recognised by the IOC.

There is room also for examination of what one might call a gigantism of the spirit, the over-estimation of the movement's importance, so noticeable at meetings of the power brokers of Olympism, and the corresponding forgetfulness that sport is in a sense a triviality. It is permissible when thinking about the future to think the unthinkable, and the book's concluding question is 'Are the Olympic Games really necessary, or have they had their day?'

Notes

1   The aspiration to universality, 'universalism' as it is called, is a complicated concept, which is used in a number of different ways. Some contexts in which it appears are, first, the belief that the Olympic movement should stretch to every corner of the globe; secondly, that people everywhere ought to be able to engage in Olympic sport, and thirdly, that sport taps some universal essence of humanity.

The word 'movement' in the phrase 'Olympic movement' is very frequently written with an initial capital: I have sought to avoid the practice, except when quoting.

2   I owe this point to Professor Tudor Hale, of the Chichester Institute of Higher Education.

3   A Marquisate was conferred upon Samaranch by the King of Spain at the end of 1991, although he does not always use the title. However the letters S.E. (Son Excellence) generally precede his name, since he was Spanish ambassador in Moscow from 1977 to 1980, and is still accorded the designation of 'His Excellency'.

I

Baron Pierre de Coubertin and the revival of the Games

The ancient Games were revived by Baron Pierre de Coubertin (born in Paris, 1 January 1863; died in Geneva, 2 September 1937) in 1896. This chapter describes Coubertin the man; briefly looks at some of the earlier festivals in the nineteenth century which described themselves as 'Olympic' and relates how Coubertin pushed through his own far more ambitious project.

Coubertin the man

Politics has been inseparable from the modern Olympic Games since the decision was taken at the Sorbonne in Paris in 1894 to revive them after a lapse of at least fifteen hundred years. Had the instigator of the decision, Baron Pierre de Coubertin, not been a natural politician of no mean skill, the decision might never been been taken, and even if it had been taken the Athens Games of 1896 might still never have been held without Coubertin's energy and determination.

Coubertin was an aristocrat, who could have taken to formal politics or to the army, but who decided to become an intellectual. In those days it was still possible for a man to be expert in a great variety of fields. Coubertin studied history, literature, education, sociology and many other subjects, and wrote voluminously on all of them.

His passion was for education, and in particular for sports education (*pédagogie sportive*), and in 1883 his first visit to England convinced him that Thomas Arnold's methods at Rugby School, where he had been Headmaster from 1828 to 1842, had been responsible for the great growth in England's power in the nineteenth century and should be exported to France.[1] Thereafter one of his major tasks was to persuade the French to introduce physical education in schools.

T

But he was not interested in just any physical education. His studies of classical history had convinced him that this aspect of education had reached its highest point in ancient Greece, where the gymnasia of Athens had created what he called a triple unity: between the old and the young; between different disciplines and between people of different types – the practitioner and the theoretician, the man of science and the man of letters. This union of many aspects of life was the central lesson to be learned from the Greek gymnasium, which was by no means to be confused with the modern type of gymnasium which was springing up everywhere.[2]

The original Olympic Games took place every four years at Olympia, in the Kingdom of Elis. They survived from 776 B.C., when there was only one event, the 200 metres, until at least A.D. 261, and possibly until 393, when the Emperor Theodosius ordered the closure of pagan centres.[3] Coubertin's scholarship had a romantic tinge and with his idealised vision of Greece it was natural that he should come to believe that the Olympic Games represented the finest expression of sporting achievement and aspiration. He tells us that the religion of athleticism, which he celebrates in some splendidly purple passages, had its ceremonies at the Pythic, Nemean, Isthmic and other Games, but that the most illustrious were those held at Olympia.[4]

Though his prose was sometimes purple, his reasoning was hard-headed. Sport promoted physical health, which was essential if nations were to win wars – a powerful argument in a France still smarting from disastrous defeat in the Franco-German war. Sport also brought the classes together, which could only be desirable in the new age of democracy (by which he seems to have meant social equality). This is not to say that he was a warmonger, nor indeed a passionate democrat, but war was an occasional necessity, and democracy a fact of life. Furthermore, to bring the classes together was not the same thing as to mingle them.

It was not primarily because he was an internationalist that Coubertin pursued the Olympic ideal; rather, he saw this as the best way of promoting sport of the finest type, his efforts to balance intellectual and physical education in French schools having failed.[5] It seems that it was not until 1889 that he decided to try to revive the Games; thereafter he spent five years preparing the ground for the International Congress of sportsmen which took place in 1894.[6]

Coubertin has been much criticised on a number of counts. For example, David Young, an American scholar primarily interested in the ancient Olympic Games, says that he completely misunderstood them, and so based his case for the modern Games (of which Young thoroughly approves, though he thinks they often succeed despite their ideological base) on misconceived evidence. Young argues that Coubertin wrongly believed that the Games were limited to amateurs and, moving to broader ground, believes that he was in any case a part of a much more general nineteenth-century movement to take over sport from the working classes and place its direction in amateur, and upper-class, hands.

The second accusation may well have substance, if what is meant is that Coubertin was unconsciously part of that movement, but not if it is alleged that Coubertin was in any sense consciously trying to disadvantage the working class: the evidence is quite the other way. The question of amateurism is more complicated. He does indeed seem to have believed that the early Games were limited to amateurs (if one excludes their trainers, whom he saw as a harmless kind of professional), but he also deplores the gradual onset of professionalism among the athletes, which in his view destroyed the games morally. At this point we enter a difficult dispute between specialists. On the one hand are those, like Young, who argue that the Games were for professionals from the very beginning: on the other hand scholars like Pleket (whose work Young greatly respects) believed that professionalism only became a factor in the Archaic period, conventionally held to have ended with the second Persian invasion of Greece in 480 B.C.[7]

The difficulty about coming to any conclusion is that the evidence is limited, but it appears to be common ground that the winners, although receiving no more than an olive wreath at Olympia and the other major festivals, were richly rewarded when they returned to their native cities. The point at issue is whether this happened from the beginning of the Games, or from some later period.

Coubertin's work predates this controversy. He may have been wrong to think that there had ever been a golden age of pure amateurism, but he certainly knew that the Games had eventually gone down hill. Yet he also propagated the entirely un-Greek idea that 'The important thing at the Olympic Games is not to win, but to take part; for the essential thing in life is not to conquer, but to struggle well'.[8] He may also have exaggerated the importance of the so-called 'sacred truce', which did not prevent wars or bring an end to one which had already broken out, but did have the more limited advantage of allowing athletes free passage to Elis for the Games.

On a more theoretical level, Coubertin may have been misguided in thinking that sporting contact between young people of different nationalities reduces the danger of war by promoting understanding. At least he did not believe that playing games together necessarily leads to people liking one another; indeed he thought such a belief infantile. But he did think that people could learn to respect one another, and that acquaintance must necessarily precede respect.[9] His successors in the Olympic movement have not always been so measured in their pronouncements. For example, Carl Diem said at the IOC's fiftieth anniversary that although the smoke of war had befogged the Olympic flame, it had not been put out. The profound point of the anniversary ceremony was to strengthen the certain truth that in future Olympism would continue to exercise its conciliatory power for the good of humanity.[10] The modern Olympic movement certainly sticks to this belief, though some of its members may do so in a spirit similar to that in which the Church of England remains attached to the Thirty-Nine Articles of Religion, which a Priest in that Church must sign.[11]

Although Coubertin insisted that the modern Games should follow what he believed to be the ancient example, and be limited to amateurs, he wrote in 1894 that English rowing had an out-of-date notion of 'amateur' and that he believed the English oarsmen's exclusion of the working class to be a monstrous aberration.[12] He would not allow work-people or anyone else to be paid for their sporting endeavours, but he thought it right that they should receive compensation for what would nowadays be called 'broken time' and used disrespectfully to refer to amateurism as 'this admirable mummy'.[13] Furthermore, although the 1894 Congress had reached a definition of amateurism, he seems to have believed that the definition should be open to change with circumstances. In an article published in 1909 he wrote that the movement should proceed very slowly towards a definition of 'amateur'.[14]

It is probable that Coubertin supported, to use a modern catch-phrase, 'sport for all' and at the same time believed in élite sport as the supreme test. His three passions can be summed up as love of country, education and love of sport. Many later commentators have rightly said that he misunderstood the Greek Games, and so had based the modern Games on false premises. It is true that he misunderstood, or even invented, what he called Olympism, yet he was determined that the modern Games should be thoroughly modern. Like his current successors he was attached to ceremony, the Olympic Flame and flag and so on, and had a high idea of the respect due to the personages of the Olympic movement, yet in much of his thinking he was entirely down-to-earth. He would not have disagreed with those who say that in evolving new guidelines the modern movement has no need to be the prisoner of the past. The Olympic movement may in part have compensated for his unhappy private life and for the lack of official recognition of his educational work, yet he seems also to have been disinterested to an outstanding degree and after his retirement from the presidency in 1925 he never attended the Games again.

The forerunners: 1) Much Wenlock

There had been an English 'Olimpick' festival as early as 1620, and Coubertin's were not the first Games in the nineteenth century to regard themselves as in the Olympic tradition. Games had been held in Greece in 1859, 1870, 1875 and 1889 (the last two were not at all successful) and from 1850 annual 'Olympian Games' had been held at Much Wenlock, in the English county of Shropshire.

It may seem surprising that a small town in Shropshire, with about 2,500 inhabitants a hundred and fifty years ago, and not many more now, should have played any part in the foundation of the modern Olympic Games. Nevertheless, a number of authorities[15] agree that Dr William Penny Brookes, the moving spirit of the Much Wenlock 'Olympian' Games, had some influence on Coubertin's thinking, and Britain's Princess Royal, a member of the modern IOC, has lent her name to this view.[16]

Brookes was a fighter for causes. He was, in the usage of the day, a gentleman, which not all surgeons were, and so had access to leading figures in the county. The forerunner of the Olympian Society was the Agricultural Reading Society, which he founded in 1841, and for which he obtained subscriptions from 725 people. It was intended for all classes – though there is no record of who actually used the library – but one purpose of encouraging people to read was to help them to decide how to vote after the extension of the franchise in the Reform Act of 1832.

It was also necessary to keep people out of ale houses, with which Much Wenlock was very well supplied for its small population, and to encourage games. The Society therefore established an Olympian 'class' (meaning 'section') in 1850,[17] (there were also a philharmonic class, art class, etc.), which in 1860 broke away and re-formed itself as an independent Olympian Society, with Dr Brookes, who relinquished the secretaryship of the Reading Society, as President of the new society. The break occurred because the parish priest had referred, at a meeting of the Agricultural Reading Society, to 'representations which had been made to him by the wives of some of the parishioners, that during the week the games were held, the working men were not so industrious, were given to intemperance, and that a loss was entailed upon their families by the consequent diminution of their wages'.[18]

The Olympian Games at first were more like traditional village jollifications than conventional athletics meetings, but the programme gradually became more sophisticated. As the Games became more established Brookes was able to interest distinguished national figures, and he was never backward in coming forward, even in approaching grandees of the highest rank.

Like Coubertin, he had a passionate interest in physical education in state schools, where he thought it absurd that farm labourers should have compulsory drawing lessons but no physical training, and he used the Wenlock Olympian Society as the vehicle through which he propagated his views.

In 1871 the committee was able to congratulate the members of the Society

on the recognition for the first time of the importance of physical training in our National Elementary Schools by the Committee of the Council on Education, in Article 24 of the Code of Regulations just issued, which states that Attendance at drill, under a competent instructor, for not more than two hours a week, and twenty weeks in the year, may be counted as school attendance.

This was no more than a first step, for it did not make drill compulsory. In any case Brookes did not think highly of drill, compared with athletics.

Although your committee are of opinion that so small an amount of bodily training will not be sufficient to preserve in early life the physical stamina of the people, yet they regard it with satisfaction as a first instalment in the right direction, and feel thankful that a branch of education which they have advocated for so many years has at last been adopted by the State.[19]

Many quotations may be found to illustrate Brookes's conviction of the virtues of physical education. For example:

The encouragement of outdoor exercise contributes to manliness of character. I say contributes, for true manliness shows itself not merely in skill in athletic and field sports, but in the exercise of those moral virtues which it is one of the objects of religion to inculcate.[20]

Again, he says: 'Every year it is getting more difficult to decide what children who are educated at the expense of the State ought to be taught', and goes on to argue that England should follow the Swiss example and introduce gymnastics in schools, partly by way of preparation for war.[21]

Ten years later Brookes writes that he has been struck on various visits to France by the population's physical degeneracy and as usual he had not been afraid to approach the highest authority: 'I wrote to the Emperor pointing out the dangerous consequences to France of a continued neglect of physical education.' A gymnasium was established, but 'it was too late! The Franco-German war showed the French that a nation cannot, with impunity, neglect the bodily training of its people. England should take a warning from this disaster'.[22]

In 1862 leading lights of the Liverpool Athletic Club held an 'Olympic Festival', repeated in 1863 and 1864, and in 1865 they, with Brookes, founded a National Olympian Association (NOA), with the intention that annual Games should be held in turn in each of England's major cities. However, unlike modern cities, which vie with each other from all over the world to stage the Games, English cities of those days did not have enough enthusiasm for the idea ever to take off. Furthermore, the National Association was disregarded by the athletic 'establishment' of Oxford and Cambridge. Indeed, it appears, as the historian of the Amateur Athletic Association has shown, that the Amateur Athletic Club, the AAA's predecessor, was established as a riposte to the NOA.[23]

In 1859 Brookes's connection with Greece began when Olympic Games were held in Athens, and the organising committee, according to David Young, consulted the British Minister in Athens, Sir Thomas Wyse, as to what events should be included in the programme. He in turn consulted Brookes, who, in addition to giving his advice, caused the Wenlock Olympian Society to give £10 for presentation to the winner of a foot race. Inspired by the Greek example, he

revived the National Games that had been organised for a few years by
the National Olympian Association, and in 1877 successfully applied
to the King of the Hellenes for a silver cup to the value of £10, which
was presented to the winner of the Pentathlon at the National Games
at Shrewsbury, in Shropshire. As a local newspaper reported (perhaps
in rather exaggerated terms): 'some years ago the late King of Greece
applied to the founder of the Wenlock Society, W. P. Brookes Esq.,
for information as to how the society was conducted, the object being
to establish one similar in the country which Wenlock itself had
endeavoured to emulate.' The present King was showing his gratitude
by giving a cup in return.[24]

Brookes was soon afterwards to express the hope that the King of
the Hellenes would visit Much Wenlock. He may not have had any
serious expectation that this would happen, but the fact that he
expressed the hope illustrates his willingness to fly high.[25] For many
years, long before Coubertin had hit upon the idea, Brookes had been
urging the revival of the ancient Games upon the Greek government.
Correspondence in the Wenlock archives shows that he was pressing
this idea upon the Greek Minister in London, J. Gennadius, as early
as 1880, the year in which Gennadius became an honorary member of
the Society, though he seems never to have been able to visit Much
Wenlock.

In January 1881 Brookes, as Treasurer, and William Lawley, Secretary, announced:

Your committee has suggested the holding of an International Olympian
Festival of Athens, when the present critical state of affairs in Greece is ended
. . . The proposal has been favourably received by Greeks resident in
England, and will, no doubt, be cordially responded to by the authorities at
Athens, and by the principal Athletic Associations of Great Britain, many of
whose members would gladly avail themselves of an opportunity of visiting
the classic land of Greece: of making an acquaintance with its people; of
inspecting the interesting and important archaeological discoveries recently
made, at a great cost, by the German Government and nation; and of contending in a generous rivalry with the Athletes of other nations, in the
time-consecrated Stadium of Athens.[26]

This was no doubt written after Brookes had received Gennadius's
letter of 18 November 1880. He wrote very cordially, but had to say
that, after consultation:

while congratulating you upon all your Society aims at, and the most excellent
proposal you now make to us, we deeply regret that in the present troubles

and critical circumstances of the Kingdom it would not be possible to carry out in a befitting manner the scheme you propose. If, as we must hope, later on a more settled and satisfactory state of affairs be established in the last[?], then I have every reason to believe that such a proposal would meet with a ready and cheerful response.[27]

Clio, a Greek paper, refers back to the exchange of prizes:

Dr Brookes, this enthusiastic Philhelline, is endeavouring to organize an International Olympian festival, to be held in Athens, from which much good will arise in many respects and, we have no doubt that the Greek Government will give every facility for its realization.[28]

Brookes kept up the campaign, and it seems that he had an ally in Gennadius, though the uncertain political state of Greece made the revival of the Games problematic. In June 1886 he wrote to Brookes:

I quite agree with you that what has lately happened in Greece was for the best. It was of very great importance that we have shown we can put on the field an important force which proved its ability to fight well.

But these events [?] have made the periodical keeping of the Olympian games difficult and of late they were not regularly kept. A meeting[?] will take place next year I think.[29]

As for Brookes's relationship with Coubertin, it appears that Brookes took the initiative in approaching him in response to an appeal placed by Coubertin in a number of English newspapers, asking for help in connection with the Physical Training Congress which he was holding under the umbrella of the Paris Exhibition of 1889. In January 1890 Coubertin referred to interesting documents received from Brookes, one dealing with tilting, and the other giving details of an experiment carried out by Brookes some years earlier. In this experiment he had taken twelve boys: subjected six to a regime of drill, and the other six to gymnastics, and shown that the latter group's muscular development significantly outshone that of the former.[30]

Thereafter Brookes and Coubertin exchanged a number of letters, and in October 1890 Coubertin paid a visit to Wenlock, where a special festival was held in his honour. Despite pouring rain he enjoyed himself, and an oak was planted in his honour. He acknowledged his debt to Brookes in a complimentary article in the *Revue Athlétique*, and after Brookes's death wrote another in the American *Monthly Review of Reviews*; but thereafter he seems to have suppressed the memory of Brookes's contribution to the Olympic movement.[31] In 1891 he became an honorary member of the Olympian Society.

A cordial letter from Coubertin to Brookes in July 1892 is interesting, not only because it shows that they were by now on quite close terms, but also because it says something about the Union de Sociétés Françaises de Sports Athlétiques (Union of French Athletic Sports Societies) which Coubertin was using as the base from which to float the idea of reviving the Games, and gives an insight into his views on amateurism. He apologises for the delay in answering Brookes's last letter, but has been terribly busy. His Union has recently reached sixty-two member societies with about 7,000 members, compared with seven societies with 800 [700?] two years ago, and at their last international meeting some of the best English runners and cyclists had taken part. 'The only trouble we have is with reference to professionalism as in country towns money prizes are given very often for bicycle races in which our men are sometimes tempted to compete. Of course we don't allow it.'[32]

The prospect of the 1896 Games was received with enthusiasm by the Much Wenlock Olympian Society. On 24 May 1894 Brookes read to the members the programme of the International Athletic Congress which was to be held in Paris on 17–24 June 1894 at the Palace of the Sorbonne on the subject of 'Amateurism and Professionalism in Athletics' and on the establishment of international Olympian festivals, with letters relating to the same from de Coubertin.

The members present expressed their decided opinion that amateurs only should be allowed to compete. They were also unanimously and enthusiastically of opinion that the proposed establishment of international Olympian festivals, to be held in rotation by all nations desirous of joining the movement, will be one of the grandest and most beneficial institutions of modern days, as it will tend to increase the bodily and mental vigour of the people and to promote friendly feeling and intercourse between the different nations of the earth.

They believed that there should be no delay. The first Games should be in Paris in 1895, and thereafter they should be held annually: otherwise, if ten nations joined the movement, each would be host only once in forty years.[33] Clearly, Brookes was not without honour in his own country, for at the 1895 Much Wenlock games R. J. More, M.P., said that it was mainly thanks to Brookes that the Olympian Games were to be renewed at Athens in the following year, and afterwards at Paris and London.[34]

Brookes, who was by now aged eighty-five, was too frail to attend the 1894 Congress, but he was included in the list of honorary delegates. In June 1894 he wrote to express his interest in the Congress, in terms which suggest that he was still primarily interested in Olympic festivals as a means to promote physical education, for he wrote that he trusted that the Congress 'would lead to an expression of opinion on the importance of the bodily training of the young in Elementary schools'. Of betting he said 'the Wenlock Olympian Society does not allow open betting at their festivals, which is such a disgrace to the English race meeting that it prevents many being present who would otherwise be gratified in witnessing a good horse race'. On gate money he foreshadowed, as Don Anthony has pointed out,[35] the modern Olympic movement's overseas aid fund, Olympic Solidarity, by saying, 'I would suggest, merely as my private opinion, that any surplus fund, after defraying the expenses of the particular festival in the Capital or large town of any associated nation, should be divided between all the other associated nations, to be invested in Trustees, for certain definite purposes connected with athletic sports as may seem best to the Congress about to meet in Paris'.[36]

Nor was Brookes slow to use what influence he could in Greece. He wrote to Tricoupis, the Greek Prime Minister, that 'It is impossible for modern nations to over-estimate the advantages they are deriving from the adoption of the Olympian games of ancient Greece. My friend, Baron Pierre de Coubertin of Paris, and other advocates of physical education, myself among the number, are exerting ourselves to promote international Olympian festivals, and I earnestly hope they will be successful, and be honoured by the patronage of His Majesty, The King of the Hellenes.'[37] In December 1895, in a letter warmly congratulating Coubertin on his engagement to be married, Brookes continued on the same theme, '. . . The Greek Government should I think, gladly acquiesce in the honour France wishes to confer upon Greece by holding the first festival at Athens' and goes on, with his usual practicality, to suggest that Coubertin 'write to Baron Courcel, your Ambassador to London, and ask him to request the Greek Ambassador to London, Athos Romanos, to use his influence with the wealthy Greeks in England, and solicit their pecuniary support . . . .'.[38]

It is impossible to say how much influence Brookes had on Coubertin, but it is obvious that he had some. He had presented a prize to the

Athens Games in 1859, four years before Coubertin was born, and had been actively working for the revival of the Olympics at least by 1880, when Coubertin was seventeen. To ask for a cup, as Brookes did in 1877, does not in itself indicate a desire to revive the ancient Games, but it does show a lively interest, and even if Brookes's active lobbying dates only from 1880 it seems virtually certain that he was seeking to revive the Games well before the same idea had occurred to Coubertin. However, that is not to say that Coubertin got the idea from Brookes, of whom he appears not to have heard until Brookes wrote to him in 1890.

Despite Young's conviction that Coubertin had gleaned the idea of an Olympic revival from Brookes, it seems inherently unlikely (as MacAloon has also said) that Coubertin would not have heard independently of the Olympic movement, which already existed in embryo.[39] The most that can be said with certainty is that he and Brookes were similar men with many ideas in common. They shared a passion for physical education: some of the words used by Coubertin, especially when he writes of the need for a healthy population in case of war, echo those of Brookes; both were political animals, and no doubt Coubertin's admiration for Thomas Arnold of Rugby overflowed into other aspects of English life. Coubertin may not have been much given to acknowledging debts, but he was generous in his article about his visit to Wenlock, where he wrote that 'if the Olympic Games that Modern Greece had not yet been able to revive still survived to-day, it is due, not to a Greek but to Dr W. P. Brookes'.[40]

The forerunners: 2) the Greek Olympic Games of 1859 and 1870

Greece owed the Games of 1859 and 1870 to Evangelios Zappas, a rich merchant of Greek origin living in Romania. He was one of the many nineteenth-century humanists and intellectuals who were passionate about Greece, and wanted to see it regain its place as leader of the western cultural world. He was born in the village of Lavovo, near Ioannina, in 1800, became a Major in the army and had been involved in Greek liberation movements before becoming an extremely active farm administrator and then landowner in Romania.

On 10 January 1852 the German archaeologist Professor Ernst Curtius of the University of Berlin gave a rather romantic lecture in which he stated that the Games would be revived. This came to Zappas's ears and he proposed to King Otto I (who had been installed as King of the Hellenes by the French and Germans in 1829, after much of southern Greece had been liberated from the Turks), that an Olympic contest be held. Since it was to be entirely financed by Zappas, Otto agreed and in 1858 Zappas gave shares and money to the Greek government to establish an Olympic Trust Fund, whose purpose was to organise competitions at four-year intervals, on the occasion of Greek industrial and agricultural fairs.

The first festival took place at Athens in 1859. It was not solely, or even primarily, athletic, but a combination of fair, exhibition and athletic events, under the aegis of 'The Commission of the Olympian Festival for the encouragement of National Industry'. There were only fifteen events in the programme, a copy of which was forwarded to Much Wenlock by Sir Thomas Wyse. The first was the 'Long, or seven-fold foot-race, 4,200 feet' for which the Wenlock Prize was awarded. The others included quoits, spear throwing and ascolism, the last described by Sir Thomas as 'a Greek Game, performed by jumping bare-footed and remaining with one foot on a greased Goatskin, shorn and filled with wine, which the winner takes'. The last two events were horse races, the first for gentlemen volunteers and the second for 'Muleteers, Drivers and Coachmen'. Zappas's intention to repeat the contest every four years came to nothing, a failure which caused him great unhappiness in his last years. Nevertheless, when he died in 1865 he left the greater part of his immense fortune to the Olympic Trust Fund, in order that it might restore the Games. His request that a stadium be built at Athens was not acted upon, but in 1870 the second competition took place on a site outside Athens which had been acquired by the Fund.[41]

Later Games were held in 1875 and 1889, but it appears that they were insignificant. However, those of 1870 were serious enough for there to be some dispute about whether Coubertin's Games should be seen as the beginning of something entirely new or as the continuation of a pre-existing series. Those who wish to magnify the purely Greek achievement and correspondingly to downgrade Coubertin's, believe that Zappas's efforts and the enthusiasm which the Games evoked meant that the modern Olympic movement had been born years before Coubertin's Congress of 1894. Young may go a little far in claiming that Coubertin feigned amnesia about these earlier Games, but he naturally wanted to keep for himself the glorious title of 'Rénovateur' of the ancient Games, and so could hardly admit that the nineteenth-century Greek games had been truly 'Olympic'. Young quotes an important letter to Coubertin from Demetrios Vikelas, who became the first President of the International Olympic Committee, in which he emphasises that there would have been no international games without Coubertin:

The Zappas foundation had nothing to do with establishing *International* [Vikelas's emphasis] Olympics: the credit is yours. but the fact still remains that there have been, in Greece, Olympic Games, and that nobody could, even if he wants, eradicate the name. Nobody among us has the right to deny the name 'Olympics' to the Athens games.[42]

At least in the early days Coubertin was not amnesic about Zappas and his brother Constantine, for he records in 1895 that the glorious name of the Olympic Games had been applied to artistic, industrial and athletic events, thanks to the brothers' munificence. But, Coubertin argues, his own project was different, because international (the same line as was taken by Vikelas, in the letter quoted above).[43]

The Congress of 1894

In 1894 Coubertin arranged an international Congress, at which the decision was taken to revive the Olympic Games. However, it has been alleged that he misled the delegates by causing them to think that they were to attend a conference primarily on amateurism, at which the Games would be of relatively minor importance.[44]

To say that he misled the delegates may be an exaggeration, but he certainly displayed the neat political footwork which remains such a noticeable feature of the Olympic movement today. His own account of the genesis of the Congress, in a book published in 1931, only six years before his death, gives a full and frank account of the matter. Its tone is often almost frivolous; without a doubt he looked back with pleasure at the finesse that he had shown.

Coubertin recounts that he used the fifth anniversary of the Union des Sociétés Françaises de Sports Athlétiques (USFSA) in November 1892 to float the idea of reviving the Games. He had expected almost any response to the speech in which he argued for their revival, except the one that it in fact received. There was applause and no opposition, but also, he complains, no understanding of his desire to revive the essence or principle of Olympism. Looking back, one can see that this failure need not have been surprising, because, as he goes on, in those days sporting organisations found it extraordinarily difficult to collaborate. A man was a fencer or an oarsman or a cyclist, but did not have the Olympic ideal of being simply a sportsman.

The winter of 1892 to 1893 passed without his idea catching on at all, whereas he had expected it to make enough of an impression to assure the success of an international Congress. It was this lack of public interest in Olympism that led him initially to make amateurism the focus of the Congress. His next step was to cause the USFSA to decide at its General Assembly in the summer of 1893 that a Congress should be held and to approve a preliminary programme. In his speech to the General assembly of the USFSA Coubertin explained why the question of amateurism needed study but did not on this occasion again directly advocate the revival of the Olympic Games (as he had done in the previous November), although he did refer to the stringent conditions of amateurism that they imposed. This time his emphasis was on the need for the Union to settle the question of amateurism for its own purposes, in order that it might be able to strengthen its internal organisation, widen its influence in the French provinces, and establish relations with foreign unions.

He argued that money was threatening to corrupt athleticism: bets were struck; professionals did not run for the sake of physical and mental strength in the service of their country, but in order to earn as much as possible. Furthermore, it had to be said that if the athlete was, for example, a cyclist, money was not lacking, for once a cyclist was well known he could obtain subventions from bicycle manufacturers and from organisers of cycling meets. (These practices would now be called sponsorship and appearance money.) There had also grown up, almost everywhere, a class of individuals whose right hand certified their amateur status, while the left accepted the metal of corruption under the counter. The students of England and America would not accept this corruption of their ideals (the English reference is to the young Oxford men who had established the Amateur Athletic Association), and the Union's own leading position gave it the authority required to hold the international Congress that had been arranged for 1894.

Coubertin was disappointed that his great idea still failed to catch on after the USFSA had adopted it. He spent four months in the USA at the end of 1893, but found no one excited about his project except Professor W. M. Sloane of Princeton, who had given a dinner at which there had been goodwill and interest but evident expectation of failure. He received the same impression, but even more markedly, in

London in February 1894. Nor was there any interest in Germany, despite the efforts Coubertin made to draw the Germans in. Indeed these efforts made matters worse, because the French gymnasts were furious at his overtures to the Germans, and threatened to withdraw if the Germans did join.[45] As it turned out, there were no German representatives at the Congress, as Coubertin rather acidly observed.[46]

The programme adopted by the USFSA included eight Articles, (that is, headings for discussion), six on amateurism, one on betting and the last on the possibility of re-establishing the Olympic Games. (We may note in passing that, so far as is known, betting has never been in evidence at the modern Olympics, although certain bookmakers will take bets on events in which they have sufficient expertise to be able to judge the odds. However, it had been very much a feature of athletics meets in England, and Coubertin must have been aware of this, as he was of the general deterioration of the Olympic ideal in England.)

The suggestion that Coubertin misled the delegates to the Congress rests upon the fact that there were two programmes for it. The first had been agreed in the summer of 1893 and printed in January 1894, when it was sent out to athletic and other sporting associations all over the world. The second, Coubertin records, was published at the beginning of 1894. It contained the dates and place of the Congress, 11–24 June (eventually it lasted from 16 to 23 June) at the Sorbonne, named eight Vice-Presidents and added two new Articles to the earlier list. The most important new development, he says, was that the list was now divided into two sections, thus giving far greater prominence to the objective of reviving the Olympic Games.[47] The first section consisted of the first seven of the original eight Articles; the second contained the original eighth Article and two new ones, providing for Olympic rules and the establishment of a committee to run the Games. It was this enlarged agenda which appeared just after the Congress in the Olympic Committee's first official bulletin.[48]

It seems, therefore, that Young may well be right when he suggests that delegates learned only from their admission tickets that the Congress was to be so much concerned with the revival of the Games, for although the ten-Article version had been ready at the beginning of 1894 it was not printed until May.[49] Coubertin is no doubt correct when he recalls that the letters of invitation referred to a Congress for the re-establishment of the Olympic Games, but if they were sent out as late as the end of May there may have been a number of delegates who did not receive them in advance. Be that as it may, Coubertin claims to have known within hours of the beginning of the Congress that there would be no opposition to his project.[50]

The guiding trinity throughout the whole operation were C. Herbert, Secretary of the Amateur Athletic Association 'for England and the British Empire'; W. M. Sloane, for the American continent, and Coubertin himself for France and western Europe. His two colleagues were crucial because Herbert had an organised propaganda network through the AAA and Sloane dominated American athletics to the extent that, as Coubertin had noticed in 1889, no one could do anything without him.[51]

The delegates divided into two commissions – on the Games and on amateurism – and the report of the commission on the Games was accepted without opposition at the final session. The President of the commission was D. Vikelas, of the Société Panhellénique de Gymnastique (who, as we have seen, became the first President of the International Olympic Committee). He had, again according to Young, been recruited as a delegate to the Congress by the Société Panhellénique de Gynmastique, of which he had never heard until the invitation arrived, and swiftly promoted by Coubertin.[52]

The commission on the Games met the conditions on which Coubertin had always insisted. The Games were to be held at four-year intervals; they were not to imitate the ancient Games, but to be exclusively modern in character – what mattered was the spirit of Olympism rather than the specific nature of the events; the Games for boys between the ages of twelve and eighteen were not to be repro-duced: in the absence of birth certificates they had given great trouble to the judges. Coubertin was also to have full responsibility for the designation of an international committee whose members would represent Olympism in their countries.

The Congress decided that the first Games should be at Athens in 1896, the second in Paris in 1900, and thereafter every four years in other cities of the world. Thus was established at the beginning the peripatetic nature of the Games, upon which Coubertin was later to insist when faced with Greek demands that they should be perma-nently at Athens. Later Coubertin was to say that the choice of Athens had not been in his original plan, as he had not expected an enfeebled Greece ('les forces juvéniles de la Grèce ressuscité') to be capable of organising them. He had thought of holding them at Paris in the first

years of the twentieth century, but he had been charmed by Vikelas
into changing his mind, although even Vikelas had been somewhat
nervous about Athens's ability to arrange so important an event.
Young rejects Coubertin's account and believes that London was the
first choice of the Congress, but that Coubertin and Vikelas then
railroaded the choice of Athens, perhaps (but he is only speculating)
because Coubertin had done a private deal with Crown Prince Constantine of the Hellenes before the Congress began.

As for the commission on amateurism, the general principle of
amateurism was established, but the report of the commission was not
easily agreed, and provoked a good deal of discussion on report-back
to the full Congress. There was general disapproval (even expressed
by the delegates from England, and from Australia, where similar
restrictions obtained) of the (English) Amateur Rowing Association's
exclusion of labourers from membership, and a definition of 'amateur'
was accepted which omitted this provision. It was also agreed that a
distinction must be made between reward and compensation (for loss
of earnings), and that, very exceptionally, unions, federations and
societies might allow encounters between amateurs and professionals,
provided that the prizes offered were not in money. The question of
gate-money (Coubertin uses the English expression) preoccupied the
commission, and it was agreed that in no circumstances should any
part of it be paid directly to athletes, but only to their parent associations. However, the possibility of those associations passing on compensation to the athletes was not excluded.

There were some exceptions to the prohibition of money prizes.
These were in yachting, horse-racing and archery. The item caused
especially lively discussion, as many delegates thought it unfair to
release the rich from rules which still bound the poor. Some delegates
thought the difficulty so great that they wanted to limit the Congress's
competence to purely athletic sports, but it reached the general conclusion that money prizes were not indispensable in any sport. No
amateur in one sport could be a professional in another and in all
sports except fencing Olympic competitions were to be organised only
by amateurs.

A subject which worries many in the Olympic movement today
raised its head, namely the question of heats. The Congress decided
that in each country, and in every sport, there should be preliminary
contests, so that only true champions should take part in the Olympic
Games themselves.[53] Other principles were established which still

guide the Olympic movement. The members of the International Olympic Committee were to be the representatives overseas of Olympism, rather than their countries' representatives on the committee and each country was to establish a National Olympic Committee.

One principle which did not survive long was that, although the IOC's administration was to be permanently in Paris (it moved to its present home, Lausanne, in 1915), the presidency of the Committee should revolve, passing after each Games to the country which had been chosen to host the next.[54] Under that rule Vikelas was the first President, and Coubertin took over after the Athens games of 1896, as the Games of 1900 were to be in Paris. However, Coubertin was then asked to continue as President, and, as we have seen, remained in office until 1925.

The Games of 1896

According to Coubertin's own account, the King of the Hellenes had telegraphed to the 1894 Congress that he favoured the idea of holding the Games at Athens. Nevertheless, Coubertin experienced considerable difficulty in persuading the Greek government actually to follow the Congress's wish and hold them. A committee had been promptly set up in Paris to organise the Athens Games and had counted on the permanent commission which administered the Zappas Foundation to provide an organisation in Athens. However, the Prime Minister, Charilaos Tricoupis, was determined that the Games should not be held in Greece.

The Prime Minister's opposition was made known through intermediaries. A letter of 1 November 1894 to Coubertin from Etienne Dragoumis, a member of the Zappeion Commission, says that Greece is very honoured to be asked to hold the Games, but that it is a new country, where much remains to be done, and that it cannot afford them. He suggests that it would be much better to attach them to some great international festival, such as the one that is to be held in Paris in 1900. He refers to Paris's great resources, and suggests that 1900, the beginning of a new century, would be a good starting date for the Games.

Coubertin was wily enough to have Budapest as his second string, in case the Greeks refused to hold the Games, and even mentioned in the *Bulletin* that this alternative existed, no doubt to give the Greeks a coded warning that he was serious.[55] But he was not immediately successful. On a visit to Athens in November 1894 he spent his first day leaving cards, and on the second Tricoupis came to see him at the Hotel Grande Bretagne, where Coubertin was receiving the French chargé d'affaires. It is not clear whether the Prime Minister called by appointment, nor whether Coubertin had timed the French diplomat's visit with that in mind: it must, in any case have been something of a coup for Coubertin to have the Prime Minister call on him, rather than the other way about. He records that Tricoupis was cordial but still refused to accept the Games.

At the same time a political row was brewing in Greece about the Games. The people who most wanted them were the small businessmen and the cab drivers. Coubertin avoided commenting to the press, but accepted an invitation to give a lecture arranged by the literary society Parnassus. He spoke to an audience of seven hundred, 'from all classes of Athenian society' and, having explained the Paris Congress's thinking about the Olympic Games, ended with a eulogy of modern Greece, which received enthusiastic applause.[56] He had also taken the precaution of going to see the Crown Prince (who had accepted the presidency of the organising committee), and Prince Nicholas, the King's third son. Both had promised active and enthusiastic support.

Coubertin's lecture was well received by the newspapers. As a result Tricoupis markedly changed his tune. He still refused to commit the government, but his attitude became benevolent, and he authorised the Zappeion Commission to help organise the Games. The next step was to set up a fund-raising committee, although Coubertin noted that it was not greatly needed. However, the picture was not entirely satisfactory, since the Crown Prince, who was acting as Regent (because his father was away in Russia for Alexander III's funeral), did not think that, as Regent, he could go to its first meeting, on 1 November 1894, despite the enthusiasm that he had expressed. Nor was any help forthcoming from the Zappeion Commission.

Coubertin recalls that, once he had left Athens for Paris, one of his Vice-Presidents worked against him, and the committee left to the Prince the decision about whether the Games would be held, expecting that he would decide against them. However, he left the decision in the air, saying that he wanted time to think. This annoyed Tricoupis greatly, and Coubertin believed that it had an influence on his fall from office in 1895.[57]

The Prince then took over the committee and reconstituted it, appointing as Secretary-General a former Mayor of Athens, Timoleon Philemon, who set up a 'véritable ministère Olympique'. Everyone wanted to join the 'ministère Philemon' and gifts of money poured in, not just from Greece, but from Greek colonies in Marseilles, Alexandria and London. Special stamps were issued, whose sale yielded more than would have come from the lottery that the government had refused to allow.

Coubertin goes on to insist that in Paris he was extremely active, giving as an example his efforts to design a velodrome for the Games. As no one in Athens knew anything about the design of cycle-racing tracks he studied the one at Arcachon, and sent a preliminary sketch to Athens. He was also under pressure from the Greeks to tell them exactly how many visitors and competitors to expect at the Games. He had had to prepare the invitation list himself, and the Greeks, who, he comments, naturally thought the whole world was as interested as they were, were astonished that he could not give them the information, fourteen months in advance.

Indeed, attracting visitors and persuading athletes to participate was not plain sailing. The French archers would take no part, because they did not wish to lose their independence and appear to be an offshoot of the French National Olympic Committee. There was powerful opposition among Frenchmen, who wanted revenge for 1870, to international Games involving the Germans. So deep was the hostility that 'The French sporting press virtually ignored the Games, not only in 1896 but also in several succeeding meetings.'[58] There were few French spectators, and their athletes needed subventions to get them interested. The response from Sweden and Hungary was good, but not from Belgium, thanks to a hostile campaign by the gymnasts' federation, and in Britain there was sympathetic scepticism.

De Coubertin worked out the programme, with the aid of experts, eliminating the sports that seemed inadequate, because in those days there were no international federations (except the Cyclists, founded in 1892). He went on directing the programme until he decided that he could hand over the technical details to such federations as had grown up meanwhile.[59] In all other cases the rules were those of a national association (for example, the English Amateur Athletic Association), or were devised specially for the Olympic Games by one of the existing associations. Coubertin regretted that polo, football and boxing were omitted from the Athens programme, the last because the Paris Congress had judged it an uncivilised sport. However, cricket was to be included.[60]

Another hostile campaign, this time in Germany (which, it will be remembered, had taken no part in the 1894 Congress), was based on an interview which Coubertin was said, falsely by his own account, to have given, in which he was alleged to have said that he would do everything he could to stop the Germans participating in the Games, or coming to Athens. However, a correspondent in Berlin wrote to Coubertin that he thought his excellent letter of denial would be shown to the Kaiser: 'no one is unaware of how anxious His Majesty is to maintain good relations with France' (original in French). A few days later the German National Olympic Committee relented and eventually Philemon, who had been infected by the German hostility, also got over his irritation.

As the preparations advanced Coubertin was piqued to discover that, despite his years of effort, he was no longer needed in Athens. No one, he complains, mentioned him again, because the Greeks had become sure of success, and everyone conspired to forget France's part in reviving the Games. After all the trouble he had taken to persuade them, the Greeks were now delighted to have the Games, and assumed that they would continue to hold them every four years. Coubertin naturally decided that this was a quite unreasonable ambition: he would probably have thought the same in any case, but he would have been superhuman not to have been affected by the Greeks' undiplomatic behaviour.

Athens, he reasoned after the Games, had attracted visitors from all over Greece, but few foreigners (despite the efforts of Thomas Cook, who had been appointed official travel agents to the Games); there was no rail line to the rest of Europe, and there were few boats. He also thought that there would be endless political problems, which he did not specify, if Athens were permitted to retain the Games permanently. In short 'to locate the revived Games definitively and exclusively in Greece would be the suicide of my achievement,' (original in French).

The King had hinted at having the Games permanently in Greece, and the press wanted a law to that effect, arguing that Coubertin was stealing Greek property, and interrupting a series of revived Games which had begun in 1859. (In fact the King had done more than hint:

he had said explicitly that the Games ought to find a permanent home in Greece.) So serious was the situation that some IOC colleagues thought the IOC would have to dissolve itself. Coubertin, however, came up with a skilful compromise. He suggested to the Prince that there should be pan-Hellenic Games spaced between the Olympics. The Prince had thought of this too, and the King liked the idea, but the press were irritated, and Coubertin got some abusive letters.[61]

The only intermediate Games were held at Athens in 1906. They may even have saved the modern concept of international sport, because they were a success, whereas the Olympic Games that followed them in London in 1908 were 'scarred by loud and bitter charges of cheating and professionalism hurled back and forth between the British and the Americans'.[62] Be that as it may, they also fulfilled Coubertin's objective. As Diem says, having realised that he could not stop the Greeks from being convinced that they should permanently host the Olympics he had arranged the Athens Games as a palliative, but they provoked so much protest from other countries that no more was heard of the idea. Nobody wanted a parallel series of games – nor wished them always to be held in a Mediterranean country.[63]

Philemon's own account, in a booklet published shortly after the 1896 Games, of the politics behind them more or less corroborates Coubertin's version, except that he goes into far more detail over the difficulty of raising funds. The Crown Prince was convinced that Greece, however poor, must go ahead with the Games. The only solution was to raise funds from wealthy Greeks, both at home and abroad, but the moment was not propitious, because there had recently been earthquakes and other calamities in Greece. 'Many wealthy persons', he records, 'turned a deaf ear to the appeal while others stubbornly turned down the appeal, declaring that the matter was comic and destined to failure and the money would be spent in vain.'[64] In the end they collected three times as much as had at first been thought necessary, so to this extent Coubertin is correct when he says that contributions flowed in. However, the contributions were made slowly, but the stadium had to be rebuilt immediately. The answer was an appeal to George Averoff, who had already built the Athens Polytechnic, the Military Academy, the juvenile prison and other public buildings. Philemon went to see him in Alexandria, armed with a letter from the Crown Prince, and Averoff saved the day by paying for the stadium's renovation.

Philemon ends his account with a paean of praise to the Greek populace and manages to mention Coubertin only once. The King was even less gracious and did not mention him at all in his speech at a great banquet at the Palace in honour of the foreign athletes. (An American attended in bicycling shorts and only the Hungarians wore the regulation dark suit.) By contrast Coubertin himself proudly took credit, in his introduction to the booklet, for the revival of the Games.

I claim its paternity with raised voice and I would like to thank once more here those who assisted me to bring it into wellbeing; those who, together with me, think that athletics will emerge greater and ennobled and that international youth will draw from it the love of peace and respect for life.[65]

Much of the preceding section is derived from Coubertin's version of events, which on the whole has been accepted by later scholars. David Young, however, presents a different picture, relying largely on letters from Vikelas to Coubertin hitherto undiscovered. He does not refute Coubertin's account in all its details (though he does dispute his version of the velodrome story, and asserts that he did indeed give the interview which so enraged the Germans, and which he later denied having given). Nevertheless, Young's overall view is that Coubertin did little to help the organisation of the Games. Vikelas, Young says, repeatedly urged him to take an interest, but with little result, perhaps because Coubertin had recently become engaged, or perhaps because he was writing a book. Young does not deny that in Greece Coubertin was given virtually no credit for the Games, nor that there was a power struggle between the Greeks, who wanted to retain the Games in perpetuity, and the infant IOC, which was seen as a body seeking to make off with Greek property. But he believes that if, instead of staying in Paris, Coubertin had been on the spot in Athens, he would have been able to ensure that he was not ignored. Furthermore, Young, so much of whose work has been devoted to showing that there already existed a tradition of modern Olympic Games, has little sympathy for Coubertin's determination to retain control of them and to ensure that they circumnavigated the world.[66]

Despite Young's persuasive scholarship, it would be unwise to dismiss Coubertin's account root and branch. Apart from the major distortion imposed by his reluctance to remember that others had thought of reviving the Games, his recollections generally seem reasonably accurate, and may in large part be reconciled with Young's account. It may be that he had not lost interest in his brainchild, but was active in Paris in at least some of the ways that he describes. Yet he may well not have been delivering the goods that Vikelas wanted, and he may not have foreseen that the Greek government would disregard the IOC in favour of the organising committee.

These first Games of the modern era were of course small beer compared with the vast circus that is now the norm. They included nine sports, forty-three events, 311 participants (230 of them Greek) from thirteen countries.[67] But they certainly seem to have generated great enthusiasm in Greece coupled with a feeling that the Games belonged to Greece as of right. That continuing feeling is generally believed to have led the Athens team bidding for the centenary Games of 1996 into a state of over-confidence amounting almost to arrogance, which was one of the reasons for Athens's losing the contest to Atlanta.

Notes

1   For his views on Rugby see Coubertin's *L'Education en Angleterre: Collèges et Universités*, Paris, 1888. The chapter on Rugby is reprinted in Norbert Mueller (ed.), *Pierre de Coubertin: Textes Choisies*, Zurich, 1986, I, pp. 48–56.

2   For a fuller exposition of Coubertin's thinking see Marquis Melchior de Polignac's speech 'Baron Pierre de Coubertin' made at the IOC's Session in Stockholm in June 1947 to mark the tenth anniversary of his death. *Bulletin du Comité Olympique* (new series), 6, September 1947, pp. 12–15.

3   For details of the ancient Games see M. I. Finley and H. W. Pleket, *The Olympic Games: the First Thousand Years*, London, 1976, pp. 13 and 43 and *passim*.

4   This example is typical of his more flowery style of writing: Les temples, ce seront les *gymnases*, foyers de vie municipale assemblant adolescents, adultes, vieillards autour de cette préoccupation d'exalter la vie humaine qui est à la base de tout l'hellénisme et se reflète si nettement dans la conception d'un au-delà crépusculaire ou domine le regret du séjour terrestre.' 'Pédagogie Sportive', *Textes Choisies*, II, p. 33. (Reprinted from *Pédagogie Sportive*, Paris, 1922, pp. 11–24.)

5   'Pierre de Coubertin', a speech by Carl Diem to be delivered at the fiftieth anniversary celebration of the IOC at Lausanne, 17 and 18 June 1944, p. 6. (The text was printed in advance, and the speech duly delivered as planned.)

6   Polignac, p. 13.

7   David C. Young, *The Olympic Myth of Greek Amateur Athletics*, Chicago, 1984, especially pp. 89–102. He refers to several works by Pleket, in particular 'Games, Prizes, Athletes and Ideology', in *Arena*, 1, 1976, pp. 49–89. For a reference to the harmless professionalism of trainers in ancient

times see Coubertin's *Mémoires Olympiques*, Lausanne, n.d., but 1931.

8 For this frequently quoted remark see, e.g., MacAloon's exhaustive study of Coubertin, *This Great Symbol: Pierre de Coubertin and the Origins of the Modern Olympic Games*, Chicago, 1981, p. 5. This brilliant work covers Coubertin's life and work, up to 1896, in great detail. For the origins of the remark see David C. Young, 'On the Source of the Olympic Credo', *Olympika*, III, 1994, pp. 17–25.

9 'Demander aux peuples de s'aimer les uns les autres n'est qu'une manière d'enfantillage. Leur demander de se respecter n'est point une utopie, mais pour se respecter il faut d'abord se connaître.' Quoted by Diem, p. 13.

10 'Les fumées de la guerre ont obscurci l'éclat de la flamme, mais elles n'ont pu étouffer le feu olympique . . . Le sens profond de cette cérémonie est d'affermir la certitude qu'a l'avenir également l'olympisme manifestera sa force conciliatrice, pour le bien de l'humanité.' *ibid.*, p. 1.

11 I owe this nice observation to Christopher Richardson, lately head of Classics at Cranleigh School.

12 'C'est à coup sur une abérration que de refuser a un ouvrier la qualité d'amateur et d'assimiler le travail manuel a un acte de professionalisme. La discordance est aigue entre cette législation vétuste et notre siècle democratique. *Textes Choisies*, II, p. 560. (Reprinted from *Revue de Paris*, 15 June 1894, pp. 170–84.)

13 Diem, p. 6. Coubertin refers to amateurism as 'cette admirable momie' in *Memoires Olympiques*, p. 12.

14 *Revue Olympique*, May 1909, pp. 67–8, reprinted in *Textes Choisies*, II, pp. 576–7.

15 For example, Don Anthony, 'One Hundred Years of Olympism in Shropshire', typescript, January 1990.

16 See the Princss Royal's foreword to Sam Mullins, *British Olympians: William Penny Brookes and the Wenlock Games*, London, 1986. The President of the International Olympic Committee (IOC), Juan Antonio Samaranch, paid tribute to Brookes in his speech at the IOC's Session at Birmingham in June 1991. *Olympic Review*, 285, July 1991, p. 308. In July 1990 the Princess Royal, in her capacity as President of the British Olympic Association, attended the Games held to mark the centenary of Coubertin's visit. In July 1994 Samaranch paid a visit to Much Wenlock and planted an oak.

17 Minute of 25 February 1850.

18 *The Shrewsbury Chronicle*, 23 November 1860.

19 Olympian Society, *Annual Report* for the year to 1 March 1871.

20 *The Shrewsbury Chronicle and Shropshire and Montgomeryshire Times*, 19 October 1877, Minute Book 2, p. 14. Cuttings and other documents are pasted into the Society's Minute Books, which are preserved at the Much Wenlock Corn Exchange.

21 *The Standard*, 30 September 1878, Minute Book 2, p. 28.

22 *National Physical Recreation*, March 1888, Minute Book 2, p. 135.

23 Peter Lovesey, *The Official Centenary History of the Amateur Athletic Association*, London, 1979, p. 17–21. See also David C. Young: *The Olympic Myth of Greek Amateur Athletics*, Chicago, 1984, and a series of his articles: 'The Origins of the Modern Olympics: a New Version', *International Journal* *of the History of Sport'*, 1987, pp. 271–300; 'Demetrios Vikelas: First President of the IOC', *International Journal of the History of Sport*, 1988, pp. 85–102; 'How Times Have Changed', in *Proceedings of the United States Olympic Academy*, XIII, 21–4 June 1989; 'Myths and Mist Surrounding the Revival of the Olympic Games: the Hidden Story', in Fernand Landry, Marc Landry and Magdeleine Yerles (eds), *Sport: the Third Millennium*, Les Presses de L'Université Laval, Sainte-Foy, 1991; 'A New History of the Modern Olympic Movement: Soutsos, Zappas, Brookes, Vikelas, and Coubertin', International Olympic Academy, *Proceedings*, May 1992.

24 *The Shrewsbury Chronicle and Shropshire and Montgomeryshire Times*, 28 September 1877.

25 *Ibid.*, 19 October 1877.

26 *Address* for the year 1880 to the committee of the Olympian Society, Minute Book 2, pp. 52–3.

27 Gennadius to Brookes, Minute Book 2, p. 59.

28 Original cutting from *Clio*, June 13/25 1881, at Minute Book 2, p. 65, and translation at p. 66.

29 Gennadius to Brookes, 23 June 1886, Minute Book 2, p. 138.

30 *Revue Athlétique*, I, 1, 23 January 1890. Minute Book 2, p. 144. Reprinted in *Textes Choisies*, II, pp. 78–84.

31 *Revue Athlétique*, I, 12, 25 December 1890, pp. 705–13, reprinted in *Textes Choisies*, pp. 78–84; *American Monthly Review of Reviews*, 1897, pp. 62–5.

32 Coubertin to Brookes, 20 July 1892, Minute Book 2, p. 206.

33 *Minutes* of meeting of the Olympian Society, 24 May 1894, Minute Book 2, p. 218.

34 *The Wellington Journal and Shrewsbury News*, 8 June 1895, Minute Book 2, p. 229.

35 Don Anthony, 'One Hundred Years . . .', p. 3.

36 Brookes to Coubertin, 13 June 1894.

37 Brookes to Thricoupis, 11 June 1894.

38 Brookes to Coubertin, 14 December 1895, IOC archives, Lausanne. Brookes, who died on 10 December 1895, misdated the letter. Internal evidence shows that he intended to write 1894.

39 Young, 'Myths and Mist'; also MacAloon, *This Great Symbol . . .*, p. 139 and Chapter 5, *passim*.

40 *Revue Athlétique*, 25 December 1890. Translation (cyclostyled) by Michael Gillions, sometime Head of Modern Languages at the William Brookes School, Much Wenlock.

41 In the preceding two paragraphs I have drawn especially on Young, *op. cit.*, and on M. I. Finley and H. W. Pleket *op. cit.* I am also most grateful to Dr Karel Wendl for sight of some unpublished notes on Zappas dated 12 January 1990. The details of the 1859 Games come from the English version of the day's programme, sent to Much Wenlock by Sir Thomas Wyse.

According to Finley and Pleket, Curtius had been tutor to the future Wilhelm I, who, with Friedrich Wilhelm IV, had been in the audience at the 1852 lecture. Two years later, when Wilhelm I came to the throne of the new united Germany, the Germans agreed to bear the cost of a full-scale Olympic excavation. From 1875 to 1881 much was discovered under Curtius's direction, and promptly published each year, so that people like Coubertin were able to follow the progress of the dig.

42 Young, pp. 28 and 71–2 for the view that Coubertin continued an existing tradition. According to Young, pp. 32–4, a few people had complained that some labouring men had competed in the 1870 Games, so that those of 1875 were reserved for educated youths only. They were universally judged a failure. For the 'equally disastrous' Games of 1889 see Young, pp. 40–3. See also Young's articles listed in note 23, especially 'Demetrios Vikelas'.

43 *Bulletin du Comité International des Jeux Olympiques*, 2, January 1895, p. 3.

44 See, for example, Young, *The Olympic Myth*, pp. 179–81.

45 *Mémoires Olympiques*, and Coubertin's speech to the 1893 Congress of USFSA, *Les Sports Athlétiques*, 4, 172, 13 July 1893, pp. 2–4, reprinted in *Textes Choisies*, II, pp. 99–103. For an account of the links between the 1894 Congress and the international peace movement, see Dietrich R. Quantz, 'Civic Pacifism and Sports-Based Internationalism: Framework for the Founding of the International Olympic Committee', *Olympika*, II, 1993, pp. 1–23. Quantz speculates that Coubertin put his aspirations for world peace into the Olympic context as a result of his visit to the USA.

46 *Bulletin*, 2, p. 4.

47 Coubertin, *Mémoires Olympiques*, pp. 13–15.

48 *Bulletin*, 1, July 1894, pp. 1–2.

49 Young, *The Olympic Myth*, p. 63. Young clears up the confusion between the circular of January 1894, in which Coubertin merely referred to the desirability of re-establishing the Games, and the definitive programme of the following May, which included the ninth and tenth Articles.

50 *Mémoires Olympiques*, p. 18. For a full account of the Congress see MacAloon, pp. 164–79.

51 *Bulletin*, 1, July 1894, p. 1 and *Mémoires Olympiques*, p. 13.

52 Young, 'Demetrios Vikelas'.

53 *Bulletin*, 1, p. 4 and *Mémoires Olympiques*, pp. 19–20. The reference to 'les forces juvéniles' is at p. 19. For the choice of Athens, see Young, 'The Origins of the Modern Olympics'.

54 *Bulletin*, 2, October 1894, p. 1 and *Mémoires Olympiques*, p. 21.

55 *Bulletin*, 3, January 1895, p. 2.

56 The fact that he made the speech is rather blandly recorded in *Bulletin*, 3, p. 2, with extracts at p. 4.

57 MacAloon, *This Great Symbol* . . ., p. 196 and, for a detailed account of the 1896 Games, his chapter 9. He confirms (p. 196) that the Olympic issue played an important, if indirect, part in Tricoupis's downfall.

58 Finley and Pleket, p. 5. MacAloon, pp. 244–6, makes the same point, but adds that the London *Times* gave the Games full coverage, in its foreign affairs pages, rather than in the sports section, and gave Coubertin full credit.

59 Diem, p. 8.

60 *Bulletin*, 3, pp. 1 and 2.

61 Except where otherwise indicated the preceding passage is based on

Coubertin's 'Une Compagne de Vingt-et-un Ans (1887–1908)', pp. 131–47. See also *Mémoires Olympiques*, pp. 28–42 and Gaston Meyer, 'Paris 1900', in Lord Killanin and John Rodda (eds), *The Olympic Games 1984*, London, 1983, p. 57.

62   Young, *The Olympic Myth*, p. 75. John Rodda gives this view qualified support, but adds that the 1906 Games turned out to be disappointing because many events were not contested. 'Athens 1906' in Killanin and Rodda (eds), *The Olympic Games 1984*, London, 1983, p. 67. It is noteworthy, as an indication that the Greeks had become reconciled to not being permanent hosts to the Games, that when Lord Desborough announced that the 1908 Games were to be held in London he was able to add that a message of good wishes had been received from the Greek Crown Prince. *The Daily Telegraph*, letter from Lord Desborough and editorial comment, 24 November 1906. (Cutting in Dr Brookes's scrapbook, inserted between items dating from 1864.)

63   Diem, p. 9.

64   The booklet is ponderously entitled *The Olympic Games in 776 BC to 1896 AD: the Olympic Games of 1896*, by The Baron de Coubertin, Timoleon I. Philemon, N. G. Politis and Charalambos Anninos. It was originally printed in 1896 in Greek and French by Charles Beck in Athens and H. Lesaudier in Paris and appeared in a facsimile edition, with an English translation, in 1966. Philemon's contribution is at pp. 111–20 and the quotation at p. 116 (English version).

65   Pierre de Coubertin, Introduction to the above, p. 110.

66   Young, 'Demetrios Vikelas'. Otto Szymiczek, 'Athens 1896' in Killanin and Rodda (eds), p. 54.

67   Finley and Pleket give slightly different figures, stating that there were ten sports, forty-two events and 285 participants and add that the gymnasts were the only athletes to compete as a team.

II

The primacy of politics in the Olympic movement

We have seen that without Baron de Coubertin's political instincts and skills the Olympic Games might not have been revived and that had not his self-esteem been as vulnerable as the next man's they might have remained perpetually in Athens. Since those far-off Games of 1896 almost every celebration of the Olympics has been fraught with politics. The Games of 1916, 1940 and 1944 were not held at all, and after the Second World War West Germany and Japan did not compete until 1952, when it was thought that the bitterness of mass destruction had sufficiently subsided.

The Olympic Games have not been alone in their political involvement, but their great public exposure has meant that the stakes have been higher and the need for circumspection correspondingly greater than in other sports organisations. Nevertheless, all sports have had to take a view on questions of international politics. In bridge (known as a 'mind sport' in some countries) where some sixty nations are represented in the world championships, the problem of how to deal with the enmity between Israel and numerous other countries has been solved by ensuring that nations which will not compete against Israel are drawn in separate qualifying pools, with the hope, fortunately always fulfilled, that two incompatible nations will not both qualify for the later stages.[1]

Just as it is not possible for sports people to abstract themselves from politics, so it is impossible to keep politicians out of sport if they can discern some advantage in making use of it. It would not, for example, have been reasonable to expect to persuade a politician like President Richard Nixon, or groups of private individuals like SANROC (the South African Non-Racial Olympic Committee) not to use sport as a political instrument. The battle against apartheid was strengthened by the well-judged campaign of SANROC to force international sports federations to expel South Africa and it would have been pointless to have asked SANROC not to use the sporting weapon which lay to hand. Some teams made the decision, no less political, to go ahead with tours of South Africa despite their governments' advice. The fact that governments had to give such advice (most famously in the shape of the statement made in 1977 by Commonwealth Heads of Government, known as the Gleneagles Declaration), when many of them would no doubt have much preferred to 'keep sport out of politics' demonstrates how powerful were the forces tapped by SANROC.

Sport may look like a continuation of war by other means but, as a leading sports administrator, Sir Arthur Gold (who has experienced both sport and war), has wisely said, it is not difficult to decide which of the two one prefers.[2] However, some sports people go so far as to argue that sport actually promotes peace. If this is taken to mean that athletic competition promotes a camaraderie which inhibits hostility, there is not much evidence to support it in top level sport, and some against. High level sport is now so closely linked with large sums of hard cash that there is little room for friendship, and investigation of the idea that interaction on the sports field produces friendly feelings has shown that the thesis is by no means necessarily true, at any level. One author goes so far as to describe the relations between Olympic athletes as 'an incidental by-product of these quadrennial political festivals where athletic events happen to take place'.[3]

On the other hand, it is clearly true that sporting contacts are from time to time used by governments as the prelude to contact at a more formal level. One has only to remember President Richard Nixon's 'ping-pong diplomacy' which paved the way for his visit to China in 1972 and for the opening of diplomatic relations between the United States and China on 1 January 1978, or the new willingness of the two Koreas to speak to each other after the Seoul Olympics of 1988.

The Olympic Games may be an effective way of bringing the youth of the world together, though if that were their sole aim it could be far better achieved by spending a fraction of their cost on scholarships. However, nearly every celebration of the Games has been marked by acrimony or worse and the recollections of contretemps or disaster long outlive the warm glow of competitive interaction. A catalogue would be tedious, but it is worth remembering that other Games than those held in Berlin in 1936 have provoked international outrage. For example, 1968 saw a massacre by the Mexican government of young people who thought the Games a waste of money. Israeli athletes were murdered by Palestinians at the Munich Games of 1972, when the outgoing President of the International Olympic Committee, Avery Brundage, decided that 'The Games must go on'. In 1976 numerous African states boycotted the Games in protest against a rugby tour of South Africa undertaken by a New Zealand side. The protesters demanded that the IOC should bar New Zealand from the Games, which it of course had no reason to do, since rugby was not even an Olympic sport.[4]

The IOC has not sought political involvement, but has had it thrust upon it. South Africa's suspension from the movement (its last appearance at the Games before Barcelona, 1992, was at Rome in 1960) is probably the issue known to the widest public, but in their time the problems of the two Chinas and the two Germanies, both now settled, caused as much anguish. Such issues as whether Rhodesia should continue to be recognised by the IOC after its rebellion in 1965, or whether the IOC should recognise NOCs from both North and South Korea, attracted rather less public attention, but were no less difficult to solve.

The IOC's conduct of policy has generally been consistent, statesmanlike and above all slow. It believes that political questions must be settled by politicians, so that its leaders frequently protest against the use made by politicians of sport, while themselves being obliged to act politically. Its overall objective has been to preserve the movement's universality, if necessary by postponing choice. In those terms, South Africa's expulsion was a failure of Olympic diplomacy; the two Chinas were a qualified success because in the end both the mainland and Taiwan remained in the movement (after a long period of withdrawal by the mainland) and the two Germanies an unqualified success, because both parts of the country, once admitted, were kept in the movement through thick and thin.

The remainder of this chapter develops further the account of the questions of the two Germanies and the two Chinas, as examples of the Olympic movement's involvement in international politics since the Second World War. South Africa is discussed in a later chapter: it represented an international political problem of a different kind, although it, too, had some 'Cold War' aspects.

The two Germanies

In 1950 the International Olympic Committee provisionally recognised the West German Olympic Committee. It seems likely that the IOC was influenced by a letter written to Lord Burghley by the British High Commissioner a few days earlier, in which he expressed the most earnest hope that the new Federal Republic of Germany might be allowed to compete in the Helsinki Games of 1952. The provisional recognition given in 1950 did not, however, commit the IOC to allow West German participation at Helsinki: that decision was to be taken a year later at Vienna.[5]

At the Vienna Session (which was also memorable for the introduction of the Soviet member, Constantin Andrianov, and with him the first interpreter), the West German NOC received full recognition, but there was considerable debate about whether it was a new body, or whether it had continued to exist through the war. The main point of the debate was to decide whether the pre-war German IOC members should be allowed to remain in office, or whether new ones should be elected to symbolise Germany's break with the past. One of them, the Duke of Mecklenburg, solved the problem by retiring because of age, so that discussion focused on Dr Karl Ritter von Halt. No one attacked him personally, but there was lively feeling that a new member was needed. One argument used was that such a move would convince the athletes that a new spirit was abroad. On the other hand, the IOC's establishment was strongly in favour of von Halt. The American Avery Brundage, the IOC's President 1952–72, described him as a perfect gentleman, with whom he had taken part in the Stockholm Games of 1912, and J. Sigfrid Edstrom, the IOC's President, refused to put the question to the vote, simply declaring that von Halt remained a member. Protests led him to defer a final decision until after the discussion of East Germany's status, but he got his way, and von Halt (who had been elected in 1929) remained a member until 1964.[6]

The question of the East German NOC had only impinged upon the IOC when separate East German federations sought international affiliation. The Executive Board of the IOC had sent out a circular to international federations (IFs) in 1949 recommending the re-recognition of German and Japanese federations, but the recommendation provoked unease at the Session in Copenhagen in the following year, because it did not reflect the general feeling of the IOC membership.[7] It appears that the IOC then urged the international federations to delay their decisions until it could consider the German question in full session at Vienna in May 1951.[8] At Vienna the discussion of whether or not the East German NOC should be recognised was lively. Some members argued that the basis of the Olympic Charter was its duty to bring the youth of the world together and that they should assist the two Germanies to reunite. The IOC was not, after all, one member said, discussing the recognition of a state, but of an NOC. However, another said that NOCs could not be recognised unless they were based in 'regular' states. The Soviet Union naturally wanted an independent NOC for its satellite and Andrianov, although a new member, took a full part in the discussion, arguing that both Germanies must be equally treated, but other members thought that to recognise two German NOCs would be to entrench the division between them – and by implication between the two Germanies.

Edstrom announced after long debate that East German representatives were waiting in the next room (it is not clear whether the generality of members were expecting them, or whether Edstrom was indulging in a theatrical gesture) and after an interval it was announced that the IOC's Executive Board and representatives of both Germanies were to meet at Lausanne a fortnight later.[9] Agreement was reached at Lausanne that a united German team would be formed, but was immediately repudiated by the East Germans.[10]

A richly farcical second attempt was made at Copenhagen, in the hope that East Germany would be able to compete in the Helsinki Games of 1952. Edstrom, Brundage and Otto Mayer, the Chancellor of the IOC (the title was later changed to Executive Director, although Monique Berlioux, who held the office from 1969 to 1985, described herself as Director-General) made a special visit to Copenhagen, where they and the West Germans arrived punctually for a morning meeting. However, the East German delegation, which was known to have been in Copenhagen at least since 2 p.m., did not respond to several telephone calls, so that at 6 p.m. the IOC and West Germans left in an extremely disgruntled state, and naturally found it difficult to take the East Germans seriously in future. In the absence of any agreement it was, of course, not possible for them to compete at Helsinki. It appears that the East Germans arrived late in Copenhagen because they had had to travel via Prague, but were prevented from keeping their appointment less by exhaustion than by fear of their government, although in that case it is not clear why they ever undertook the journey at all.[11]

One of the most important discussions of the German question was held at the IOC's session at the time of the Helsinki Games. Several members spoke in favour of recognising East Germany's NOC, and Edstrom recalled the precedents of Bohemia, whose NOC had been recognised although the territory had been an integral part of the Austro-Hungarian Empire, and of Finland, which had been self-governing but annexed to Russia.[12] Brundage was, as one might expect after his experience at Copenhagen, extremely opposed to the East German Olympic authorities, whom he described as irresponsible, and von Halt recounted that all efforts to reach an accommodation with the East had failed. Every possible concession had been made, including allowing the East's team to have its own team managers, umpires, uniform, and separate lodgings, but they had refused to parade with the West.

Von Halt also had no objection to international federations affiliating local East German branches and indeed some had already done so, although most were waiting on a decision by the IOC.[13] Thus the IOC was in a dilemma, for if it delayed a decision the IFs might be pushed into going ahead without it, thereby weakening the IOC's authority. Yet it would not have been unreasonable for IFs to go ahead without waiting for the IOC, for some of them must have feared that their own authority would be weakened if they delayed recognition and thereby encouraged states to sponsor athletes directly, without reference to the appropriate IF. Once provisional recognition had been granted to East Germany's NOC, many international federations did follow the IOC's lead. For example, Burghley, who was both President of the International Amateur Athletic Federation (IAAF) and a member of the IOC, persuaded the East and West Germans into a single athletics federation, but with two addresses. But, as with the two Chinas, not all international federations followed suit, because the call from the IOC for co-operation was seen by some of the international federations as a threat.[14]

So disillusioned was Brundage with the East Germans that he asked Andrianov to negotiate with them on the IOC's behalf.[15] At the next session, held at Athens in May 1954, Brundage referred to the torrent of abuse hurled at the IOC in the East German press, but Andrianov was able to report that the East German NOC, although unrecognised, was functioning normally and that it would be wrong for the IOC to deprive East German youth of the possibility of Olympic sport, or to keep East Germany out of the 1956 Games. He added that the President of the East German NOC had wished to attend in person to present his apologies for the bad press coverage, but had been unable to obtain a visa to travel to Athens.

Von Halt reminded his colleagues of his deep commitment to a united German team, but thought that the IOC must be bound by the principle that NOCs are independent and autonomous, and considered the East German NOC a striking example of the opposite. Von Halt himself did not feel that he could resume negotiations after the attacks to which he had been subjected, including faked photographs (of what he does not say). The East German NOC was refused recognition by 31 votes to 13.[16]

At Paris in 1955, the year in which the Soviet Union released East Germany from its status as the Soviet Zone of Germany and recognised it as a sovereign state, the East German NOC was provisionally recognised, but only on condition that it co-operated in forming the single team on which the IOC insisted. Brundage reviewed the history of the IOC's unhappy relationship with East Germany. He had told its representatives that he did not think the IOC would wish to deal again with the individuals who had repudiated the Lausanne agreement, but that it might reopen the question if the NOC were reorganised and represented by more responsible delegates.

A few days earlier the NOC had duly been re-formed and a meeting had been held at which Brundage had said that he would recommend provisional recognition once a united team had been formed to compete at the Melbourne Games of the following year. The East Germans, however, had said that in view of their definite promise to co-operate with West Germany they expected immediate recognition. It was agreed by 27 votes to 7 to grant provisional recognition 'on the understanding that, should it prove impossible to form a united team from both Germanies for the Melbourne Games this recognition will lapse automatically. It is understood that after the reunification of Germany, the IOC will recognise one German Olympic Committee, standing for the whole of Germany.'[17] It would have been difficult for the IOC to grant recognition on any other terms, given that the West German response to the Soviet Union's recognition of East Germany had been to enunciate what came to be known as the Hallstein Doctrine, whereby West Germany refused to maintain or to enter into diplomatic relations with any country that recognised East Germany.

So successful were negotiations between the two Germanies that they were able, against all expectations, to enter a joint team for the winter Games at Cortina d'Ampezzo as well as for Melbourne later in the year. The athletes were to share flag, emblem, uniform and lodgings; the head of the contingent was to be drawn from the larger team, and the best athletes were to be chosen from both sides (it sounds, therefore, as if the trials themselves were not mixed). Brundage enthused 'We have obtained in the field of sport what politicians have failed to achieve so far.' He was, however, displeased by East German newspaper articles warning their athletes not to lose sight of the political question.[18]

The provisional recognition of East Germany continued and the Germans competed as a joint team at Rome in 1960 and Tokyo in 1964. There were many difficulties. In 1962, as a consequence of the erection of the Berlin Wall in the same year, both the French and the Americans refused visas to East Germans for world championships. The IOC's response was to point out that French, American and Canadian cities were bidding for the Games of 1968, and to threaten to reject them if their governments did not mend their behaviour. East Germany continued to ask for separate recognition, though with assurances that if it were not granted it would still compete on the current terms. NATO wished the joint team to continue, but the West Germans were also beginning to want a separate team of their own.[19]

When the question, having been deferred from Tokyo, was discussed at Madrid in 1965, the President said that complete recognition of the East German NOC would imply two separate teams being entered for the winter and summer Games of 1968 at Grenoble and Mexico City. The latter presented no problem, but he believed that for Grenoble NATO would refuse visas to East Germans. Thus, if Grenoble were unable to receive the East Germans it would be necessary to hold the winter Games elsewhere. The French Prime Minister Georges Pompidou had agreed that, if the Games were granted to Grenoble, the French Government would 'grant entry to all teams under existing conditions'. The IOC had interpreted this to mean 'in accordance with IOC rules', but the French were now saying that they had intended a united German team as before. However they relented and allowed entry to a separate East German team using Olympic identity cards.

A further cause of urgency was that, now that political reunification of the two Germanies was barely on the cards, twenty out of twenty-four international federations were demanding separate teams for

1968. Indeed, as Guttmann records, the IAAF had played an impor-
tant part in undermining the agreements that there should be a joint
German team by recognising a fully independent East Germany in
1964 and allowing separate teams to compete in the European
Championships in 1966. A vote was taken, and the IOC agreed by a
very large majority, with only five dissenting votes, that as East
Germany would no longer accept a joint team 'the West German
Olympic Committee will revert to affiliation for Germany and the East
German Olympic Committee is fully affiliated for the geographical
area of East Germany'. (This use of the term 'geographical area' –
sometimes the word 'territory' is used – neatly avoids commitment as
to the legal status of East Germany.) At Grenoble and Mexico City
there would be separate teams, marching under the same banner, with
the same anthem and emblems. A new affiliation for Berlin would not
be considered. East Berlin was included in East Germany and West
Berlin in West Germany.

The German question was laid to rest at the Mexico City session of
the IOC in 1968, when it was agreed that the name by which East
Germany referred to itself, the German Democratic Republic, would
be adopted in Olympic parlance. Its team made its first appearance at
Munich in 1972, and thereafter, as Riordan says, 'This sporting
autonomy and success led to mounting recognition of the GDR (German Democratic Republic) throughout the world'. Guttmann comments on how triumphant the Munich team must have felt:

When in 1972 the East Germans marched into the Olympisches Stadion in
Munich, they 'achieved their ultimate objective'; they quite literally flaunted
their flag before their hosts from the Federal Republic, who had publicly to
acknowledge East German legitimacy as well as East German athletic
prowess. For Brundage, however, it was a defeat, a reminder of the frailty of
Olympic ideals and of their inability to dam the tides of *Realpolitik*.[20]

Lessons of the German question

The IOC felt able to take a strong line with East Germany for many
years. The forces that persuaded it to abandon its insistence on a joint
team for the two Germanies were in part internal to the movement and
in part external. Internally, the international federations' interest lay
in affiliating East German federations, and as time went on they
increasingly did so. The IOC was therefore faced with its usual
problem: if it gave a lead it might act precipitately and be accused of

acting in too overtly political a manner; if it delayed indefinitely, the IFs might take decisions without waiting for the IOC, thereby undermining its authority within the world of sport.

Externally, the IOC was strongly influenced by the prevailing belief that it would not be long before Germany was reunited. This gradually became an unlikely outcome, partly because East Germany had made such effective use of sport as a means to establish a separate national identity in the eyes of the world. The West German Government had also abandoned the Hallstein Doctrine and even given up, at least in the short term, the objective of reunification in favour of an Ostpolitik which normalised relations with the whole of eastern Europe. The process culminated in an exchange of letters in November 1972 recording the two Germanies' intention to co-ordinate their requests for membership of the United Nations, followed in December by a 'Treaty on the Basis of Relations between the Federal Republic of Germany and the German Democratic Republic'. It is true that the treaty was accompanied by a letter from West Germany stating that 'this Treaty does not conflict with the political aim of the Federal Republic of Germany to work for a state of peace in Europe in which the German nation will regain its unity through free self-determination', but this can at the time have hardly been seen as more than a prudent reservation without much real force. The Treaty led in March 1974 to a protocol by which the two states agreed to exchange 'Permanent Representations'. These, although not called embassies, were more or less indistinguishable from them.[21]

Once the policy of normalisation had been firmly established, there was no point in the IOC's continuing to press for a joint German team at the Olympic Games, or to stick to its routine proviso that agreements made would automatically lapse once Germany was reunited. Indeed to do so would have been to blow futilely against the wind of politics. Instead the IOC made prudent use, as it did in the Chinese case, of the distinction that it had invented between a 'territory' and a country.

But in the long run both the IOC and the West German government have been proved right, for Germany was reunited in 1989 with startling suddenness.

The two Chinas

The first Chinese IOC member was elected as long ago as 1922, and the IOC thereby recognised the Chinese NOC.[22] In 1932 China sent one athlete to the Los Angeles Games, but at the Berlin Games of 1936 they had fifty-four participants in seven sports. In 1948 at London they managed twenty-six, in five sports.

General Chiang Kai-shek was a signatory of the Charter of the United Nations in 1947 and China received one of the permanent seats on the Security Council. At that stage Taiwan was no more than a province of China, which is the status still officially accorded to it by Beijing, and there was no question of its having any independent existence as a state. After the war between nationalists and communists most (or at least some: the accounts vary) of the NOC fled to Taiwan in 1951 and continued to be recognised. According to Brundage it had simply changed its address, and the change had been duly registered.[23] However Killanin (who was to become President of the IOC in 1972, after the Munich Games) states that there is no trace at Lausanne of the change ever having been recorded.[24] Meanwhile, in the Cold War the USA and its allies and the United Nations recognised what we now call Taiwan as the 'Real China' and went along with its claim to sovereignty over the whole of China, although that is not unlike recognising the 'government' of the Isle of Wight as having jurisdiction over the whole of Great Britain. Of course the Soviets and their satellites recognised the mainland, which adopted the name 'People's Republic of China' (PRC).

On the Olympic front nothing was heard at Lausanne for some years after the Second World War. But in 1952 the President (Edstrom) told the IOC Session that the mainland's All-China Athletic Committee had informed him that it supervised all sport in China and functioned as an NOC, and that he had told the committee how to proceed in order to be recognised. The Taiwanese were also signalling their interest in the Olympics, for Erik von Frenckell (the IOC member in Finland) said that he had recently been told by the Chinese (i.e. Taiwanese) Minister in Helsinki of his surprise that the Chinese Olympic Committee had not been invited to the forthcoming Games, which were to be held in Helsinki later in the year.[25] Brundage thought the first step should be to establish contact with the Chinese members, one of whom lived in New York and the others in Hong Kong and Shanghai.[26]

Since both Chinas had said that they intended to send athletes to the 1952 Games at Helsinki, the Helsinki Session was faced with an awkward decision. On the one hand there was the rule of only one NOC per country, and Taiwan (often referred to as Formosa) was already recognised; on the other, if there were two distinct governments in China, should not both their territories be allowed to participate in the Games? Twenty-two members voted for no Chinese team being invited to Helsinki, and twenty-nine for both, for those events for which they were recognised by federations. Brundage acknowledged that the IOC was breaking its own rules by allowing participation by a territory without an NOC, but argued that the circumstances were exceptional.[27] Much time and eloquence were expended, but in the event the discussion had been a farcical waste of energy. Only one athlete from the PRC presented himself at Helsinki, and none from Taiwan, which withdrew in protest once it had learned of the resolution to admit the PRC despite its lack of an NOC.[28]

In 1954 the IOC at last recognised the NOC of the People's Republic, while maintaining its recognition of Taiwan's. The Beijing committee was known as the 'Olympic Committee of the Chinese Republic', changed in 1957 to 'Olympic Committee of the People's Democratic Republic of China' and Taiwan retained the title 'Chinese Olympic Committee'. Since the rules stated that there could be only one NOC per country, the IOC might be thought to have been implying recognition of two countries by recognising two NOCs, but it got over the difficulty (as it did later in the case of the two Germanies) by introducing the idea of recognising territories under the control of an NOC, rather than insisting that an NOC have a nation behind it.

At the beginning of 1956 the third Chinese IOC member, Shou Ti-tung, who had been elected in 1947 and who supported the Beijing government, asked that the Taiwan Olympic Committee be erased from the list of NOCs. This proposal got short shrift from the President, Avery Brundage, who said that it was out of the question to exclude Taiwan on political grounds. Later in the year the PRC withdrew from the Melbourne Games in protest at Taiwan's continuing membership and in 1958 it withdrew from the Olympic movement and from all international federations. Shou Ti-tung resigned from the IOC with an abusive letter dubbing Brundage 'a faithful menial of US imperialists'. (The Taiwanese members remained in office until the mid-1950s.) That summer the PRC bombarded Quemoy and Matsu and the United States despatched reinforcements to Taiwan.[29] Thereafter the PRC was lost in the throes of the Great Leap Forward and the Cultural Revolution, and played no part in Olympic affairs for some years.

Of course the communist bloc IOC members wanted Taiwan expelled and the PRC reinstated. In 1959 the IOC agreed that the Taiwan committee could not continue under its present name, since it did not administer sport on the mainland. It would therefore be struck off the register under that name, though if it chose to reapply for admission under another the application would be considered.[30] This decision was generally misunderstood by the press, which thought Taiwan had been expelled, with the result that there was uproar in the USA.

In 1960 it was reported to the IOC that the Taiwanese NOC had proposed that, as it was recognised by the United Nations as the Republic of China, its NOC should be known as the Olympic Committee of the Republic of China. This was accepted for the future, but the Taiwanese were told that at the Rome Games they must compete as Taiwan (Formosa).[31] The team duly carried a name board 'Formosa' during the opening parade, but displayed a placard 'under protest'.[32] In 1968 the name 'Olympic Committee of the Republic of China' was reaffirmed by the IOC.

The PRC's return to the fold

In 1971 the United Nations recognised the PRC and expelled Taiwan, giving Taiwan's seat on the Security Council to the PRC. In 1972 President Nixon visited China, the way having been prepared by the 'ping-pong diplomacy' mentioned earlier – an officially blessed visit by an American table tennis team.

Events in the Olympic world marched in tandem. In 1971 the IOC resolved that the PRC would be welcome back if it respected Olympic rules, although it also laid down that Formosa would not be excluded. The mainland Chinese began to rejoin international federations, in order to build up to the five required for Olympic eligibility, a policy which posed problems for federations of which Taiwan was a member. If they decided to make the major shift in policy involved in recognising the PRC they risked endless squabbles between the two Chinas. If they did not, they would cut themselves off from competition with the mainland.

The dilemma was particularly difficult for federations which had a rule against competition with non-members, as was well illustrated in 1973, when the American State Department wanted to sponsor ten swimmers to go to the PRC. But the Amateur Athletic Union, which governed swimming in the United States, was a member of FINA (the international swimming federation), which did not recognise the PRC, and did not allow competition against non-members. The result was that if the swimmers had competed against the Chinese the AAU would have had to suspend them or itself be suspended from FINA and in that case no US swimmer would have been able to take part in any international event. The Senate, which was already holding hearings on American sport, asked FINA to make an exception, which it could not do. In the end the storm in a teacup had been for nothing: the ten swimmers had nothing to lose because they had already decided to end their swimming careers, and so were able to carry out the visit to China.

The Chinese question was much discussed at the Varna Congress of the Olympic movement in 1973, the first since 1930. In October 1973 the Asian Games Federation voted to admit the PRC to the Tehran Asian Games and to expel Taiwan. This was proposed by Japan and Iran. Thereupon some international federations said they would withdraw from the Asian Games if the PRC were admitted at the expense of Taiwan. After the Varna Congress the IOC warned the Asian Games Federation that it risked the loss of IOC patronage if it expelled Taiwan, but the IOC did not in fact withdraw its patronage because it wanted to develop sport in Asia, and many international federations agreed with Taiwan's expulsion.[33] It may seem illogical, as Geoffrey Miller comments, for the IOC not to have withdrawn its recognition, but the decision has to be seen in the context of Killanin's conviction that by one means or another China must be brought back into the Olympics. Killanin records that he even arranged for Chinese representatives at the Asian Games to attend an Olympic seminar, a gesture of acceptance which he believes they understood.[34]

Killanin also reveals that discreet contacts had been maintained with the mainland behind Brundage's back all through the 1960s. Eventually Brundage got wind of them, and responded in 1970 by forcing the election to the IOC of a Taiwanese member, Henry Hsu, in the same year. This he did by falsely informing the session that Hsu's election had been recommended by the Executive Board. However, even if the election had gone to a vote the wily Brundage would have won, since he had a majority of the IOC members behind him.[35]

By April 1975 the PRC was in membership of the required number of international federations, and applied for IOC membership, stipulating however that it would join only if Taiwan were expelled. The strength of its political case lay in its now being the Chinese member of the United Nations, although the IOC was naturally reluctant to admit that a sporting decision should be governed by political arguments. The immediate decision to be made was whether the PRC should be allowed to participate in the 1976 Games at Montreal. There was considerable discussion at the session in May 1975, when Alexandru Siperco, the Romanian member, proposed that Beijing's NOC be recognised as the sole representative of China; that the recognition of Taiwan be withdrawn and that the mainland be assisted to frame its statutes in a form acceptable to the IOC in time for the 1976 Games. Dr Hsu pointed out (incorrectly, since the USSR had done the same) that it was unprecedented for an applicant to attach conditions to its application; that the Taiwanese government was recognised by many states, including the USA, as the government of China and that it was clear that the mainland did not control sport in Taiwan. In any case, he demanded to know, how could the IOC expel an NOC which it had recognised for fifteen years?[36] In the same month, at the IOC's meeting with the NOCs, forty-two delegates spoke. Twenty-five favoured dual membership; seventeen wanted Taiwan to be expelled and there were vitriolic Chinese attacks on Brundage and the IOC.[37]

The Montreal crisis

No immediate decision was taken. Killanin announced his intention to visit both Taiwan and the PRC, but the situation was raised to new heights of crisis by the Canadian government. Canada had adopted a one-China policy in 1970 and recognised the PRC as the sole representative of all Chinese. It would not accede to the Chinese request to refuse entry to the Taiwanese team, but did say that the word 'China' must not appear in its name, and that it might not use its flag or anthem. At the Montreal Session, where the Chinese question occupied the IOC for days (they seem to have spent far more time on it than on the African boycott), there was considerable indignation.

Killanin had first to apologise to the assembled members for the late circulation of information, which had been delayed because fifty activists demanding the independence of the Jura had occupied the headquarters at Lausanne and removed the Director and staff from the premises. Having got this embarrassing explanation over he pointed out that the Canadians were in breach of the undertaking given in 1970, when they had been awarded the Games, that no recognised member country would be denied entrance. He had had no inkling of their intention to refuse entry to the Taiwanese team until 28 May. James Worrall, the senior Canadian member, was mortified by his government's attitude, and said that he and the Canadian NOC would never have supported Montreal's candidature if they had known that their government would behave as it had.

Some members of the IOC argued strongly that the Games should be cancelled, but it was eventually decided to go ahead with them, by 57 votes, with 9 abstentions. Some thought the Games should be moved to the United States or Mexico, which was considered impracticable, or held without the Olympic label, which it was thought would weaken the IOC's control. It was also suggested that the opportunity should be taken to stop the practice of marching under national flags and to invite all NOCs to use the Olympic flag instead, but this idea, which if pursued would have represented a major step back towards the traditionalists' conception of the Games, made no progress once it became clear that at least some NOCs would reject it: indeed, Killanin thought that it would give NOCs an excuse not to participate in the Games.[38]

The Canadian decision was very unpopular in the United States. Ronald Reagan and President Ford intervened, with an eye to the Presidential race, in Ford's case very possibly producing the opposite effect to that which he had intended by strengthening the Canadian Government's resolve. According to Killanin the United States Olympic Committee had been instructed to follow its government's policy and withdraw from the Games if Taiwan did not compete, and such a withdrawal would have invalidated the television contract. It is not clear why Killanin should have thought that the United States government was in a position to instruct USOC, but the American member, Julian Roosevelt, did say that if the United States team were to go home it would be difficult to keep the US government out of USOC's administration in future.

The Taiwanese refused the IOC's offer to permit it to march in the opening parade as Taiwan – Republic of China, under the Olympic flag, and threatened to withdraw, which made the IOC fear that others might follow their example. However, after Killanin had negotiated with the Canadian government the latter agreed that Taiwan might retain its own flag and anthem, provided its team paraded as 'Taiwan'. This was a breakthrough, and Killanin believed that Taiwan should have accepted the compromise. However it refused and the Canadians would not allow the counter-compromise proposed by Taiwan that they parade as 'Republic of China – Taiwan'. By 11 July all efforts had been exhausted: the Executive Board of the IOC gave in and said it would propose to the full IOC that Taiwan should compete as 'Taiwan' under the Olympic banner and the IOC approved the Executive Board's recommendation by 58 to 2, with 6 abstentions.[39]

The Canadian government remained unrepentant in the face of uproar in the United States and general disapproval throughout the Olympic movement. It insisted that it had given plenty of warning of its intention to exclude the Taiwanese. Its policy had been adopted in 1970, and it had refused to allow Taiwan to attend the World Cycling Championships of 1974 and the pre-Olympic boxing, both at Montreal. One charge was that the Chinese had threatened to go elsewhere for their wheat. The government flatly denied this (and Killanin accepts that the charge was mistaken) and said that in any case Canada supplied only 1.5 per cent of the PRC's wheat.

Espy comments that the IOC should have known that there would be trouble in store at Montreal. 'To be unaware of Canada's consistent policies, or to believe that the IOC was somehow invincible and supranational, showed serious lack of political acumen.' Yet the Canadian action over something so trivial as a name destroyed everything the athletes had worked for.[40]

In fact the Taiwan team solved everything by packing its bags and going home the day before the Games.

Solutions

The solution was only temporary. In 1977, by now determined to settle the Chinese question before it could pose any threat to the Moscow Games, Killanin paid his delayed visit to China (but put off his visit to Taiwan until after a crucial Session at Montevideo in April 1979). In 1978 three members of the IOC (Lance Cross of New Zealand, Roy Bridge of Jamaica and the Romanian, Alexandru Siperco) followed, although Siperco went only to the PRC. According to Killanin his government had forbidden him to visit Taiwan.[41]

Juan Antonio Samaranch, who succeeded Killanin in 1980, made his first major appearance in the saga in 1978, when he reported at Athens on his own recent visit to the PRC and said that the IOC must do everything in its power to allow the PRC to be recognised. As a first step the NOC of the Republic of China should be asked to change its name. The Marquess of Exeter (formerly Lord Burghley), who, having been President of the International Amateur Athletic Foundation from 1946 to 1976, was well versed in the China question, agreed that only one of the Chinas could be called 'China', but pointed out that there were precedents for dependent territories having their own NOCs, such as the American Virgin Islands and Puerto Rico. Dr Hsu made a significant, though little remarked, concession by observing that both parts of the divided country were entitled to recognition.[42] However much his government was still insisting on all or nothing, he at least was prepared to recognise reality.

At Montevideo Killanin reported that he had visited China without much success and Cross reported on his team's visit to China and Taiwan, giving five reasons why he could not support the recognition of a single NOC for the two Chinas. One of the difficulties at Montevideo was that the IOC could not get Taiwan and China together round the same table. Taiwan caused the difficulty, in a way reasonably, since its delegation insisted that its purpose in coming to Montevideo had been to consult the President of the IOC. However, Killanin subjected the delegation to quite harsh questioning, implying that the Taiwanese were playing politics with what should have been a solely Olympic question. This was of course true, although Killanin also understood perfectly well that the PRC was making political capital from the whole issue, and was not really so naive as to believe that a question so fraught with politics could be kept on a 'purely Olympic' level.

Nevertheless, at Montevideo some signs of compromise began to appear, possibly in response to João Havelange's remark that it would be to the glory of the Olympic movement if there could be two Chinese IOC members, one from the PRC and one from Taiwan. Mr Ho, for the mainland, made the crucial point that the PRC would only accept the title 'Chinese Olympic Committee' for itself, but would accept 'Chinese Taiwan Olympic Committee' for Taiwan, with the proviso that the Taiwanese committee would be regarded as a local body with delegated powers, and that the compromise would be temporary. Frantisek Kroutil of Czechoslovakia referred to the opposition of both

Austria and Hungry in 1912 to Bohemian participation in the Games, which had been solved by the Bohemian team marching at a distance behind the Austrian team, and with its own flag. Perhaps the two Chinas could do something similar? The observation was pertinent (if somewhat esoteric), since this was the first time that the PRC had shown any willingness to allow Taiwan's NOC to include the word 'China' in its title. Beside that change of position, all talk of delegated powers and temporary measures was mere face-saving.

Killanin persuaded the Executive Board to accept a resolution, which proposed to 'reintegrate' the Chinese Olympic Committee and to 'maintain recognition of the Olympic Committee whose headquarters are located in Taipeh'. All matters pertaining to name, anthem and flag were to be the subjects of further study. When this resolution was presented to the full IOC it was (no doubt to Killanin's considerable annoyance) amended from the floor, so that the motion finally carried at Montevideo, by 36 votes to 30, recognised the Chinese Olympic Committee located in Beijing and maintained recognition of the Chinese Olympic Committee located in Taipeh. Thus, both bodies were to be permitted to describe themselves as Chinese. The Executive Board was authorised to solve the problems associated with names, anthems, flags and constitutions.[43]

The matter was remitted to the next meeting of the Executive Board, which met at Nagoya in October 1979. Killanin, who had at last visited Taiwan on his way to Nagoya, was by now thoroughly tired of the Taiwanese manoeuvrings, and considered that 'the course ahead was to get China back in and let Taipei remain members, if they wished, on our terms'.[44] After the Nagoya meeting a postal vote was taken on a resolution that the PRC's NOC be recognised as the Chinese Olympic Committee, with the PRC's flag and anthem. The emblem and statutes had been approved. Taiwan's NOC was to be known as the Chinese Taipeh Olympic committee (as it still is), with a different anthem, flag and emblem from those then in use. They were to be approved by the Executive Board by 1 January 1980 and its statutes submitted by the same date.

The ballot paper was sent to all 89 members, and brought 81 responses: 62 in favour; 17 against and two spoiled papers. In his memorandum accompanying the ballot papers Killanin urged members to forget the various political pressures which had been brought upon them. In this he showed some inconsistency, since in the preceding paragraph of his memorandum he had reminded them that

Avery Brundage had used the argument that the government in Taiwan, and not that in Beijing, was recognised by the United Nations. The situation was now, Killanin said, reversed, and he asked members to bear in mind the precedent created by his predecessor.[45] In April 1981 it was reported that the name, flag and emblem of the Chinese Taipeh Olympic Committee had been approved.[46]

The international federations and China: the example of the IAAF

The problems faced by the international federations in their dealings with the two Chinas were exactly similar to those of the IOC. For example, the IAAF, the most important of the international federations (though football might dispute the title), had been aware of the problem for years, and had in part got over it by allowing member federations to take part in competitions where the non-member PRC was taking part. In 1976 the IAAF had sent an angry telegram in support of Taiwan's participation in the Montreal Olympics, in which it affirmed that 'Our member is recognised as the sole governing body for athletics in the country or territory'.[47]

The question became active in 1978, the year in which the political wind changed decisively when the United States dropped its recognition of Taiwan and switched to the PRC. By then nine IFs recognised the PRC and sixteen were still loyal to Taiwan.[48] Some IFs were torn apart over the issue, for example the cyclists, whose woman President had accepted a personal invitation to Taiwan. The IAAF had recognised the PRC in 1954 and Taiwan in 1956, whereupon the PRC had resigned. The decision facing the IAAF in 1978 was whether to admit the PRC to full membership, at the price of expelling Taiwan. The federation was naturally reluctant to expel a member which had been in good standing, first as Taiwan and since 1970 as the Republic of China, ever since 1956. On the other hand China was still adhering to its policy of not belonging to any international federations of which Taiwan was a member, and the IAAF did not want to cut itself off from the athletes of the world's most populous country.

There were major discussions at the IAAF's Council in April and October 1978 and at three meetings in 1979. According to Primo Nebiolo, who was to become President of the IAAF in 1981, Killanin was waiting on a decision from the IFs and it was agreed that the Republic of China (meaning, of course, its NOC) should be asked to change its name to Taiwan. The problem was to find a way to let

Taiwan athletes compete which was acceptable to China. It was argued that before expelling Taiwan they should find out whether China wished to join, but Nebiolo, with his eye on the Moscow Olympics, was in favour of expelling Taiwan, not playing for time. It was finally agreed, by 7 to 5, with 2 abstentions, to expel Taiwan if China applied. The action would not be intended to be punitive, but would be taken in order to allow the PRC to provide opportunities for the overwhelming majority of Chinese athletes. A further motion, to recommend to Congress that the PRC be the sole Chinese representative, was just carried, by 10 votes to 9.[49]

The IAAF's decision naturally encouraged the PRC to believe that, if enough other IFs followed its lead, Taiwan would automatically lose its recognition by the IOC because it would lack the necessary five international affiliations. Taiwan, however, did not take its troubles lying down. As its relations with the United States and other nations fell away so it became ever more important for it to gain what international political mileage it could from sport, and the IAAF was soon notified that the Taiwan Athletic Association intended to issue a writ in England alleging that the IAAF Congress had acted *ultra vires*, and would seek an injunction against its suspension.[50] The action was successful and at its meeting at Dakar in April 1979, the IAAF Council, whose defence had been that it should never have admitted Taiwan in 1956 and was seeking to rectify the mistake by expelling the territory now, learned that the court had ruled that the Republic of China Track and Field Association remained a member of the IAAF with all the rights and privileges of membership, and that the Congress resolution was void and of no effect. The court had not yet given an injunction, as it had thought it very likely that the IAAF would act on the declaration. The IAAF's lawyers advised against an appeal and considered that the judgement should be accepted. The costs so far amounted to about £12,000. The decision provoked consternation among the Council members, who seem genuinely not to have understood why an international body should be subject to English jurisdiction just because its headquarters were in London.[51]

The Council learned at its meeting in Montreal in August 1979 that the IOC's Executive Board now wanted to recommend that there should be a Chinese Olympic Committee and a Taiwan Olympic Committee, on condition that the latter had a new anthem and flag. This was two months before the Executive Board actually took the decision at its Nagoya meeting, and the IAAF decided to await the result of that meeting. If the recommendation were adopted as fore-seen, then the IAAF would be able to recommend its Moscow Congress to follow suit, and in that case there would be no need to appeal against the English court.[52] In due course the IAAF was able to follow the IOC's line and the crisis was at an end.

News of the London court's decision was received at the beginning of the IOC's Montevideo meeting, where sympathy for Taiwan was reinforced by fears that it might also sue the IOC in the Swiss courts. In fact two cases were attempted. One, brought in Lausanne by the Taiwan Olympic Committee, 'could not' in Killanin's words, 'be proceeded with because of legal technicalities'. Another, brought by Henry Hsu, the IOC member in Taiwan, was still pending when Killanin handed over to Samaranch, and was dropped thanks to the latter's diplomacy.[53]

More recent events

Killanin was naturally disappointed that both Chinas boycotted the Moscow Games, but he records with pleasure that their representatives sat together and talked amicably at the Baden-Baden Congress of the Olympic movement in 1981.[54] However, the PRC's sporting relations with the rest of the world have had their ups and downs.

In 1983 the PRC severed all sports ties with the United States in retaliation for the asylum given to their tennis player Hu Na. Samaranch did not think this would affect the PRC's participation in the Los Angeles Games and, to the great joy of their organiser, Peter Ueberroth, he turned out to be right. Overall, Ueberroth says, the relationship had been good, although in 1982 the float of the oil company ARCO (a LAOOC sponsor) in the Rose Bowl parade had flown the Taiwan national flag instead of its Olympic flag, and had not flown a PRC flag at all. The PRC had immediately stopped ARCO's off-shore drilling rights for several months.[55] Such difficulties not-withstanding, the PRC's Olympic credentials have become so well-established that Zhenliang He, who was elected to the IOC in 1981, reached the Executive Board in 1985, and has since held numerous other posts including a period as a Vice-President of the Board.

Despite the massacre of students in Tiananmen Square in 1989, there was never any danger of a boycott of the eleventh Asian Games in September 1990. As David Miller wrote in a justifiably emotional article, the Games would go ahead without the slightest twinge of conscience for the students who had died for democracy in Tiananmen Square. 'Sport, as always, rises above tragedy in a euphoria of self-interest.' A senior official of the Hong Kong Olympic Committee had even described the China situation as 'nothing serious'.[56] In September 1989 the Chinese Olympic Committee announced that it would bid for the Games of 2000.[57] It just lost to Sydney, but at the time of writing (April 1995) it remains possible that it will bid again, for the Games of 2004.

Conclusion

The two Germanies and the two Chinas are prime examples of the inability of the Olympic movement and sport in general to avoid involvement in great questions of international politics. Sometimes the involvement entails the expenditure of inordinate amounts of time and energy on essentially trivial contentions, such as the precise name to be accorded to an NOC. Yet those trivial-seeming questions are often symbols of deeper disputes, so that by giving way a contestant may lose ground at a more genuinely important level. In any case time-wasting is often elevated by diplomats to an art of meticulous petifogging, and in this respect Olympic officials do not differ from their governmental equivalents.

Notes

1   I am indebted for this observation to Patrick Jourdain, Editor, The International Bridge Press Association.
2   I am grateful to Sir Arthur Gold for permission to quote this remark.
3   Roman Czula, 'Sport as an Agent of Social Change', *Quest*, 31, 1979, p. 48. See also, for example, C. Roger Rees, 'The Olympic Dilemma: Applying the Contact Theory and Beyond', *Quest*, 37, 1985, pp. 50–9; Richard G. Sipes, 'War, Sports and Aggression: an Empirical Test of Two Rival Theories' (extracted from a 1973 article in *American Anthropologist*), in D. Stanley Eitzen (ed.), *Sport in Contemporary Society: an Anthology*, New York, 1984 (first edn 1979), pp. 46-57.
4   The Olympic movement's involvement with the major international issues of modern times has been well documented in Richard Espy, *The Politics of the Olympic Games*, Berkeley, 1979. (Reprinted with an *Epilogue 1976–80*, 1981.)
5   44th Session, Copenhagen, 15–17 May 1950, *Minutes*. General Robertson's letter is at Annexe 3.
6   45th Session, Vienna, 7–9 May 1951, *Minutes*.

7 44th Session, Copenhagen, *Minutes*.
8 Espy, p. 33. I have made extensive use of Espy's valuable sections on the German question.
9 45th Session, Minutes.
10 50th Session, Paris, 13–18 June 1955, *Minutes*. Espy, p. 34, adds that the East Germans were demoted by their government for having made the agreement. If this is correct Brundage's frequent diatribes against the East German representatives may have been less than fair.
11 46th session, Oslo, 12–13 February 1952, *Minutes*; Espy, p. 35, and Allen Guttmann, *The Games Must Go On: Avery Brundage and the Olympic Movement*, New York, 1984, p. 153. Guttmann's valuable account of the German and Chinese questions is at pp. 142–57.
12 Neither Austria nor Hungary had wished Bohemia's NOC to be recognised, but it had been allowed to take part in the 1912 Games. See pp. 51–2.
13 47th Session, Helsinki, 16–27 July 1952, *Minutes* and Espy, p. 52.
14 Espy, pp. 52–3.
15 48th Session, Mexico city, 17–18 April 1953, *Minutes*.
16 49th Session, Athens, 11–15 May 1954, *Minutes*.
17 Paris, 1955, *Minutes, loc. cit.*
18 51st Session, Cortina d'Ampezzo, 24–5 January 1956, *Minutes*.
19 Espy, pp. 76 and 78–9.
20 63rd Session, Madrid 6 8 October 1965, *Minutes*; Espy, p. 108 and Guttmann, pp. 156–7; James Riordan, *Sport, Politics and Communism*, Manchester, Manchester University Press, 1991, p. 113, where he also gives a valuable 'league table' of medals won by East and West Germany.
21 The documents are conveniently assembled in *Documentation Relating to the Federal Government's Policy of Détente*, Bonn, Press and Information Office of the Government of the Federal Republic of Germany, 1974.
22 Another account states that the China National Amateur Athletic Federation was recognised in 1924 as the Chinese NOC. Confusingly, the Olympic Directory gives the date of the mainland NOC's foundation as 1910. I have made use in this section of two summaries of the Chinese question as it affected the Olympic movement, one in English and the other in French, both kindly made available by the archivist of the IOC, Dr Karel Wendl. I have also drawn heavily on Espy, and on the relevant sections of Geoffrey Miller's *Behind the Olympic Rings*, Lynn, Massachusetts, 1979 and Allen Guttmann, *The Games Must Go On*.
23 55th Session, Munich, 24–8 May 1959, *Minutes*.
24 Lord Killanin, *My Olympic Years*, London, 1983, p. 109.
25 An IOC member is always referred to as the member *in*, rather than *for* a certain country, to underline the now somewhat mythological view, which was established at the 1894 Congress, that members are akin to ambassadors of the IOC to their countries, rather than those countries' representatives on the IOC.
26 Oslo Session *Minutes*, 12–13 February, 1952.
27 47th Session, Helsinki, 16–27 July 1952, *Minutes*.

28 IOC summaries. Espy, p. 37, adds that the mainland team arrived too late to compete. According to Brundage, as reported in the *Minutes* of the 48th Session, Mexico City, 17–18 April 1953, far more than one mainland athlete took part at Helsinki, since he states that Chinese athletes had participated in swimming and football. Both appear to be mistaken. The Chinese arrived too late to take part in the opening ceremony, judging by the list of participating countries in *Bulletin du Comité Olympique*, 34–5, September 1952, p. 50, but the *Official Report* of the organising committee of the Helsinki Games does not record any Chinese participation in football, although it does list a lone Chinese swimmer.

29 Espy p. 45; Geoffrey Miller p. 162; 51st Session, Cortina d'Ampezzo, 24–5 January 1956, *Minutes*.

30 Munich, 55th Session, 25–8 May 1959, *Minutes*.

31 57th Session, Rome, 22–4 August 1960, *Minutes*.

32 Espy, p. 66, says the display of the protest placard was momentary. However, it continued for long enough to be photographed. Killanin regrets that no disciplinary action was taken against the Taiwanese NOC for this political demonstration in the Olympic arena.

33 Espy, pp. 147–50.

34 Geoffrey Miller, p. 166; Killanin p. 113.

35 Killanin, p. 111.

36 76th Session, Lausanne, 21–3 May 1975, Annexes to *Minutes*, pp. 64–7.

37 Espy, p. 151.

38 78th Session, Montreal, 13–19 July 1976, *Minutes*.

39 Espy pp. 152–3; Montreal *Minutes*; Killanin, p. 134.

40 Espy, p. 155, Killanin, p. 133.

41 Killanin, p. 113.

42 80th Session, Athens, 17–20 May 1978, *Minutes*, Annex 37, p. 112.

43 81st Session, Montevideo, 5–7 April 1979, *Minutes*.

44 Killanin, p. 114.

45 Resolution and memorandum reprinted in *Olympic Review*, 145, November 1979, pp. 626–9.

46 *Olympic Review*, 162, April 1981, p. 211.

47 IOC, 78th session, Montreal, 13–19 July 1976, *Minutes*, Annexe 4, p. 63. The IAAF, like the IOC, prudently allowed itself, following a change in its rules in 1968, to recognise territories as well as countries.

48 Geoffrey Miller, pp. 166 and 170.

49 IAAF Council meetings, Seoul 14–16 April 1978 and San Juan, Puerto Rico, 3–4 October 1978, *Minutes*.

50 IAAF Extraordinary Council, London, 19 January 1979. (The Taiwanese NOC had previously sued the International Badminton Federation, whose headquarters, like those of the IAAF, were in England. Geoffrey Miller, p. 169.)

51 IAAF Council, Dakar, 26–8 April 1979, *Minutes*.

52 IAAF Council, Montreal, 2–4 August 1979, *Minutes*.

53 Killanin, p. 116.

54 *Ibid.*, p. 110.

55 *The Times*, 9 April 1983 and Peter Ueberroth, *Made in America*, London, 1986, p. 232.
56 *The Times*, 21 September 1989 – David Miller, Beijing.
57 *Ibid.*, 22 September 1989.

III

Power and authority in the Olympic movement

The Olympic movement consists of the International Olympic Committee (IOC), the National Olympic Committees (NOCs) and the international federations (IFs), with their many regional associations and offshoots, all existing in a state of sometimes uneasy, and always delicate, symbiosis.

The IOC is a self-electing, self-regulating body, consisting on the whole of individuals (mostly men, with a few women since 1981) who are rich or well-born or powerful, or all three. As in other regulatory bodies whose members are unpaid (Britain's Jockey Club is a good example) the need has been felt in recent years for more members who are young and businesslike enough to make effective contributions to the growing committee work, and efforts have been made to find people who fit these requirements.

Nevertheless, of the ninety-six members at the beginning of 1995 sixty-two were aged sixty or over.[1] Juan Antonio Samaranch, the President since 1980, reached his seventieth birthday in July 1991, and the punishing routine of constant meetings and travel that he sets himself has taken its toll. It had been expected that he would retire after the Barcelona Games of 1992, but he decided to offer himself for yet another term, and was unanimously re-elected. This new term has already included the centenary Congress of the Olympic Movement, which was held in Paris in August/September 1994, and will take Samaranch on until the Atlanta Games of 1996, after which he may keep his promise to retire.

Since its foundation in 1894 the Committee has had only seven Presidents, several of whom have been larger than life in one way or another. In modern times the American Avery Brundage has been perhaps the most remarkable. A man of ruthlessly authoritarian and reactionary opinions, he ran the movement almost as a private hobby from 1952 until his retirement at the end of the Munich Games of 1972. In those days the movement's staff and activities were far less extensive than at present, and Brundage was able to finance it largely from his own fortune. Although the movement was not rich when Lord Killanin succeeded Brundage at the end of the Munich Games the IOC was able to pay his expenses: he was the first President to be unable to forego them, although, like all Presidents, he served without salary.

Killanin is a shrewd and amiable peer who, as his memoirs show, had a high estimation of the importance of his office and a strong sense of protocol. He did not attempt to control the IOC's day-to-day business, but left much of it to his full-time Executive Director, Madame Monique Berlioux, who (when there were still no women members of the IOC) ran the headquarters in Lausanne, while Killanin continued to operate from his fairly modest house in Dublin.[2]

President Samaranch

Samaranch, who had long had his sights on the Presidency, achieved his heart's desire in 1980, immediately after the Moscow Games. His management style has been entirely different from Killanin's; soon after his election he took up residence in Lausanne, and concerned himself with every detail of Olympic life. There was no room for Madame Berlioux, who was opposed to the growing commercialisation of the movement, under a President who was presiding over the developments that she so much deplored. They got continually on each other's nerves, but she survived for a surprisingly long time, until finally Samaranch sacked her, with virtually no notice, though with a generous retirement package, at the IOC's session in East Berlin in 1985. Samaranch used Richard Pound (a young Canadian tax lawyer who had been elected to the IOC only in 1983) to inform Madame Berlioux that she was to 'resign'.[3] Her nephew, Alain Coupat, survived as Samaranch's *chef de cabinet* until 1989, since when the President has relied increasingly on his new part-time Director-General, François Carrard, who before his appointment was already the IOC's lawyer.

A new President does not take up office until the end of the Games which mark the commencement of the new Olympiad (the four-year period ending with the Games) in which he is elected, so that it was Killanin, rather than Samaranch, who had to deal with the American boycott of the Moscow Games. However, Samaranch's life as President has not been easy: he had to heal the wounds in the movement after Moscow and limit the damage caused by the Soviet boycott of the Los Angeles Games of 1984. Furthermore, the Games of 1988 were a source of nightmarish uncertainty from the moment in 1981 when Seoul was chosen to host them.

Samaranch has suffered even more keenly the ups and downs of his native Barcelona's preparations for 1992, although it is often thought that his life's greatest triumph was to see Barcelona win the nomination. (Of course he had played no overt part in winning the Games for his native city, but he had propagated the idea as long ago as 1978 or 1979, while he was still ambassador in Moscow, in conversations with Narcis Serra, the then Mayor of Barcelona, who later became Minister of Defence). However, once Barcelona was chosen, the city's slow progress gave him constant anxiety, which led him frequently to express his worries to the Prime Minister, and even to the King. Terrorism, bad luck or incompetence could have rendered them a fiasco, but as it is he can look back on the Barcelona Games as the summit of his career.

History will no doubt establish Samaranch as the IOC's pivotal President. He has been unkindly described by distinguished *Times* journalists as (like the post-war Labour Prime Minister, Clement Attlee) someone who might emerge from an empty taxi, and as probably the only man in the world who looked like his passport photograph.[4] He may also, as has often been said, be too concerned with public relations, yet his background in business, politics and diplomacy prepared him ideally for the demands of his highly political office and he has presided over fundamental changes in the movement's nature. The wealth now associated with top-level sport has brought about a proliferation of interest groups within the movement, all competing for the spoils, and the finesse with which Samaranch has placated and controlled the IFs and NOCs and managed to maintain the IOC's position at the movement's centre has earned him world-wide admiration.

Samaranch had a successful career in both local and national politics under General Franco. How attached he was to Franco and his Fascist politics is impossible to establish, though there has been a recent attempt to discredit him, but he seems to have belonged to no particular faction within the Falange, and always says that he saw his career in loyal and national government as in a sense non-political, because it was concerned with sport.[5] Some Spanish politicians of those days soon faded away, but Samaranch avoided the mistake of thinking that he could simply continue as a member of the political class after the death of Franco and the restoration of the monarchy in 1975, and instead has made his name in sport and business.

Samaranch's business career, largely in banking, made it possible for him to indulge his passion for sports administration. There has been no difficulty in combining the two: even as President of the IOC he has been active in business, and in 1990 became chairman of the largest savings bank in Spain, through a merger between the Caixa de Pensiones (then the third largest) and the Caixa de Barcelona.

Samaranch, a great devotee of roller hockey, which was a 'demonstration sport' at the Barcelona Games in 1992, attended the Olympic Games for the first time in 1952, became a member of the Spanish Olympic Committee in 1954 and its President from 1967 to 1970. Some accounts say that it had been his dream from youth to become President of the IOC, and that he had worked for it tenaciously, even to the extent of learning foreign languages as an adult. However, he was not well known in sporting circles outside Spain, until in 1966 Brundage proposed him for membership of the IOC. He rose quickly in the movement, as Brundage had forecast, serving as a member of the Executive Board from 1970 to 1978 and as a Vice-President from 1974 to 1978.

In 1977 he was appointed Spain's first ambassador to the Soviet Union. At that time there were commercial and cultural relations between the two countries and, with his passion for news, Samaranch may have realised sooner than most people that full diplomatic relations were about to be established. It has often been said that he asked the King for the appointment in order to build up his position within the Olympic movement with a view to eventually becoming President. A more recent version of the story, not incompatible with the first, is that he was sent to Moscow because he had started a political party in Barcelona which he had refused to amalgamate with the ruling Union Centro Democratico. Thereafter, in Samaranch's own words, 'Suarez [the leader of UCD] and the King thought I was the right man, and also that it would be diplomatic to end the two-party situation in Barcelona'.[6]

Although he had never before been a diplomat, it could still be said that his was a suitable appointment, in that, thanks to his sporting interests, he was one of the few Spaniards who had Soviet contacts. He worked hard as ambassador, helped Moscow to organise Games, which were successful (barring the boycott), and made good friends in Moscow and in the Soviet bloc generally, particularly with Serge Novikov, one of the nine deputy Prime Ministers of the Soviet Union and later head of the organising committee for the 1980 Games. At the same time he was physically close enough to Lausanne to stay in touch with what was going on at the Olympic movement's headquarters. In 1980 Samaranch fended off other candidates (of whom the most serious was Marc Hodler, an IOC member since 1963 and President of the Swiss Ski Federation since 1951) and was duly elected President of the IOC in succession to Lord Killanin.

He also seems to have formed close alliances with Mario Vázquez Raña, the Mexican president of the Association of National Olympic Committees, João Havelange, President since 1974 of the international football federation, FIFA, and Horst Dassler, the chairman of Adidas, the sports gear manufacturer. According to Aris, he was instrumental in opening the Soviet bloc to Adidas, and: 'Dassler and Havelange not only taught Samaranch an immense amount about the nature of Sportsbiz (a useful term invented by Aris) but they helped him get his job. . . . It was Dassler who delivered the Third World while Havelange controlled the Latin bloc.'[7]

According to an unsigned profile of Havelange in *The Independent*, another of the businessmen who helped Samaranch up the ladder was Colonel Marceau Crespin, an old Gaullist with strong sports connections, who was head of Coca-Cola in France (and who is also said to have assisted the rise to power of Jean Marie Balestre, the high priest of motor racing). According to this account, Havelange gave Samaranch his final push towards the presidency of the IOC after an interview between the King of Spain, the Spanish organising committee for the 1982 World Cup and Havelange himself. This was Havelange's first pay-off for the Third World votes which had enabled him to defeat Sir Stanley Rous for the presidency of FIFA, his victory having been brought about by the expansion of the World Cup from sixteen to twenty-four teams, which had been engineered in order to make African and Asian participation possible. It had been known that the expansion would raise the World Cup's costs and lower its profits, but the arguments goes that these disadvantages were worth while for the King and Samaranch, because Samaranch gained Third

World votes in return for backing the expansion. All this may present a startlingly labyrinthine picture, but it has become the common change of speculation about sports politics.[8]

IOC Membership

Election to the IOC is an honour much desired by men and women who have made their names in the practice and administration of sport. The duties are not demanding, except for those who take a serious interest in committee work. But even for those who are not much involved in central administration there are meetings to be attended of such bodies as ANOC (the Association of National Olympic Committees), which provide interest, as well as pleasant outings and the opportunity to see old friends and associates. Furthermore, sports administration is for some of its practitioners an occupation somewhat akin to publishing in providing a combination of creativity, hard-headed business and vicarious excellence. One cannot forever go on running races, or riding them, but one can go on as an administrator into old age.

Membership of the IOC does not in itself bring financial rewards, although it has often been alleged that such firms as Adidas could 'deliver' votes in the competition to host the Games. Bidding committees have been said to offer jobs to relations of undecided members, or to hold out such inducements as free surgical operations. The journalist David Miller, commenting on a meeting which was to take place in Lausanne to discuss how the bidding process could be simplified and abuses eliminated, recounts how a minority of members will make money by taking a round-the-world ticket to visit the bidding cities, and then send a bill to each city for a first class fare from their home bases.[9] At a trivial and generally uncorrupt level, any well-travelled member will accumulate numerous presents, and will usually feel able to keep them (though they would surely protect themselves against gossip if they did not), and Britain's Princess Royal sets an example by accepting nothing. Some of the presents are attractive, many hideous, and some, like banners and commemorative medals, are harmless mementos.

However, although for the majority of members there is no financial reward, even the rich enjoy free travel. Since the main power of the run-of-the-mill IOC member is to vote for the host cities for the summer and winter Games, the proliferation of candidates since Seoul (whose only rival was Nagoya in Japan) meant until recently that the member who believed it to be his or her duty to visit all the bidding cities could have an agreeably busy schedule, and be treated like a Prince along the way. Of course, not all members enjoy travelling: some could not afford the time to visit all the bidding cities, and so may have to decide to visit none; again, the Princess Royal is an example. Others are infirm or too heavily occupied with other business, and for them travel may well be a sacrifice, rather than a pleasure. Nevertheless, members would not willingly give up the power to award the Games to a supplicant city, which may explain why the latest attempt to limit their visits (to be discussed below) is not more radical.

In principle a member operates without regard to political considerations, though in many cases the claim is obviously false. Furthermore, we have seen in Chapter I that a member (again in principle) does not represent a country on the IOC, but is the IOC's representative to the country. The distribution of IOC membership between countries is much debated, because at present many countries are not represented at all, and most of those that have held the Games are allotted two members, with the result that there is ample room for disaffection among the unrepresented.

The IOC was somewhat enlarged, bringing it up to a symbolic hundred, at its 103rd Session, held in Paris in September 1994, immediately after the centennial Congress. Twelve new members were elected, and the President was accorded the right to co-opt ten members, instead of two, as at present. It was expected that he would use this new power at the next Session, in order to increase the number of IF presidents , of whom at that time seven were members of the IOC. The discretionary members must come from different countries and be approved by the Session, and those who are selected by reason of their office will remain members as long as they hold the office.[10]

The manner of election of new members also causes dissension. It appears that Samaranch has virtually sole say about who is to be proposed for membership, and it is almost unknown for one of his candidates to be rejected. So tight is his control that some stronger-minded members complain that there is no opportunity to debate a candidate's suitability, and that nominations just go through 'on the nod'. This may be part of what Princess Anne had in mind when she told David Miller that she saw the IOC as a one-man band.[11] Of

course the President will take extensive soundings, as may be seen
from Denis Howell's account of why he was passed over in favour of
Mrs Mary Glen-Haig, when Samaranch's enquiries apparently
extended as far as the Queen's husband, the Duke of Edinburgh.[12]
However, the President's control over nominations to the IOC seems
not to be a new phenomenon: one reason for Killanin's papers remaining under seal until his death is that they contain so much correspondence about possible members. Killanin did at least consult, whereas,
as he told Aris, before his presidency 'What normally happened was
that the president made decisions off the top of his head which were
then ratified by the full session of the IOC. It was run like an
international jockey club.'[13] One might add that, although the
comparison may be unjust to the Jockey Club of the 1990s,
Samaranch's Caixa de Pensiones is perhaps a not dissimilar institution
to the IOC as described by Killanin.

The Executive Board and commissions

It is not surprising that day-to-day business has to be left to an
Executive Board – it is not possible to envisage a committee of one
hundred members being an effective decision-making body.
Membership of the Board is greatly prized, both by those members
who see it as the highest office to which they can aspire, and by some
who have their eyes on the succession to Samaranch. The Board is
elected by the Session (that is, the IOC's annual full meeting) and
elections, although fiercely contested, are strongly influenced by
Samaranch. However, although he can help his friends to make their
careers within the movement by assisting them to gain office in such
bodies as the ANOC or by nominating them to IOC commissions (as
committees are called), he cannot bank on having his own way at the
Board. Both its, and his, freedom of manoeuvre is also limited by the
need to have a good geographical spread among the members.

The President's power is even greater when it comes to commissions, since the Olympic Charter reserves to him the right to set them
up, determine their membership and terms of reference, decide when
they shall meet and dissolve them when he considers that they have
served their purpose.[14] Appointments to these bodies are highly
valued, and are therefore useful pieces of patronage, for although they
do not bring financial reward they do offer opportunities to travel, and
within the extended Olympic family they confer a prestige which is

often prized more highly than money. Often an appointment to a commission may serve to keep an experienced Olympian close to the centre of the movement; for example, after Charles Palmer had been defeated by Sir Arthur Gold for the chairmanship of the British Olympic Association, Samaranch appointed him to the powerful Programme Commission of the IOC, which decides which sports are to be included in the Games. The appointment may not have pleased all his British colleagues, but it would clearly have been foolish to waste his talent.

At a more exalted level the gift of the gold medal of the Olympic Order represents patronage which seems to be appreciated even by heads of state, though it must be said that the choice of recipients has sometimes been unfortunate. At Baden-Baden Amadou Mathar M'Bow, then Secretary-General of UNESCO (with which the IOC has had troublesome demarcation disputes), received it; subsequent recipients have included Nicolae Ceauşescu of Romania (1984) and Erich Honecker of East Germany (1985).

When he travels Samaranch is treated with a deference at least equivalent to that accorded the Secretary-General of the United Nations, especially in poor countries, which owe so much to the IOC's fund for sports development, known as Olympic Solidarity. In Korea he became an extraordinarily popular figure because he was seen as the saviour of the Games for Seoul, who had triumphed over the protests that the decision to hold them there had provoked. His popularity was marked by the announcement in September 1990 that he had been awarded the first 'Seoul Peace Prize' of £300,000, which he at once donated to the new Olympic museum's construction fund.

Throughout the movement Samaranch's web of patronage and influence maintains him as a virtually unchallenged monarch, but such a network of influence does not sustain itself automatically: it requires constant maintenance and the judicious choice of friends. Those friends must be made not only within the IOC, but in the NOCs and IFs, which themselves, as Samaranch's own career illustrates, provide ladders to power in the world of sport. It is often unkindly said that Samaranch surrounds himself with a 'Latin Mafia': indeed, he is believed to have no use for Anglo-Saxons, whom he calls 'Sassenachs' and has been heard to ask 'What have the Sassenachs ever done for sport?' The names most frequently associated with him are those of Mario Vázquez-Raña, João Havelange and Primo Nebiolo. Raña is independently rich from the ownership of newspapers in Mexico, but the other two have made their own ways. Until 1991 (when Raña was elected by only a small number of members and with many opposing him) only Havelange was a member of the IOC, but all of them take their positions extremely seriously. For example the IOC put out a press release on 30 October 1990 merely to record the fact that Samaranch had received Havelange, and that they had 'discussed subjects concerning their two organizations in an atmosphere of total cooperation and friendship'.

In the crises of Olympic life it is noticeable that these men (especially Raña and Nebiolo) are in Samaranch's entourage. For example, after Moscow announced its boycott of the 1984 Games, these two accompanied Samaranch to an acrimonious meeting of Soviet bloc sports leaders at which he sought to reassert the unity of the Olympic movement: in 1980 and 1984 Raña was the IOC's intermediary with President Fidel Castro of Cuba; Raña's ANOC issued the supportive 'Mexico Declaration' in 1984, when the award to Seoul of the 1988 Games was coming under fire; Nebiolo was early in his support of Barcelona's candidacy for 1992 and Havelange was described by John Goodbody as 'an outrageously enthusiastic supporter'. Samaranch could, according to this account, afford to remain neutral because Havelange was doing the lobbying for him. Samaranch had even had to restrain Havelange's enthusiasm for promoting Latin officials when in 1982 it looked as if Anglo-Saxons were going to lose effective representation on the Executive Board, and Samaranch had to ensure that an American was elected to it in order to preserve appearances.[15]

The three pillars of the Olympic movement

There is a constant tension about the balance of power between the IOC, the IFs and the NOCs, particularly over the choice of host cities for the Games, which is decided entirely by IOC members, though with the benefit of ample advice.

It is even said that the IOC is redundant and that the IFs and NOCs could adequately run the Olympic movement between them. This may seem a surprising assertion, since the IOC decides which IFs are to be recognised, and which are to take the further step of being admitted to the programme of the Olympic Games. Both these steps are eagerly desired by IFs, because they immediately make a sport better known and more popular, and so increase its ability to raise funds. To be able to bestow or withhold these gifts is therefore a great source of power for the IOC.

However, it can equally well be argued, and sometimes it is even hinted by the Presidents of such important federations as the IAAF, that, without the IOC, IFs would simply concentrate on their own World Championships and the Games would fall away. Indeed Park Seh-jik, the chairman of the organising committee of the Seoul Olympics, observes that the international federations 'thought of the Olympics as nothing more than a collection of the world championship contests of the various events, all held simultaneously in Seoul.[16] A step towards seriously weakening the Olympic Games was taken when the campaign long waged by Primo Nebiolo, President of the IAAF, to hold IAAF World Championships every two years, instead of four, came to a successful conclusion at the IAAF's Congress in Tokyo in August 1991. Despite this demonstration of power by Nebiolo, the IOC's reply to any suggestions that it could become redundant is that, although without it the IFs might benefit in the short term, in the long run the world of sport would collapse into chaos, because there would be no supreme regulatory body.

The NOCs join with the IFs in complaining about the IOC's power. Though neither they, nor the IFs, contest the IOC's ownership of the Games, they have long believed that they should have more say in the IOC's decisions by being given greater representations on the Committee. Complaints have been heard for at least the past ten years, to the effect that every NOC should have a seat on the IOC. More recently similar suggestions have emanated from the IAAF, on the ground that their (and other IFs') members are the people most directly affected by the choice of city. A further demand voiced by the IFs is that they should have some share in the IOC's marketing income from the TOP programme (to be discussed in Chapter IV). This complaint is not shared by the NOCs, which already participate in the programme through the Olympic Solidarity fund.

Certainly, IFs could break away from the Olympic movement if they wished, though it would only be worth while for the richer ones to do so. It must therefore be asked why they in fact remain within the movement. The reasons, no doubt, are partly matters of calculation, and partly idealistic or even irrational. On the one hand the sports administrator who contemplates going it alone knows that he may not succeed, and that in breaking away he will forfeit for ever the chance of becoming an IOC member himself. (This must have been a powerful factor in Nebiolo's thinking, since for many years it was his dearest ambition to achieve IOC membership, an ambition that was at last satisfied in 1992, though only after the change in the rules that allowed Samaranch to co-opt two members.) On the other hand, there is the intangible magic of history; the fact that the IOC has prestige of a unique kind in the world of sport; an attachment to the ideals upon which the Olympic Games were founded.

There may not be much evidence that élite sport promotes friendship between peoples – perhaps more is gained from the twinning across Europe of small provincial towns – yet it may be that the old ideals still have a powerful atavistic force. The reasons for the potential rivals' continuing (if uncertain) loyalty are complex but, whatever they are, the IOC does not stay at the top of the sporting pyramid without continuous effort. The process is political. It demands resources, which are channelled worldwide through Olympic Solidarity, an understanding of human motivation and the prudent manipulation of power.

The IFs' concern for greater representation on the IOC is to some extent motivated by a desire for personal aggrandisement on the part of the leading personnel in these bodies and that is a motive which cannot be argued away. But it also rests upon a genuinely felt need for the IFs to play a more direct part in evaluating the technical aspects of the various candidate cities' bids than they do at present. There are, of course, counter-arguments. For one thing, not all IF Presidents are in favour of such a change in the composition of the IOC. When it chooses a host city the IOC has at its disposal the reports prepared for it by the IFs and NOCs, as well as those of its own evaluation commission, not to mention the information and opinions gained from the numerous formal and informal contacts which take place between IOC members and figures in other organisations, and from such reports as may be rendered by Samaranch's personal emissaries. Many IOC members are in any case expert in at least one sport, and it is hard to see that they would benefit by having further sources of advice built in to the structure of their committee, when they can so easily obtain it as things stand.

The clinching arguments should be as follows, although it appears that they are being ignored. First, significant enlargement would make the IOC still more unwieldy than it is at present, so accelerating the tendency for power to be concentrated in a few hands. Secondly, the ordinary members would, as was suggested above, strongly resist any further dilution of their power to choose between rival bidding cities, the only real power left to them. This power has already been diminished by the new regulations that have come into force for choosing the host city for the winter Games of 1998, and which there is no reason to believe will be significantly altered thereafter. According to this dispensation an 'electoral college' will produce a short-list of four bidding cities, and until that list has been published no city will be allowed to invite IOC members on visits. Such visits will be most strictly controlled from Lausanne, as to the months during which they take place, their number and duration (not more than one visit, to last a maximum of three days), and the degree of lavishness which their hosts will be permitted to display. Compare the relative frugality to which the IOC now aspires with the intense activity undertaken by Leopold Rodes, a leading member of Barcelona's team, who visited ninety members an average of seven times each![17]

Two aspects of the IOC's response to threats to its dominance have been to consult the IFs and NOCs more fully than in the past and to follow a policy of divide and rule, by recognising a plethora of organisations through which the interests of the IFs and NOCs are articulated. The ANOC brings all the NOCs together, and has itself spawned local associations in Africa, the Americas, Asia, Europe and Oceania. The federations also are heavily organised. There is an association of all federations which have been recognised by the IOC, whether or not they have been admitted to the Games (ARISF), and a General Association of International Sports Federations, which contains all IFs, whether recognised or not (GAISF). There are two more associations, specifically for Olympic sports, ASOIF for the summer federations, and its winter equivalent, AIWF.

There may be something to be said for these bodies, since without them common interests might not be formulated, nor effective pressure groups formed, but at least two of them originate in the demands of internal politics rather than in functional necessity. Samaranch admits that he stimulated the creation of the summer and winter associations in order to reduce the power of the late Tom Keller, President of FISA, the International Rowing Federation, who he believed was building up too powerful a base as president of GAISF. He adds that, now that Dr Kim (of whom more in the context of the Seoul Olympics) is President of GAISF, that body is drawing closer to the IOC, but he does not suggest that the newer associations might now be abolished.[18]

Yet a movement devoted to spending money economically might decide to re-amalgamate them, although it is certain that rival caucuses (mainly concerned with the division of the proceeds of the sale of television rights) would persist within them. Similarly, it is hard to see why the regional associations of NOCs could not just as well meet at the same time as ANOC's main meeting, or just before it, as hold special conferences of their own. (They did so in December 1994, when ANOC held its General Assembly in Atlanta.)

The IOC and the host cities

The IOC will not look seriously at a candidate city unless it is able to demonstrate that it has the backing of all levels of government, and that arrangements have been made to cover any eventual loss. The IOC has also strengthened the contract which every bidding city is required to sign, despite opposition from the old guard, in advance of the decision as to which city is to hold the Games. The contract confirms the IOC's ownership of the Games and the right to exploit them (which is in any case laid down in the Olympic Charter): it confirms the division of television rights between the local organising committee and the IOC and the latter's share in the marketing programmes and ultimate control over them. Detailed contracts between the IOC and the host city began with Los Angeles in 1984 and Seoul in 1988, but these were signed after the Games had been awarded. However, under Samaranch the new procedure was adopted of signing in advance by all the cities competing to hold the Games of 1992.

Naturally, candidate cities have been unhappy with these arrangements, but have felt unable to combine to resist them for fear of antagonising the IOC. The reasoning behind the IOC's firmness is that it has been found that cities have ignored aspects of the contract once the Games have been awarded, or interpreted it in ways unacceptable to the IOC, and the purpose has been to ensure that the IOC's interpretation will prevail in future. There was a nice example at the June 1990 meeting of ANOC, when NOCs were demanding from Barcelona more free facilities than it was prepared to give. Right was probably on Barcelona's side, but Vázquez-Raña, the President of ANOC, remarked bitterly on the humility with which candidate cities approached the IOC and the arrogance with which they behaved once the Games were in the bag. On the other hand, Rana is hardly the right person to talk about arrogance and humility: at the Seoul Games he demanded twenty personal invitations, and no fewer than ten cars.[19]

This chapter has shown that the Olympic movement is a hotbed of politics, as the passenger on the Clapham omnibus has always suspected. Yet it would not be fair to blame the movement. Like any sub-culture it breeds its own rivalries and power blocks and, as in any large organisation, much of the managers' energy is spent on keeping all the potentially conflicting interests in some sort of balance.

Notes

1 Four were over eighty; twenty-five in their seventies; thirty-three in their sixties; twenty in their fifties; twelve in their forties and two in their thirties. Honorary and retired members are not included in these figures.

2 Lord Killanin, *My Olympic Years*, London, 1983.

3 Neil Wilson, *The Sports Business: the Men and the Money*, London, 1988, p. 16.

4 *The Times*, 17 July 1980, John Hennessy, Moscow and *The Times*, 16 December 1988; Simon Barnes.

5 Vyv Simpson and Andrew Jennings, in chapter 5 of their controversial and very successful *The Lords of the Rings*, give a lively account of Samaranch's period under Franco. Unfortunately, they quote hardly any sources, and do not really put Samaranch into the context of Spanish politics at the time, so that it is difficult to evaluate what they say. At various points in the book it is possible to compare their statements of fact with those made by David Miller (see next note). They broadly agree, but their tone throughout is shrill, ungenerous and disapproving, and sometimes they seem determined to ignore the realities of political life.

6 David Miller, *Olympic Revolution*, p. 24.

7 Stephen Aris, *Sportsbiz: Inside the Sports Business*, London, 1990, p. 160.

8 *The Independent*, 9 June 1990.

9 *The Times*, 9 January 1991.

10 'Decisions of the Session', *Olympic Review*, 322, October 1994, p. 405.

11 *The Times*, 18 October 1989.

12 Denis Howell, *Made in Birmingham: the Memoirs of Denis Howell*, London, 1990, pp. 290–1.

13 Aris, p. 158.

14 *Olympic Charter 1991*, clause 24:5.

15 *The Times*, 24 October 1986, John Goodbody.

16 Park Seh-jik, *The Seoul Olympics: the Inside Story*, London, 1991, p. 146.

17 Miller, p. 232.

18 *Ibid.*, p. 28.

19 *Ibid.*, p. 142.

IV

Financing the Games

This chapter examines some aspects of the complicated subject of Olympic finance. It discusses the movement's rise to riches with the growth of income from the sale of television rights and the ways in which that income is divided. There follows an account of the IOC's marketing programme, introduced in order to reduce dependence on television. The chapter concludes with a section on the part played in Olympic sport by Adidas, the firm of sports gear manufacturers which has exercised great influence over the movement's commercial development, and has even been thought capable of influencing the choice of host city for the Games.

The rise to riches

Samaranch often says that the IOC has 'semi-diplomatic status', but in fact it is recognised in Swiss law as an international Non-Governmental Organisation. It is therefore something like a non-profit-making sports club, whose international dimension gives it certain tax advantages and allows it to employ foreigners without the usual necessity, very strict in Switzerland, of obtaining work permits for its employees.

The IOC's detailed accounts are not available, but from the condensed statement of financial position included in its *Report for Olympic Year 1992* it appears that expenditure for 1992 was $20.65m. Income is not broken down on an annual basis, but for the four years of the Olympiad 1989–92 it was $157.1m. The IOC's total assets at the end of 1992 stood at $125m, including $48m of designated funds, most of which were earmarked for the Olympic museum. Undesignated funds at the disposal of the IOC were $76.8m, but this figure was expected to go down to below $50m at the end of 1993, with the transfer of the Olympic museum to a new Foundation. Even so, the IOC has clearly achieved what one may assume to be its minimum aim, namely, to have enough in reserve to be able to survive, even if one set of Games has to be cancelled.

The IOC headquarters in Lausanne is a beautiful, indeed magnificent, but not ostentatious, building beside Lake Geneva, designed by one of the Mexican IOC members, Pedro Ramirez Vazquez. About ninety-six people work there, and in some smaller office buildings in the city. A further fifty-one work at the splendid new museum at the other end of Lausanne. The general atmosphere is one of hardworking affluence, and it is hard to remember that in its early days the IOC was not a rich organisation.

The television age

Television started the Olympic movement's rise to riches, which has more recently been reinforced by massive marketing programmes. There had been television at the Berlin Games in 1936 and in London in 1948, but it did not at that stage benefit the movement commercially. In 1952, at its Oslo Session, Lord Burghley asked that the IOC itself should make provision for television, and that the number of cameramen be restricted. He was told that negotiations were already taking place with an American firm, and that the rules for cameramen would be the same as at the London Games of 1948.[1] In 1955 the IOC's President, Avery Brundage, informed the Paris Session that estimated receipts for the year were 31,000 Swiss francs, against estimated expenses of 45,000. Although he was exceedingly rich, and had treated the Olympic movement as a hobby, he said that the IOC could not continue to spend fifty per cent more than it received.[2] At the Cortina Session in 1956 Lord Burghley picked up the same theme again and said, speaking from his experience as President of the IAAF, that many international federations

suffered from the same evil as the IOC, namely from want of money. Were it possible for us to obtain subsidies [from television companies] on a friendly basis, we could let the International Federations reap the benefit of this. The latter in their turn, may feel more inclined to give us satisfaction in the matter of the world championships.

(He was referring to the IOC's fear that some IFs might organise world championships in the same year as the Olympic Games.)[3]

The attitudes expressed in the 1950s would nowadays be seen as naive, but television soon began to turn the Olympic movement into a business, though at first the sums raised were trivial by modern standards. The first rights were sold in 1960 to the American network CBS for $440,000, which allowed it thirty-five hours' coverage of the winter and summer Games. None of this came to the IOC, and even when ABC paid $4m for the summer Games of 1968 in Mexico the $150,000 given to the IOC was an *ex gratia* payment. Thereafter it changed its rules to protect its ownership of the Games and their exploitation, and when Killanin succeeded Brundage in 1972 at the end of the Munich Games, it had $2m in hand (a loan from the Munich organising committee), which had grown to over $45m by 1980, when Samaranch became President.[4]

It had been agreed that from 1972 the organising committee should receive two-thirds of the television rights and the IOC one-third, of which it would pass on one-third to the National Olympic Committees and a third to the international federations. The IOC received over $2m as its share for 1972 (and a further $945,000 for the winter Games) and so was able to pay off its debt to Munich and to survive until 1976.[5] After Munich the IOC was well enough off to allow it not to touch the sums promised for the summer and winter Games of 1976 at Innsbruck and Montreal until after those Games had been staged. It was therefore not necessary for insurance to be taken out against the Games not taking place, whereas this had been necessary before Munich, because the IOC had had to spend some of the money in advance.[6]

ABC paid only $7.5m for Munich. In those days 'The telecasts still garnered relatively small audiences, and the advertising community could barely stifle a yawn.' The Munich kidnappings turned the Games into major news and 'Even commercial advertisers realised a grisly profit: they had paid low rates in anticipation of the usual low Olympic ratings and were the unintended beneficiaries of the skyrocketing audiences as the crisis wore on'. ABC bought the Montreal rights for $25m, Roone Arledge, the head of ABC's negotiating team, having made use of what became known as 'the ABC closer'. That is, he made a much higher offer than ever before, but allowed only twenty-four hours for its acceptance or rejection.[7]

With the Games' growth as a television spectacular the IOC has behaved prudently and steadily taken more power unto itself, in order to protect its share of the proceeds. Its leaders have become understandably nervous lest the market collapse and leave the movement in unaccustomed poverty. The IOC, which already insisted that it owned the Games and all rights to exploit them, has therefore asserted the exclusive right to negotiate their sale, though still in consultation with the organising committee of the host city.

It is estimated that in the Olympiad 1993–6 television will provide 48 per cent of the Olympic movement's total income, though this figure conceals a considerable difference between television's share of the income attributable to the winter Games at Lillehammer in 1994 (68 per cent) and of that generated by the summer Games at Atlanta in 1996 (35 per cent). The continuing interest of the IOC is to preserve the market by not being greedy, whereas organising committees are determined to make the most they can during their short periods of glory. Pride also plays its part, and for organising committees it has become the ultimate status symbol to sell the American rights for a record sum. After Seoul the IOC believed that the ceiling had been reached; Pasqual Maragall, the Mayor of Barcelona, thought he knew better, and turned out to be right. Another record was set, and yet another by Atlanta.[8] It should be added that the sums paid for television rights in the Olympics are not always rationally determined. Indeed, paying huge sums for them has always been seen by the television companies as a loss leader, and 'the networks have allowed the Olympics to become so emotional an issue, so much a matter of pride and self-importance, that they no longer measure it by any reasonable business standard normally applied to programming decisions'.[9]

The division of the spoils

The sale of television rights benefits the whole movement. The precise division of the proceeds changes frequently, but in 1992 it was as follows. First, 10 per cent of United States rights (Barcelona $400m and Albertville $243m), or approximately $64m, was deducted from the worldwide total of about $930m for the benefit of USOC. From the remaining $866m a top slice of 20 per cent, or $173m, was applied to the organising committees' technical costs; of the remainder ($693m) two-thirds were divided between the organising committees and the remaining third went to the IOC. The IOC's share was divided equally between the IOC itself, the IFs and the NOCs (through Olympic Solidarity). Thus, each of the three constituents of the Olympic family received one-ninth of 80 per cent of the total television rights (after USOC's share had been deducted), giving an IOC share of $77m. (This last is confirmed by the IOC's report for 1992.)

From 1994 onwards the 20 per cent for technical expenses is not being taken out before the division is made, but will be paid by the organising committee from its enhanced share of 60 per cent of the total. The Olympic family's share has also risen – to 40 per cent – but it has become responsible for the 10 per cent of United States rights paid to the USOC.

The IOC's disbursements to NOCs are made through the Olympic Solidarity fund, partly in the form of subventions to assist with the expense of sending teams to the Games ($14.657m in 1992) and partly on projects, such as training coaches, for the general improvement of sport in the recipient countries ($11.043m). Each participating NOC receives the same basic subsidy of $8,000 and $800 for each athlete up to six. By contrast, the training projects underwritten by Olympic Solidarity are allocated on merit, but an element of political calculation does enter into the division of the percentages of the budget destined for the different continents. The amounts spent by Solidarity and the formulae governing their distribution are naturally principal concerns of the ANOCs and its regional subsidiaries.

The issues within and between the associations of winter and summer federations also relate to money. The winter federations receive the same amount between them as does the much larger number of summer federations, which naturally does not please the latter. The summer federations nowadays divide equally the portion of the television proceeds allocated to them by the IOC, but formerly the IAAF took the lion's share with 25 per cent, because of the high proportion of revenue from ticket sales generated by athletic events. This was whittled down to 20 per cent at the Moscow Games, and drastically reduced at Los Angeles, when Primo Nebiolo, the President of the IAAF, agreed, just before his election as President of ASOIF, that the IAAF should receive no more than any other summer federation. There has been speculation that if Nebiolo were to lose the presidency he would press for the restoration of what some regard as IAAF's rightful share in the television rights, but the smaller federations correctly identified their own interests when he came up for re-election in 1989 and only six of them voted against him. No doubt there were some sighs of relief, even from people who disapproved of him as President, and the possibilty of a painful renegotiation was averted. Not surprisingly, he was again re-elected in 1991.

The Olympic Programme (TOP)

Television is only part of the total marketing effort, which in the Olympiad 1993–6 is expected to generate over $2.5bn, of which $525m is attributable to Lillehammer. The IOC's intensive efforts to diversify have ben so successful that, while television's share of Atlanta's revenue will have dropped to 35 per cent, sponsorship will have risen to 35 per cent. If the Atlanta and Lillehammer Games are taken together, sponsorship should still account for 34 per cent of total revenue, but television's share goes up to 48 per cent.

Marketing the Olympics long predates television. Kodak advertised in the programme of the 1896 Games and by 1920 (Antwerp) the programme was so full of advertisements that there was little room for material relating to the Games themselves. Licensing of products started at Stockholm in 1912, and thereafter marketing grew apace: at Tokyo (1964) the organising committee even allowed a special brand of cigarettes, named 'Olympia', and earned $1m from them. In 1976 this, still relatively small-scale style of marketing peaked at Montreal, where there were no fewer than 628 sponsors and suppliers. Olympic marketing finally left the age of innocence at Los Angeles in 1984, when the 'private enterprise Games' were entirely funded by the private sector. The marketing was still largely limited to the United States, but most of the sponsors were international corporations.

The most important apple in the IOC's marketing basket, the apple of the Marketing Director's eye, is The Olympic Programme (always abbreviated to TOP, except in the contract with host cities, where it becomes 'the international programme').

TOP's origins lie in the 86th Session of the IOC at Delhi in April 1983, which decided that the movement was becoming too dependent on television. Events moved swiftly, and on 1 June 1985 the IOC, with SLOOC (the organising committee for the 1988 Games at Seoul) and the United States Olympic Committee (USOC) jointly handed marketing over to ISL (International Sports and Leisure), a subsidiary company of Horst Dassler's Adidas (51 per cent) and the Japanese advertising agency Dentsu (49 per cent).

ISL produced a scheme, 'The Olympic Programme', whereby

certain categories of product (no exhaustive list has been published) were identified, and a single company would be given worldwide rights to use the Olympic marks for products in one or more of those categories, to the exclusion of all other companies in that sector. In practice, fields of interest have been defined by participating companies in such a way as to exclude as many potential rivals as possible, which has led them to buy rights in a whole set of categories. For example, in the second TOP programme Mars purchased rights not only to confectionery but also to snacks, ice cream, milky drinks and rice.

It is at first sight surprising that USOC should have been a separate party to the agreement. The explanation must be seen against the background of USOC's great economic power and its perennially uneasy relations with the IOC, which will be discussed later in this chapter. At the last ditch the IOC could resolve this unhappy state of affairs by withdrawing its recognition of USOC, but the victory would be pointless. The Olympic movement would be irretrievably split and the American companies which dominate TOP would pull out. As things are, the IOC can present it as something of a triumph to have persuaded USOC into TOP at all, while USOC may have seen joining the scheme as a sop which it could afford to throw to the IOC while protecting its own interest by obtaining a high proportion of the programme's proceeds.

The scheme is not as original as is sometimes thought, since Dassler had, through an earlier company, SMPI (Société Monégasque du Promotion Internationale) made very similar arrangements for the football World Cup in 1978 and 1982 and for the IAAF at its inaugural World Championships at Helsinki in 1982. Once the IOC had accepted TOP it started negotiations with NOCs, and persuaded 153 out of the then existing 156 to agree to the new arrangements in time for the Seoul Games of 1988. In some cases NOCs already had very satisfactory contracts with companies, which they had to give up because the essence of TOP is that only one company in any single product category (for example, Coca-Cola in soft drinks) is given exclusive worldwide rights. In those cases the NOCs in question were able to negotiate substantial compensation in return for loss of income. A good example is the British Olympic Association, which had a thriving link with American Express, which it had to jettison when Visa entered TOP.

There is considerable commercial secrecy under the TOP regime.

Each NOC negotiates with ISL, acting on behalf of the IOC, the share of total TOP income that it is to receive and no NOC is told what percentage goes to any other. It is, however, known that the United States Olympic Committee takes a first slice of the total proceeds, which is believed to be as much as 20 per cent, and that the minimum received by any NOC was $20,000 in TOP III and is to rise to $40,000 under TOP IV (Nagano, 1998 and Sydney, 2000). An NOC receives its share of the TOP proceeds, whether or not it participates in the Games, whereas it does not receive any assistance from the Olympic Solidarity fund if it fails to participate.

The programme is limited by politics in that some product categories, like cars and aircraft, are deemed to be too bound up with national sensibilities for any single company to be chosen. In any case, many NOCs already have successful local arrangements in such categories, and would not readily give them up.

TOP companies acquire extensive rights to use the Olympic marks on products and packaging, and in advertisements (but not inside the stadia, where no advertising has ever been allowed, except at Paris in 1924), on letterheads, point-of-sale material, posters, corporate communications, etc. They may also use such designations as 'Sponsor of the IOC' or 'Worldwide sponsor of the Olympic Games'.[10] Organising committees offer TOP sponsors the right to use their emblems and mascots, and give them preferential advertising in their publications and the opportunity to buy the best tickets and accommodation.

As products become more similar, companies increasingly look for points of differentiation which are exclusive and therefore cannot be copied. Thus, the Olympics provide one of the best imaginable vehicles for worldwide advertising. They also provide a unique opportunity to promote feelings of security in potential customers and to entertain important associates. Olympic entertaining is corporate hospitality *par excellence*, something like a worldwide Derby or Grand National. In consequence it is not surprising to learn that Visa put $14m into the Calgary/Seoul sponsorship programme and spent $25m to advertise its involvement. Similarly, 3M, one of America's largest companies, attempting to raise its image outside the United States, put $15m into the Olympic package, with a further $50m in worldwide back-up.[11]

The first TOP programme did not live up to ISL's expectations in all respects. For one thing, it attracted only nine companies, which between them paid a little over $100m.[12] The nine were Coca-Cola (which has been associated with the Olympics since 1928; it was the first respondent and got the franchise for all other hot and cold drinks as well as its main product); Visa; 3M; Brother; Philips; Federal Express; Kodak; Time Inc. and Panasonic. Evidently some companies which might have participated did not relish having to buy rights in such minor territories as Chad (although, of course, rights in such a territory would not be very expensive). Aris quotes American Express (in the *Wall Street Journal*): 'We didn't want to waste our money buying rights to countries where we don't even have a presence.'[13] Nor would a company necessarily wish to undertake an Olympic promotion in all its major territories at once. In commercial terms it is said that an Olympic promotion is always right in the United States, because of that country's obsessive patriotism, which in the Olympic context shows itself in a frantic interest in the number of medals won by Americans. That does not mean that a simultaneous promotion in, for example, Germany would necessarily be judged a correct strategy by a multinational company's marketing experts.

Another difficulty was that some of the lesser international sports federations felt that TOP made it less easy for them to sell the rights in their own championships, which of course do not form part of the Olympic marketing programme. This consideration does not affect the more powerful federations, which are well able to market their championships.

TOP II and III

Olympic etiquette does not permit the commercial negotiations to start again for the next Games until the current ones are over. After Seoul similar arrangements were made for the Barcelona Games in a new programme, known as TOP II which attracted twelve companies. To establish TOP II, ISL had to complete new deals for various product categories with each NOC. The companies recruited included all the Seoul nine save Federal Express, plus EMS (courier service replacing Federal Express), Ricoh, Mars and Bausch & Lomb, and between them the twelve produced $175m for Albertville and Barcelona taken together (the breakdown between the two is not available).

Ten companies have been recruited for TOP III, for the Olympiad culminating in the Games at Atlanta in 1996. When the number of companies rose to twelve the IOC's marketing department was pleased, but it now sees the reduction to ten as part of a planned concentration of sponsorship in as few companies as will produce the optimum income. The ten are Coca-Cola, Visa, Kodak, Time/Sports Illustrated, Matsushita/Panasonic (survivors from TOP I); Bausch & Lomb from TOP II; and United Parcel Service, Xerox, IBM and John Hancock insurance (all new to this level of Olympic sponsorship). It is estimated that Lillehammer and Atlanta will produce over $300m between them, of which over $40m will have been contributed by Lillehammer. The entry level for some companies has also risen to $40,000.

The division of the proceeds of TOP is different from that of income from television. In 1992 half was paid to the organising committees (two-thirds to Barcelona and one-third to Albertville); 6–8 per cent to the IOC and up to 42 per cent to the USOC and other NOCs (the detailed figures of distributions to NOCs are, as we have seen, not published). In 1996 the distribution is to change again, with 56 per cent to Atlanta (including an unknown amount destined for USOC), 14 per cent to Lillehammer, 20 per cent to NOCs and 10 per cent to the IOC. TOP payments are made directly to NOCs. These TOP payments are for NOCs to spend as they like, rather than through Olympic Solidarity for specific programmes, because they are essentially made as compensation to NOCs for rights foregone in their own territories. The NOCs' share takes the form of its flat fee; a standard payment of $400 per athlete in 1992 , and in about thirty major economies a negotiated fee, whose amount is a commercial secret.

TOP is only part of selling the Games: the estimated yield from all types of Olympic marketing, including television, during the four-year period is in excess of $2.5bn. (The detailed estimates are: 48 per cent television; 34 per cent sponsorship; 10 per cent tickets; 4 per cent licensing; 4 per cent coins.) In addition to TOP, host cities conduct their own marketing campaigns, as do NOCs in all categories of goods that have not been handed over to TOP: Lillehammer's non-TOP sponsorship revenue was estimated at $70m, well above the income generated by TOP. The IOC receives 5 per cent of all sponsorship revenue raised by the host cities (3 per cent up to and including 1992) and reserves the right to vet all their contracts. Some observers believe that the IOC (especially Richard Pound) is anxious dramatically to extend its commercial control by extending something like the TOP programme in such commercially active Olympic countries as Britain, France, Japan, Australia and perhaps West Germany (the last has not been very active in the past). However, Britain wishes, as no doubt do other countries, to go on selling its own logo locally, as well as getting what it can from the TOP programme, although it could perhaps do just as well by handing over to the IOC its present right to make local sales.

The commercial relationship between NOCs and IOC is not without difficulty: NOCs need to be able to guarantee their sponsors exclusivity in their own territories, whereas the IOC, through TOP, guarantees it worldwide. There is, unfortunately, always a danger of overlap between the rights granted by the IOC, and those given by an individual NOC in its own territory, and the danger will necessarily grow if the IOC proceeds with the idea of further expanding its own marketing activities.

A similar danger arises from the IOC's developing interest in licensing goods on its own account, apparently without the prior authorisation of NOCs. (This is different from the encouragement it gives to organising committees, following Lillehammer's success in this field, to conduct their own licensing campaigns.) The dangers are precisely of the kind encountered by Los Angeles in 1984, namely that, if the sale of rights centrally by the IOC is not co-ordinated with local sales by NOCs, a confused market may be created. This is exactly what TOP is designed to avoid, and it would be ironic if the IOC were to cause in the field of licensing the confusion which it has, on the whole, skilfully avoided in TOP.

Apart from television rights, TOP and licensing, the IOC derives income from coins and from its share of local sponsorship programmes arranged by the two host cities' organising committees. Funds from all these sources in the four years to the end of 1992 were, according to the IOC's report for that year, over $1.9bn, of which the IOC retained a little below 7 per cent (under $133m) for the general administration of the movement, the remainder being passed on to the Games' organising committees, the IFs and the NOCs.

The United States Olympic Committee and the IOC

As has already been suggested, the USOC has long been a thorn in the flesh of the IOC.

USOC was established by a federal statute of 1948, which protects

USOC's exclusive right to use the Olympic rings in the United States, and even the right to use the word 'Olympic'. In 1978 there followed the Amateur Sports Act, which settled the long-running feud between two rival athletic organisations, the National Collegiate Athletic Association and the Amateur Athletic Union, and established the right of athletes to 'due process'. This meant that for an athlete in any discipline who had a grievance against his or her association or federation the ultimate sporting authority became USOC, although this did not take away the athlete's final right of recourse to the courts.

As we have seen, USOC is entitled to receive 10 per cent of the fees received for American television rights. However, it is no longer satisfied with this formula, and hard negotiations have taken place between it and the IOC.

USOC's case rests on two facts about broadcasting in the United States. First, to receive broadcasts is held to be part of the general constitutional right of communication, so that no one would tolerate having to pay to receive radio, and few to receive television. (However, the point is somewhat weakened by the fact that NBC, once it had acquired the North American television rights in the Barcelona Games of 1992, decided to put out some of its coverage over pay television. The decision provoked public protests, to the effect that no one had previously had to pay to watch the Olympic Games, to which NBC replied that the public had never before been offered such extensive coverage.) USOC claims that it is the only NOC to receive no government funding, and that over 90 per cent of its revenue comes from commercial sponsorship. (The first claim is over-stated, since USOC rents its headquarters, an old Air Force base, from the federal government for a dollar a year. Furthermore, donors to USOC receive tax credits on their gifts.) Since it receives only 10 per cent of the Olympic television revenue, the remaining 90 per cent represents a dramatic loss of the advertising and corporate space potentially available to it as a source of funds. The consequential questions, therefore, concern the extent to which USOC should be involved in the negotiations over television rights, with a view to retrieving some part of what it calls 'lost revenues'.

USOC argues that all parties would benefit if it were involved. At present the whole Olympic scene is complicated by the fact that, under the law of 1978 governing USOC, any American citizen has the right to compete in trials for all Olympic events. Thus the rights to the Olympic trials are an asset saleable separately from those to the

Olympic Games themselves: for example, in 1988 NBC had the rights to the Games, but USOC sold the rights to the trials to ABC for about $3 million. These trials rights, it is argued, would be more valuable if tied to the Games, and it would also be possible to market packages tying them to rights in other competitions.

There is, therefore, a case, USOC believes, for the sale of television rights to be negotiated in North America in partnership with USOC. So strong is the case thought to be that there have been stirrings in Congress. In 1990 there were hearings before various Congressional Committees, including the Commerce Committee, and there are Congressmen who have been willing to press for legislation to prevent the seepage of what is seen as American money into the Olympic movement at large.

USOC does not demand a specific enhanced percentage, but believes that the united intention of all parties should be to maximise return from the television rights. A starting point would be to establish the needs of the organising committee, and thereafter to establish a formula for sharing. One obvious counter-argument is to ask why, if USOC takes a hand in the negotiations for its local television rights, should not every NOC do the same? To this USOC replies that most NOCs are much better off receiving a share from the IOC than they would be on their own, but that there can be no objection to any NOC that has anything substantial to sell being similarly involved. Thus, the British Olympic Association might well benefit from being involved in the sale of its own television rights.

The power of business: the role of Adidas

The growing commercialisation of the Games has inevitably bred close relationships between the Olympic movement and certain companies and none has been closer than the one with Adidas. The story of its formal connection with the Olympic movement starts in 1983, when, as we have seen, the IOC was by no means rich.

The IOC had anxiously discussed the problems of long-term finance as long ago as 1974.[14] In 1983 it set up a committee (New Sources of Finance Commission), consisting of Adrien Vanden Eede, Colonel Don Miller and Richard Palmer, the Secretaries-General of the Belgian and United States NOCs and of the British Olympic Association, to look at ways of diversifying revenue sources, because Samaranch's great fear was that the television companies could collude to keep the price down or that a future boycott could destroy the United States television market. The committee decided that the IOC needed outside help, and fixed on Horst Dassler, the chairman of Adidas, to market the 1988 Games through Adidas' subsidiary company, ISL. This company was 51 per cent owned by Adidas and 49 per cent by the Japanese advertising agency, Dentsu. When it made its presentation to the IOC in New Delhi in 1983 it had a staff of only five, but Samaranch and Richard Pound knew Dassler well and were never in any doubt that he was the man to whom they should turn.

Dassler had for years devoted himself to extending his influence in international sports circles. According to Aris, he had started in the late 1950s by spending millions in cash and equipment to induce athletes to wear Adidas kit. The frantic drive for sales had originated in a row between Adolf Dassler, Horst's father, and Adolf's brother Rudolph, shortly after Rudolph had completed a year in prison for having been a member of the Nazi party. (This, however, can hardly be the whole reason for his imprisonment.) Adolf also quarrelled with Rudolf, for reasons unknown, and after the quarrel Rudolph sold out to Adolf and started a rival sports gear firm, Puma, in 1948. The story of their cut-throat rivalry appeared in an article entitled 'The Shoe Wars' in *Sports Illustrated* in 1969, which revealed, against the background of the 1968 Games, the extent of the under-cover payments to athletes (which would have been pointless without television).

After these revelations Dassler was rebuked by Brundage (until then the authorities had been turning a blind eye) – but 83 per cent of winners at the 1968 Games had used his shoes and equipment, and criticism meant nothing to him. Instead he turned his attention from the athletes to influencing federations with cash or by underwriting their programmes and helping his friends to rise within them. Thus he acquired influence and contracts, becoming official supplier to the Russians, the East Germans and much of the Third World.

The contract made between ISL and the IOC at New Delhi made an already powerful man much more so, and brought to the IOC Dassler's network of friends in the IFs, without whom it would have been hard to put into effect the IOC's plans to sell worldwide advertising rights to a limited number of companies.[15] It appears, too, that Monique Berlioux's reluctance to have ISL associated with the IOC in any role other than that of consultant was an important cause of her sudden downfall.[16]

It will, of course, probably never be known for certain how much influence Dassler had on the choice of Olympic cities, but the rumours were persistent during his lifetime. For example, in October 1986 David Miller repeated a story which had appeared in *La Vanguardia* that Adidas could guarantee thirty votes for Barcelona: Miller did not disagree with the basic idea, but thought fifteen votes would be nearer the mark. He recalled, too, that Dassler had supported Seoul in the last forty-eight hours before the vote. He added that it was a pity that Denis Howell had condemned Adidas's influence a few months before the beginning of Birmingham's campaign.[17] Neil Macfarlane, formerly Britain's Minister for Sport, agrees that Dassler swung the IOC from Nagoya to Seoul.[18] However, David Miller appears later to have changed his mind, and to have put the swing down to environmental protesters who lined the streets at Baden-Baden.[19]

Usually Samaranch is respectfully treated by the press, but he faced a tough session with *L'Equipe* after Barcelona had been awarded the Games, in which the interviewer asked why the IOC had not reacted to *La Vanguardia*'s allegations about Adidas. This was not much better than being asked when he had stopped beating his wife, and Samaranch naturally said that any suggestions of impropriety were totally false; that the IOC's contract had been given to ISL only because Dassler had done so much for sport, especially in the Third World, and that in any case it would not necessarily be renewed after 1988.[20] (At the IOC Executive Board's meeting at Berlin in September 1991 ISL's contract was renewed until 1996, to cover TOP III and the Atlanta Games.)

Since Dassler's death Adidas has maintained a much lower profile. The sales of such items as sports shoes can be volatile because they depend to a considerable extent on fashion, and are very liable to cheap imitation, as well as legitimate competition. In 1989 the firm lost DM130m ($86.7m) worldwide, and for a time it looked as if Adidas were a spent force and unlikely to re-emerge as a major player on the field of sports politics. After many ups and downs it passed at the end of 1994 into the full control of Robert Louis-Dreyfus; he had been its chairman since April 1993, after the withdrawal of the controversial Bernard Tapie. The company was expected to report a pre-tax profit of more than DM100m in 1994, against DM34m in 1993 and a loss of DM150m in 1992.[21]

Conclusion

Perhaps it is fitting to end this chapter on Olympic finance on a note of doubt. The ambiguity of Dassler's relationship with the world of sport must strengthen the misgivings of people who disapprove of the Games' conversion to a commercial spectacular. But for those who do not disapprove, and who see the Olympic marketing programme as similar to that of any other commercial organisation, Dassler was a natural ally. Without him the Olympics' present prosperity might have been long delayed.

Thus in a single relationship the arguments both ways are symbolised and summed up. On the one hand, a purity of intention which does not readily accommodate itself to the world of commerce. On the other hand, enterprising capitalism which sees the fears and doubts of the purists as merely anachronistic.

Notes

1   46th Session, Oslo, 12–13 February 1952, *Minutes*.

2   50th Session, Paris, 13–18 June 1955, *Minutes*.

3   51st Session, Cortina d'Ampezzo, January 24–5 1956, *Minutes*.

4   Neil Wilson, *The Sports Business*, London, 1988, pp. 17–18. However, there is a remarkable conflict of evidence between Wilson and Aris, who states that 'in 1980 the official record shows that the IOC's reserves had dwindled to no more than $241,000'. A possible explanation is that Wilson is taking into account sums held by the IOC on behalf of IFs and NOCs. Stephen Aris, *Sportsbiz: Inside the Sports Business*, London, 1990, p. 160.

5   Monique Berlioux, 'The History of the International Olympic Committee' in Lord Killanin and John Rodda (eds), *The Olympic Games 1984*, London, 1983, p. 43.

6   75th Session, Vienna, 21–4 October 1974, *Minutes*.

7   David A. Klatell and Norman Marcus, *Sports for Sale: Television, Money, and the Fans*, New York, 1988, pp. 164 and 165. According to Geoffrey Miller, *Behind the Olympic Rings*, Lynn, Massachussetts, 1979, p. 150, the IOC's share of the 1975 television rights was $7.05m.

8   Television continues to generate ever higher fees, although the rises become less dramatic when dollar inflation is taken into account. NBC paid $300m for the American rights to the Seoul Games, which in total raised $408m from television rights. Against the experts' forecasts, NBC paid $400m for the American rights at Barcelona, and $243 for Albertville, and yet more records have been made by the same company's $456m for Atlanta and by CBS's $295m for Lillehammer and $375m for Nagano (1998).

The European Broadcasting Union's payments for European rights have also increased dramatically, from $90m for Barcelona to about $250m for Atlanta. It must, though, be doubted whether the EBU will continue the upward trend when it comes to Sydney (2000), whose time zone is inappropriate for European live viewing. Total yields from recent television rights have been: Albertville (winter 1992) $290m; Barcelona (summer 1992) $635.56m: Lillehammer (winter 1994) $355m. Total television fees raised by June 1995 for Atlanta were $900m.

In this section I have drawn freely on the IOC's 1994 *Olympic Marketing Fact File and Marketing Matters*, summer 1994. I am also much indebted to Mr Michael Payne, one-time ski champion and now head of the IOC's marketing department, who patiently answered my questions.

9 Klatell and Marcus, p. 186.

10 Marketing documents, as in note 8. For the increased TOP payments to NOCs, see *Olympic Review*, XXV, 1, February/March 1995, pp. 30 and 33.

11 David Miller, *The Times*, 16 September 1988.

12 Wilson, p. 27.

13 Aris, p. 178.

14 International Olympic Committee, 75th Session, Vienna, 21–4 October 1974, *Minutes*.

15 Aris, pp. 162–8. I have drawn heavily on Aris's valuable chapter on the Olympic Games. The article which he cites on the payments made to athletes was 'Shoe Wars' by John Underwood in *Sports Illustrated*, 10 March 1969. For a further account of Dassler's rise see Vyv Simson and Andrew Jennings, *The Lords of the Rings*, London, 1992.

16 Wilson, p. 16. However, Berlioux would have fallen anyway. The disagreement over ISL was a symptom of a much deeper difference of understanding of the true role and nature of the Olympic movement.

17 David Miller, *The Times*, 15 October 1986 and *La Vanguardia*, 6 October 1986.

18 N. Macfarlane, *Sport and Politics*, London, 1986, p. 70.

19 *The Times*, 16 September 1988.

20 *L'Equipe*, 20 October 1986.

21 *The Times*, 27 December 1994.

V

Bidding for the Games: the British experience

This chapter goes into the bidding process, with particular reference to the failed bids by Birmingham to host the Games of 1992 and of Manchester to be chosen for 2000. It will be seen that the bidding process does not differ greatly from year to year, though attempts are periodically made to cut down its complexity and expense. What does vary is the number of candidates. There were six for the Games of 1992, six for 1996 and five (three others having dropped out) for 2000, but there had been only two for 1988, and for 1984 only Los Angeles. Such a paucity of candidates shifts the balance of power between the IOC and the host city, so that the IOC is now determined that there shall in future always be a good choice of aspiring host cities.

The bidding process

The Olympic Games have until lately been awarded by the IOC six years before the year in which they are to be held. The 1992 Games were awarded to Barcelona in 1986, and the decision between the six contenders for 1996 was made at the IOC's Session (annual meeting) in Tokyo in September 1990, when it chose Atlanta. The timetable has now changed: so great an event have the Games become that host cities are chosen seven years ahead. At the Birmingham Session in 1991 Nagano, Japan, was given the winter Games of 1998 and in September 1993 Sydney was chosen as host for the summer Games of 2000.

Until 1992 the winter and summer Games were held in the same year, ever since the first winter Games were held at Chamonix in 1924, and the choice from both sets of candidates has been made at the same Session of the IOC. However, at the 91st IOC Session in Lausanne in

1986 it was decided to stagger them. The year 1992 was the last time both summer and winter Games were held in the same year, at Barcelona and Albertville respectively. Thereafter the winter games moved into their new cycle and were held at Lillehammer, Norway, in 1994. The new procedure carries with it the disadvantage that the Olympic movement will be more continuously than ever in a turmoil of campaigning and lobbying, but it is thought that it will be possible to maximise revenue by separating the two sets of Games, as well as spreading them more evenly over the four-year period.

The purpose of a city's campaign is to gain the votes of as many as possible of the hundred members of the IOC. It is necessary to pay heed to a member's second and third preferences, as well as his or her first, since if no city gains a majority on the first round of voting the one with the fewest votes is eliminated, and a second vote is taken. It may be necessary to hold numerous rounds before a decision is reached and once members have seen their first choice eliminated they will feel free to give their vote on subsequent rounds to another candidate, or to different ones as the voting proceeds. There is also some anecdotal evidence that some members change their allegiance even if the city for which they first voted is still in the race. It is therefore desirable for every member to have a first-hand opinion of every bidding city, and each city does all it can to persuade each member to pay it a personal visit. This is not necessarily done in the hope of capturing his or her first preference, but in order that he or she will have a clear impression of the city's strengths, in case the second or even lower preference becomes relevant. (It should be noted that evidence is difficult to gather, as the voting takes place in private. The figures for each round are published, but nobody knows how any individual member voted. Nor are members' own accounts of how they voted necessarily reliable, since there is a natural propensity to claim afterwards to have voted for the winner.)

To lobby a hundred IOC members does not sound an especially demanding task, but it has been becoming more complex as the number of bidding cities has grown and, in the campaign for the winter Games especially, it must sometimes be difficult for IOC members to remember which candidate is which. There is in any case far more to the lobbying process than soliciting the members' votes. Each international federation (IF) must be satisfied that the facilities for its sport are adequate; National Olympic Committees (NOCs) must be assured that their interests are covered, as must the numerous associations of IFs and NOCs. There must be national and local support for the bid; the technical aspects must be satisfactory, as must security, transport and accommodation for the athletes and the 'Olympic family' and the facilities for the press and television need to be sufficient for world wide coverage. (The 'Olympic family' commonly refers to the IOC and its entourage and to the great number of representatives of international federations, NOCs and so on who always surround the Games.) A bid which is 'technically' good provides excellent sports facilities, secure accommodation, good communications, etc.

Although no one but the IOC members can make the final decision, they are in touch with other sections of the sporting world; some have been athletes themselves; many hold, or have held, office in a federation or NOC, and most of them are political animals. Thus their decisions will be influenced by a multitude of considerations, ranging from the opinions of contacts in the NOC and IFs to their notions of where it would be agreeable to spend two weeks in summer, and most of them will have a lively awareness of the wider political considerations. A few members may also be willing to accept gifts of more than nominal value, though of course there can be no guarantee that they will then deliver their votes.[1]

Financing the games

Even to bid for the Games may cost as much as $25m, not including contributions in kind, such as air tickets or cars on loan. The bill may be met from governmental funds, as at Moscow, where the 1980 Games were held, or from privately raised money, as at Los Angeles (1984), or from a mixture of the two, as at Barcelona.

Once the Games have been awarded, a city has to move into an immensely higher gear and develop an organisation capable of spending billions of dollars on the plans which have been presented to the IOC in outline in the bidding document. The question then arises of what is to happen if the Games make a loss.

In a state-directed economy, where the costs have been borne by government to start with, there is no particular problem: the state merely continues to pay the bills. However, in a capitalist economy, there arise at least two problems. First, there is no rule of thumb by which it can be decided what is to count as a cost specific to the Games. Secondly, after Los Angeles had shown that it was possible to make an enormous profit on the Games ($215m) it has become a matter of pride to outdo Los Angeles, so that there may be a temptation to overstate the figures for public consumption.

Montreal, by including in the profit and loss account capital items, such as a new airport, managed to make a loss on the 1976 Games and has left taxpayers with huge bills to pay off. South Korea, an authoritarian capitalist state, was anxious to outdo Los Angeles and declared a profit of $497m, but this figure included $347m cash donations and advance premiums for apartments built in the Olympic village, and sold after the Games to private owners. However, when it came to calculating the profit for the purpose of dividing it between the various branches of the Olympic movement, Seoul asked that the $347m be excluded, and Samaranch agreed.[2] Barcelona had never been expected to make a large profit, and in the end made $3.27m. However, it should always be borne in mind that such figures are virtually meaningless, because of the varied accounting conventions that are used by different cities.

Why host the Games?

In a sense the prospect of profit is irrelevant. It is not the potential profit that makes a city believe that the award of the Games confers a great benefit, but the fact that the winner immediately becomes known worldwide and is given a kick-start into development. Very often the improvements would have happened in any case, but are accelerated, just as when the Queen of England travels by train the station at which she alights may expect to get a coat of paint. Bidding committees may over-estimate the advantages of holding the Games, but they all believe them to be tremendous.Nor, if one compares the cost of bidding with that of prime-time television advertising, is it very great. This is particularly true of 'cities' (some of them are little more than villages) which bid for the winter Games: in some cases bidding is an effective and cheap way of promoting a little-known ski resort.

Birmingham's bid

When a British bid for 1992 was first discussed both Sir Denis Follows, the chairman of the BOA, and Denis Howell (the former Minister for Sport who later was to lead Birmingham's bid) believed

London to be the only runner. James Callaghan, the Prime Minister, agreed early in 1979 that Howell should include a commitment that the government would assist the bid financially in the sports pro- gramme which he was to draw up for the Labour Party's election manifesto. However, Labour lost the election, so nothing came of it. When Manchester announced its candidature most of the leaders of the Birmingham Council decided that Manchester could not be allowed to bid without a challenge from Birmingham.

At first Birmingham wanted an Olympics spread across the British Midlands, a plan about which Howell was privately sceptical, partly because the diffusion of events over a large area at the Los Angeles Games had been much criticised, and partly because the Olympic Charter required the Games (with the exception of rowing and yachting) to be awarded to a single city. Richard Palmer, General Secretary of the BOA, agreed with Birmingham and the team pro- ceeded to draw up purely Birmingham-based proposals, which included a plan for several small Olympic villages to be placed alongside the National Exhibition Centre, so that for most of the events the athletes would be competing within walking distance from their villages. This had obviously good security implications.

At this stage all Birmingham was trying to do was to sell itself to the BOA as Britain's candidate: bidding for the Games themselves would come later – if the BOA were convinced. As with any bidding city, the key to getting votes was to show the BOA members the site well before the vote, which was to be taken at the Café Royal in London on 12 July 1985. The Birmingham team also had to win over the national officers of participating sports. The two most influential British Olympic journalists, David Miller of *The Times* and John Rodda of *The Guardian*, were unenthusiastic, yet Birmingham's bid was technically so good and its team lobbied so well that it gained 25 votes, against Manchester's 5 and only 2 for London.

Financial support for the bid came from industry, but the appeal to the City of London produced only £35,000 'which was quite dis- graceful – one more sign that the City cares little for life north of London'.[3] For the purpose of convincing the government Birming- ham worked on a profit figure of £50m (although earlier they had been thinking of as much as £200m), which was accepted by the Treasury and by the Birmingham City Treasurer. At that point the new Prime Minister, Margaret Thatcher, authorised Kenneth Baker, the Secre- tary of State for the Environment, to sign the letter to the IOC guaranteeing the Birmingham bid, and guaranteeing the entrance into Britain of the members of the Olympic 'family'. (It was a great disappointment to Birmingham that the Prime Minister did not sign the letter herself.) The government also agreed to cover any loss over £100m, should there be a catastrophe against which insurance could not be obtained, like boycott or war.

The Birmingham team then embarked on the exhausting business of lobbying the Olympic movement, against the formidable competition of Amsterdam, Barcelona, Belgrade, Brisbane and Paris. Birmingham, like any bidding city, had to send representatives to all the main Olympic events, starting with the IOC Session, and continuing through the regional and continental assemblies. At all these a stand would be erected and receptions be given (more of them than current regulations allow) for IOC members and anyone else in a position of influence. The team also took advice on the delicate matter of gifts, and found that it was the invariable practice to give them to IOC members, not only when they visited bidding cities but also at other gatherings of the Olympic movement. Birmingham decided to follow the custom, but 'modestly, expressing our friendship and respect'.[4] One can only hope that this nonsensical custom will lose its grip, if the IOC will only keep to its guidelines.

With one exception the IOC members who visited Birmingham all said how much they approved of the city's slogan 'Give the Games back to the athletes'. However, in the end this perfectly unexceptionable slogan seems to have done Birmingham damage because certain members of the IOC could not stomach the suggestion that the Games might have ever been taken away from the athletes, and because Birmingham overdid the use of the slogan in its final presentation to the IOC. Another disadvantage for Birmingham was that, while Howell himself was smooth and ambassadorial, the homespun genuineness of certain of his colleagues jarred on some IOC members, who were unaccustomed to such cheerfully informal invitations as 'Brothers, come and sit down'. Another great difficulty was the British Government's attitude to South Africa. Its stand against sanctions caused the Commonwealth Games of 1986, which Birmingham had hoped to use as a shop window, to be boycotted by twenty-one of the forty-seven members of the Commonwealth, and those that attended were overwhelmingly white. Of course, IOC members were not impressed to be told about Birmingham's multiracial character.[5]

When it came to the vote in Lausanne on 17 October 1986,

Birmingham did very poorly, despite its technically superb bid, as the
table of voting shows.

Round	1	2	3
Barcelona	29	37	47
Paris	19	20	23
Brisbane	11	9	10
Belgrade	13	11	5
Birmingham	8	8	
Amsterdam	5		

Birmingham is thought to have done badly because most of its team
were unused to the corridors of international power, though an
exception must be made for the team leader, Denis Howell. Birmingham had also to contend with the city's rather dull provincial image; it
was, so Howell says in his memoirs, let down by some IOC members
who had promised to vote for it; the bid was not endorsed with any
great enthusiasm by the British government, which was represented
at the final vote only by the low-ranking Minister for Sport, Richard
Tracey, who in any case arrived too late to have much time for
last-minute lobbying. By contrast France and Spain sent their Prime
Ministers, Jacques Chirac and Felipe González. That is not to say that
Birmingham would necessarily have gained by the British Prime
Minister's presence. Howell had not asked that she should attend in
person, but had merely urged that the government be represented,
perhaps because he feared the possible results of a number of the
Prime Minister's actions, including her stand against sanctions
against South Africa, the permission that she had given to the
Americans to bomb Libyan targets from bases in Britain in April 1986
and the attempt to boycott the Moscow Games of 1980.[6]
    There were naturally many post-mortems. John Rodda commented
that Birmingham's team had found that the campaign was giving their
city such marvellous publicity that they had drifted from the target,
and sent people to championships where there would be few or no
IOC members. He went on that during the evening after Chirac's
powerful speech commending Paris's candidature Barcelona's supporters had panicked and shifted their votes for the winter Games
from Falun (Sweden) to Albertville (France), which Rodda thought in

some ways the worst candidate of all.[7] Their thinking was that if the
winter Games were awarded to a French contender it would be
unthinkable also to give France the even greater prize of the summer
Games. According to David Miller, Chirac's presentation had been
applauded for two minutes; afterwards Guy Drut, the Paris cam-
paigner and a former hurdles gold medallist, had admitted that Paris's
bid had been killed by the support given to Albertville.[8]

Rodda's considered view was that Birmingham had fought a
crudely naive campaign around a solid technical base. 'Their bid
showed signs of leaning leftwards and carried exaggerated claims
more usually found in a general election campaign. The extent of the
hype was illustrated when on the morning of the voting so much
money was placed on Birmingham with a London bookmaker that
they had to make them 2–1 second favourite.'[9]

The second attempt

After Barcelona had won, thoughts immediately turned to the Games
of 1996. Manchester was waiting in the wings to compete against
Birmingham. It offered new blood in the shape of Bob (now Sir
Robert) Scott, Manchester's charismatic team leader, a theatrical
entrepreneur in Manchester, and the son of a distinguished diplomat,
Sir David Scott. He was anxious to learn from Birmingham's mis-
fortunes, and recognised that the main difference between Birmingham's campaign and those of Paris and Barcelona had been the extent
of government involvement. 'You can hardly', he said, 'compare
Jacques Chirac with Richard Tracey.'[10] Howell sourly records that he
and the rest of the Birmingham team got little congratulation from the
BOA for their efforts, and he is bitter that he got no support against
Manchester from leading BOA members, like Mrs (now Dame) Mary
Glen-Haig, Lord Luke and Charles Palmer. He thought the IOC
would find it incomprehensible if the BOA deserted Birmingham.[11]

In his campaign against Manchester Howell set much store by his
achievement at the IOC's Session in Istanbul in 1987 of having beaten
off great opposition to persuade the IOC to hold its 1991 Session in
Birmingham, but the BOA was not greatly impressed by his having
secured the 1991 Session for Birmingham. Nor, indeed, was David
Miller. It was true, he wrote, that Britain had not hosted an IOC
Session since before the war, and the rivals this time had included
Budapest, Monaco, Moscow, Nairobi and Riyadh but, he went on, 'A

session carries no special significance, other than emphasise a nation's international sporting presence.'[12] Nor had Howell had as much help as he had hoped for from his own side. Lord Luke had not even stayed to the end of the Istanbul meeting to vote for Birmingham and in the end it won by only one vote over Budapest. It may even be that the decision was a matter of chance, since Howell says that he had heard that the elusive Magvan, having left the room temporarily, had not realised that Moscow had been eliminated, and went on voting for it, thus spoiling his paper.[13]

Despite Howell's determined lobbying, the BOA switched from Birmingham to Manchester by 20 votes to 11. The change was received with ill grace by Birmingham, but it is easy to follow the BOA's reasoning. There was no real difference between the plans Birmingham prepared in outline for 1996 and those it had drawn up in detail for 1992. Unkind gibes had been made that the National Exhibition Centre at Birmingham, in which many of the sports were to be held, was not much more than an enormous shed which would leave no legacy to Birmingham in the shape of new sports facilities once the Games was over. In short, the Committee could see little reason to expect Birmingham to do any better in the voting for 1996 than it had four years earlier.

Manchester's bid

After a sometimes acrimonious campaign, Bob Scott's victory speech was delightfully magnanimous. 'Denis would be a hard act to follow. Denis has been a credit to British sport, a trail-blazer.'[14] Denis Howell, in return, at first took defeat well, and stated: 'Our warmest congratulations to Manchester. They will carry our best wishes. Obviously we are disappointed because we thought we had a superb bid. But now we have to give Manchester every help we can'[15] However, he did not stick to these good intentions and by the time of the Seoul Games it had become clear that Manchester would have to go to the Session without any advice or support from Denis Howell, despite his former promises of both. When Howell went to Seoul to see how they were handling the 94th Session, in preparation for Birmingham having the 97th in 1991, members of the Olympic family were naturally disconcerted that Howell was being, to put it mildly, grudging about Manchester.[16]

Scott was always realistic about the possibility of failure, though he heeded the one piece of advice Samaranch gave him, which was not to advertise the fact that he was prepared to try more than once, because that would only encourage IOC members to vote for other candidates. From the start he had a clear idea of what Manchester was trying to do. The first task was to set the bid's overall direction and philosophy. It was to be private-sector-led, 'laid-back' in style, and had to gain national support, especially in London. Its theme was to be urban regeneration and revitalisation of the whole north-western region with the Games as the catalyst of renewal, though it would also be rooted in the region's industrial history, celebrating the centenary of the Manchester Ship Canal. Above all, it would leave a legacy of venues placed to meet the needs of the population for the next thirty years. To get these venues built would entail persuading Local Authorities and Development Corporations of their long-term desirability, whilst making it clear to the IOC that they were being built especially for the Olympic Games.

When working out the team's programme, Scott learned from the mistake Birmingham had made in diffusing its effort. His sole objective was to gain a majority of votes in September 1990, so that the prime targets must be Olympic gatherings where IOC members were likely to be present. (One of the most important turned out to be the IOC's Session at Puerto Rico in August 1989.) It would also be possible to go to endless cups and championships, but they would be of little value if none of the IOC members were to be there.

The team had three clearly defined sets of activities. First came preparing the technical bid. From the beginning Manchester realised that the technical bid does not win votes, but it can lose them: in other words, members will use a real or perceived deficiency to eliminate a city from the running. Secondly, there was the international task: this was the most important and difficult activity. It was essential to keep the team small (aided by a broader panel of helpers and Olympic celebrities like Daley Thompson, the decathlete, and Sebastian Coe, the runner) so that its members could become personally known to and trusted by the IOC members, and it was vital to know the latter as individuals and to study their individual needs. Thirdly, the slogan 'Driving the Dream' was not merely a slogan but the name of a set of activities, designed to generate local and national enthusiasm, and to establish Manchester firmly in the popular mind as a venue for the year 2000, should it fail in 1996.

The campaign fell naturally into three phases. First, in 1988, the team had to come to terms with the Olympic environment, learn its language and make initial contacts; then came the phase of getting to know the members; finally it was necessary to persuade them to visit Manchester, preferably as late in the campaign as possible – ideally in the spring or summer of 1990. Great attention was paid, as by every bidding city, to the detail of their visits. For example, a send-off would be arranged in their countries of origin; there would be a VIP reception at Heathrow; use would be made of private aeroplanes, helicopters, Rolls Royces; there would be a police escort; carefully thought-out entertainment, inexpensive but pleasant presents and in general the creation of an atmosphere of luxury and respect, without subservience. Later Scott summed it up: 'The secret is to seem like an old friend while not appearing a nuisance.' So birthday cards and enquiries about golf handicaps were legitimate, but Manchester would not follow the example of one team bidding for the 1994 winter Games, whose members had all turned up in stifling Seoul dressed as Eskimos.[17]

Bob Scott was able to obtain major contributions to Manchester's campaign fund from companies (plus one private individual, the Duke of Westminster) and financed the remainder of the cost of the bid from gifts in kind. By October 1989 sixteen companies had given £100,000 each and the total sum raised was £2,160,000. Members of the team had already met seventy-seven out of ninety-three members of the IOC; a successful presentation had been made to the Executive Board, and a dinner party, attended by Princess Anne, had been given in Seoul on the first night of the Games.

The international task took Manchester's team far and wide, notably to the Annual Congress of Pan-American NOCs in Puerto Rico, where the most important event from Manchester's point of view had been a private 'audience' with Samaranch, who had stressed that a north-western bid, to include Manchester and Liverpool, would not be viewed as a weakness, even to the extent of there being two Olympic villages. Armed with that assurance, it was possible to get on with preparing the bid on a regional basis. Samaranch also told Scott that Princess Anne's leadership was crucial if the bid were to succeed.

The international federations are naturally of great importance to the success of any bid. The team picked up the feeling among them that the IOC would probably vote for Athens on sentimental grounds, but that the IFs were not happy about the Greeks' ability to organise the Olympics. However, one difficulty which faces all organising cities is that the IFs are slow to work out details of what they want. As Samaranch plaintively asked: 'What can I do when there is uncertainty in some minds, for instance, as to what is a canoe and what is a kayak.'[18]

Scott later developed an extremely subtle (albeit risky) line in public references to Athens's candidature: his policy was to be deferential and even to say that they had a moral right to the Games, but that if the IOC decided against them, Manchester was the best of the rest. It was not, in other words, up to Manchester to point out the political instability, environmental pollution or administrative incompetence of the Greeks, although Nicholas Winterton, the MP for Macclesfield, was to say, rather pungently: 'Any athlete who wants to go to Athens instead of Manchester will need a respirator.'[19]

Meanwhile Manchester did its best to enlist the government's support, and the first indication of its favourable stance came in a letter from the Minister for Sport, Colin Moynihan, who was a Junior Minister in the Department of the Environment. A successful meeting was also held with north-western Conservative MPs, and Mrs Lynda (now Baroness) Chalker, Minister of State at the Foreign Office, was enthusiastic, but puzzled about how she should form a view as to the desirability of Britain's holding the Games. The team was reasonably satisfied with the progress of its relations with government, though they would presumably have gone even better if Britain's Minister for Sport had not been so junior in the hierarchy: a more senior Minister would have been in a far better position to guide the government's thinking on the Olympic Games, and on sporting issues in general.

In the end Mrs Thatcher wrote an excellent letter to Samaranch on 10 November 1989. Apparently, when the letter was first drafted for her, the Prime Minister asked her officials to rewrite it more robustly, and even after the draft was changed she added a few words of her own to strengthen it further. It seems unlikely that she would have written as enthusiastically on behalf of Birmingham.

One of the principal objectives of any bidding city is to attract important visitors. So far as Manchester was concerned, the visit to end all visits was paid by Samaranch on 10 July 1989, rather early for Scott.[20] He combined the visit with watching tennis at Wimbledon, and had modified an extremely important trip to North Korea in order to accept an invitation to dinner at Buckingham Palace with the

Princess Royal, who knew exactly how to treat him with the friendly deference due to his age and importance in the Olympic movement. He arrived at Manchester by helicopter (perhaps not a good touch, as he does not like helicopters). The police provided a band at the airport, an escort for his 'motorcade', a visit to their headquarters (it became clear as the campaign progressed that a visit to the police command centre was a strong selling point with IOC members), and the present of a policeman's helmet. Fifteen mayors in robes and chains turned out to greet him (emphasising the regional unity behind the bid), and at lunch he met industrial barons, all of them supporters of the bid. Only Ian Wooldridge in the *Daily Mail* spoilt the tone of the press comment by pointing to strikes, trouble in the National Health Service, the disaster at Hillsborough football stadium: so unlikely did he think a Mancunian victory that he offered odds of 66–1 against, compared with even money for Athens. As he pithily put it: 'Moscow in 1980 staged a magnificent Games because anyone opposing the concept could be arrested or shot.'[21]

Manchester continued to campaign through the summer, and right up to the decision in Tokyo in September. This time the British Government had realised that the IOC would not be satisfied with a junior minister, and had sent Chris Patten, the Secretary of State for the Environment, and head of the ministry which at that time housed the much more junior Minister for Sport. But to no avail: in a hard-fought contest between Athens and Atlanta, from which Atlanta emerged the victor, Manchester gained only eleven votes in the first round (when only Belgrade did worse, with seven), and five in the second, after which it dropped out. Yet it would be a mistake to see the defeat as a disaster. For the relatively small sum of not more than £3m Manchester was placed on the world map. Although many of the facilities for an Olympic Games were still to be built, the bid gave impetus to projects of modernisation and improvement which were necessary if Manchester was ever to be transformed from a run-down post-industrial city, with its roots in the Victorian age, into a modern city able to face the twenty-first century with confidence, and to vie with Birmingham for the title of Britain's second city.

Once Atlanta had been chosen for 1996 the Olympic movement again began to look ahead, this time to the Games of 2000 and London returned to the lists against Manchester. Some members of the BOA were doubtful about entering the competition at all, but eventually it recognised the value of the bidding experience and knowledge of the highly complicated Olympic world that Manchester had already gained, and stuck with Manchester.

The British Olympic Association's choices

As soon as it was clear that Atlanta had won the right to hold the Games of 1996, Sebastian Coe, the runner and aspiring politician (he had recently been adopted as prospective Conservative candidate for Falmouth), announced, with what seemed to many people to be indecent haste, that he was organising a bid on behalf of London for 2000. The fact that Athens had lost to Atlanta clearly improved London's chances, since if Athens had won it would have been unlikely that the IOC would choose a third European city in a row, Barcelona having been host to the Games in 1992.

To counter the criticism that a politician could hardly devote the required time to running a bid, Coe soon made it clear that his major commitment was to politics, and that his involvement with the London bid was in order to give it a good start rather than to stay in charge. There was opposition to the London bid from Manchester, as one would expect, and from BOA members, who were annoyed that Coe had allowed them to read about the bid in the newspapers, instead of consulting them in advance. Nor was his association with Peter Lawson welcomed, because Lawson was Secretary of the Central Council for Physical Recreation (CCPR), which has for years played a central part in the feuds and divisions which bedevil British sport.

Bob Scott let it be known that it would be helpful if the BOA made up its mind before the Birmingham IOC Session scheduled for July 1991, and towards the end of November 1990 it was announced that there would be a special BOA meeting in London on 19 December 1990 to decide if Britain should field a candidate for 2000. By now another London group had its hat in the ring; this was the London Regional Council for Sport, an amalgam of representatives of the thirty-three London Councils that had belonged to the old Greater London Council and of representatives of sport. In addition, Tarmac, the building materials company, was expected to announce its interest imminently, and Bernard Sunley, the building contractor, was believed to be interested. Despite his unpopularity with the BOA, Coe was not without friends: his supporters included Daley Thompson (decathlete), Gary Lineker (footballer), Virginia Wade (tennis player) and Adam Faith, ('pop' star).[22]

There was also a battle within the CCPR as to which city to support. Some members resented Lawson's backing London, thereby seeming to forget that the CCPR was a national body.[23] Within the BOA there were also doubts: an element within it, led by its President, Sir Arthur Gold, questioned the British capacity to bid at all.[24] At its December meeting it decided unanimously that it would hear bids, but would not back any city simply for the sake of having a British entry: none would be backed if none had a good chance internationally. The decision between candidate cities would be made in April 1991.

The Times was by now firmly in the Manchester camp. Miller pronounced that it had 'a springboard start'. For one thing, it was working closely with the Greater Manchester Council, whereas since the demise of the Greater London Council there was no local authority to back London, and a real problem as to what authority could underwrite the bid.[25] This point was developed some months later by another *Times* correspondent, who reported that the BOA was demanding that cities should obtain signed statements of support from their civic authorities, but that the Corporation of London (which must be by far the richest authority in the capital) had said: 'The Corporation would not be prepared to contribute financially to staging the Olympics in London. Nor would it be prepared to sign the agreement.'[26].)

By now the three London groups had solidified: they were Coe's London Olympic 2000; Tarmac; and the London Council for Sport and Recreation (LCSR, apparently another name for the London Regional Council for Sport mentioned above). Cooper & Lybrand, the accountants who had written a feasibility study for Coe's group, were trying to bring all three together and for a short time they succeeded, but the alliance soon fell apart.

Meanwhile the government very properly insisted that the decision was a matter solely for the BOA, though the tone of Baroness Blatch's answers to questions (for the Department of the Environment) in the House of Lords on 14 January 1991 suggests that she may have wished that she could declare a preference for Manchester. (After the bid it became clear that Chris Patten, who, it will be remembered, had been present in Tokyo for the decision in respect of 1996, had always favoured Manchester, though he had of course not felt able to say so.) Kate Hoey, Labour MP for Vauxhall and Shadow Minister for Sport, was brought in as mediator but by making it clear that she thought only London had a chance internationally she annoyed Bob Scott, who wrote to Neil Kinnock (at that time leader of the Labour Party) to express his dismay.[27]

The unwelcome publicity given to London's disunity soon caused Tarmac to drop out. The unity talks broke down on 5 February 1991, when it became clear that the difference between the remaining factions rested on a fundamental divergence of view about the underlying purpose of the bid. Coe emphasised the Games' importance as a festival of sport, and thought existing facilities could be used, while LCSR saw them as a vehicle for urban renewal, for which new facilities were essential.

Very soon Peter Lawson resigned from London 2000. His position had been complicated by the fact that he was seen in some quarters as the Duke of Edinburgh's man, because the Duke was, and remains, a keen President of the CCPR, although no supporter of a London bid. His departure seems to have cleared the logjam, and only eight hours before the BOA's deadline London agreed on a joint board of six directors, with Coe as president and a chairman to be appointed. The way was now open for London and Manchester to submit proposals to the BOA by mid-March, for decision in April. Manchester's confidence in the outcome was indicated in a reaction to London's new unity from Richard Parry, Scott's second in command: 'Excuse me while I yawn.'

The BOA insisted that any city, if it were to be chosen, must guarantee to have built, or be in the process of building, three stadia by the time the IOC voted in 1993. The stipulation was welcomed by Scott, who was of the school of thought that saw the Games as a vehicle for urban renewal. He believed that the Games would resemble the 1951 Festival of Britain: 'It will mark a new beginning, not just for sport but for British society. As an Olympic city the old image of Manchester would simply evaporate.'[28]

The Times came out for London in a leading article because Manchester 'lacks the prestige to overcome the claims of Berlin or Johannesburg [a very early mention of Johannesburg in the Olympic context] which can trade on their status as symbols of reconciliation'.[29] Yet David Miller, the paper's chief sports correspondent, seems to have differed, for on the following day he pointed out that Manchester had powerful support. Samaranch inclined towards it, as did the Princess Royal (a member of the IOC) and the Evaluation Commission of the BOA. Furthermore, Manchester's bid seemed to have a more solid financial base, and the siting of London's proposed

venues did not emphasise the glamour which foreigners might associate with the capital: 'a press village east of Barking and
redevelopment of east London Docklands is not quite the gracious
portrait of London familiar on airline advertisements around the
world'.[30]

In the event Manchester won the contest by 25 votes to 4. The BOA
had not thought either bid perfect, but Manchester's had solid local
support, and the city possessed more facilities than did London. Its
presentation to the BOA had been far more impressive than
London's, and there was a widespread feeling that London's new-
found unity might not last and that the lack of a single London
authority was a grave handicap.

Bob Scott, as always master of the graceful phrase, said that it was
an 'extraordinary event in his life to beat Sebastian Coe in a race'. The
Association of London Authorities (representing thirteen councils,
mainly Labour; the other twenty were in the mainly Conservative
London Boroughs Association) was less graceful in defeat than Scott
had been in victory, and said that the decision was a sad indication of
the state of London. The government was to blame for the capital's
'crumbling infrastructure'.[31]

Had the BOA not remained faithful to Manchester, having only a
few years earlier jettisoned Birmingham, it would have invited ridi-
cule on the grounds of chopping and changing. In any case, the
decision was made easy by the fact that several groups had fought
among themselves for the official London nomination; the BOA had
insisted that it could not deal with more than one group from any one
city (just as internationally the IOC will not deal with more than one
candidate from any country); the two main London groups coalesced
into one only after the first deadline had passed, and were widely seen
as likely to fall apart again in times of stress.

Developing relations with government

Now that Manchester had won, its team could turn its attention to the
tasks of ensuring whole-hearted support from the government, con-
solidating local and national support for the bid, replenishing its
almost exhausted funds and preparing the immense documentation
required by the IOC. In all these connections the Duke of
Westminster, however out-of-date Dukes may be thought, came into
his own as an active chairman. He led the fund-raising effort for the

bid, which was expected to cost over £5m, compared with nearly £3m for 1996, and personally gave £50,000, as well as later pledging a further £100,000, and lending a painting by Velázquez for the opening in June 1993 of Samaranch's pet project, the Olympic museum at Lausanne. An early indication of the government's attitude came in the form of an immediate letter of congratulation to Manchester from the Prime Minister, John Major, which also gave a boost to Manchester's ambition to be seen as a truly national bid, rather than one local to the north-west.

In July 1991 it was announced that Major had agreed to meet Manchester's team in September, and early in August a new poll showed that more than three-quarters of those questioned in the north-east were already in favour of the Olympics being held in Manchester.[32] The first meeting with the Prime Minister took place on 11 September, amid speculation that, if his preliminary response were not encouraging, Manchester might not persist with its bid. Although nothing solid came out of this first meeting, the portents were sufficiently good for Manchester to continue. The Prime Minister gave Manchester a long list of questions, and the Department of Education and Science was instructed to report on how the strategy of Manchester's campaign should be devised and what facilities were needed if the bid were to succeed. At this stage three Departments of State were involved: Environment, (DoE), Education and Science (DES, where the Minister for Sport was now a Junior Minister, his portfolio having been transferred from the DoE), and Foreign and Commonwealth Office (FCO), with DoE leading.

Manchester was sufficiently encouraged to sort out the legal aspects of the bid. The key point was the relationship between the three major players, the bid committee, the BOA and the city council. The relationship was embodied in a company on whose co-ordinating committee sat three representatives of each interest. The city's new determination to gain something from the bid and, *a fortiori*, from the Games, if they were awarded, was signified by the fact that the company was wholly owned by the city, which would also have underwritten any losses incurred by the bid, whereas in the previous attempt they would, at least nominally, have been the responsibility of trustees.

On the governmental front a great step forward was taken when the Foreign Secretary promised to back the bid and even agreed to establish a special unit within the FCO. Ambassadors and High

Commissioners were instructed to give Manchester every support, and arrangements were finalised for a co-ordinating office within the FCO, under the command of Sir Michael Pike, a former ambassador, who had volunteered his services. Manchester's budget for the Olympics was £973m, of which 40 per cent would be spent on the Olympic village. No poll tax money was to be spent, as Graham Stringer, leader of the Council, stressed, for it was important that no section of the local population should be alienated. Although public money was not to be spent directly, public resources were to be expended in less noticeable ways, for a good deal of officials' time would necessarily be committed, and municipal land would be made available.

On 16 December the 'crunch' meeting took place at 10 Downing Street, with a line-up of Ministers and officials which immediately showed the bid team (whose members had not known in advance who would be present) that serious business was in prospect. The Prime Minister was supported by Kenneth Clark (Education), David Mellor (Chief Secretary to the Treasury) Michael Heseltine (Environment), Chris Patten (by this time Leader of the Conservative Party, but present because of his experience of the Olympic movement at the Tokyo Session of the IOC) and Robert Atkins, Minister for Sport, and a friend of Major, who seems to have played an important part in persuading him to back the bid. The civil servants included the Secretary of the Cabinet, Sir Robin Butler, and two Permanent Secretaries: Sir Terence Heiser (DoE) and Sir Terence Burns (Treasury).

On the morning of the meeting a *Times* leading article came out very positively in favour of Manchester. Having mentioned in passing that there were thirty marginal seats in the Olympic catchment area, it urged the Prime Minister to do his sums carefully. If the Games cost no more than the budgeted £1bn they would be a bargain: if they cost £10bn they would not.[33] Despite the positive atmosphere no definite commitment was made at the meeting, beyond £2m for further studies. Manchester was asked to rework its figures, which did not match those prepared for the government, over the next eight weeks. After two months of very intense work, in partnership with civil servants, the team was able to produce satisfactory figures, and the Prime Minister announced that £55m of public money would be committed for expenditure on a gymnastics hall, a velodrome, clearing the site of a new stadium (expected to cost £170m) and

associated developments. In addition, £2m would be contributed
towards the cost of the campaign.

It had not been possible to start serious fund-raising until the
government's position had been clarified, and the team, which now
had to be enlarged, was also mindful of the need not to cut across the
BOA's own fund-raising efforts for the British Olympic teams. However, by the time that the bid was officially launched on 3 March 1992,
twenty-four companies were already backing it. The private sector
had given £1m of the £5m required for the bid (compared with a little
under £3m the last time), and must now match the £2m subscribed
from public funds. The government was committed to give a total of
£360m if Manchester's bid succeeded, leaving the remainder of the
budgeted £1bn to be raised from the private sector.[34]

Manchester's second campaign

Manchester was now able to get on with its campaign to capture the
hearts and minds of the ninety-four voting members of the IOC, and
of the National Olympic Committees and International Federations
without whose support no bid can hope to succeed. Like its
competitors (Sydney, Beijing, Berlin, Istanbul, Brasilia, Tashkent,
Milan – the last two dropped out early on and Brasilia before the vote
was taken), Manchester had to take a full part in the expensive and
often inefficient merry-go-round of sending representatives to a great
many Olympic gatherings as the campaign wore on. Some sort of
contact was made with nearly all the IOC members and no fewer than
fourteen international federations held meetings in Manchester
during the bidding period. As well as being stalked at international
events, IOC members were invited to Manchester, as to every other
bidding city. By then the IOC was making another attempt to impose
guidelines designed to curb the extravagance of such visits and Scott
co-ordinated the chairmen of all the bidding cities' teams in an
unofficial self-policing group.

It was also necessary to conduct a national campaign, of a much
more diffuse nature, in order to persuade the general public of the
plausibility of a bid by Manchester. National, as well as international,
federations had to be involved; Manchester needed to be visible at
major sports events in the UK; relationships had to be built up with
sports magazines and closer links still had to be forged with the BOA,
as well as with the Sports Council's International Affairs Unit and its

Regional Directors. It may seem strange that time and energy had to
be expended on establishing good relations with other sports bodies in
Britain, but we have already seen that the sports scene is fragmented,
whereas the IOC naturally demands widespread and unified support
for a bid.

By July 1992 it was clear that Manchester's 'product' had improved
enormously since the city's previous attempt, but that it was still not
well enough understood, nor well enough marketed. Four reasons
were distinguished for Manchester's still lying only in the middle of
the field of contestants. First, it was more difficult to market Manchester than Sydney or Beijing; secondly, the bid was perceived as
being dominated by Bob Scott; thirdly, the government's support and
the Prime Minister's enthusiasm were not well enough known; and,
finally, there were forces in Britain which were either opposed to the
Olympic Games, or which misunderstood them. There were also
quite widespread accusations of an Anglo-Saxon conspiracy against
the IOC, accusations which had been fuelled by the publication of
Lords of the Rings, a sensational account of the Olympic movement
(largely of its shortcomings) by two journalists.'[35]

The government's support for the bid continued enthusiastic. In
April 1993 the Prime Minister even paid a visit to Samaranch at
Lausanne to advance Manchester's cause, against the advice of some
officials, who saw it as unbefitting a Prime Minister's dignity to pay
court to the leader of what amounted to a private club. Later, after
some hesitation, he agreed to go to Monte Carlo for the IOC Session to
present Manchester's case in person.

Thanks to the Foreign Secretary's backing and to Sir Michael
Pike's efforts, Ambassadors and High Commissioners were in most
(not all) cases extremely helpful: it was agreed that whenever a Manchester representative visited an IOC member the Head of Mission
would be informed in advance, so that he and his staff could be
involved in the arrangements, and in some cases the Head of Mission
handed over Manchester's official bid document to the local IOC
member.

Bob Scott had been afraid of Manchester's campaign peaking too
soon, and had always seen the last six or seven weeks as crucial.
However, by July 1993, two months before the vote, fifty-five IOC
members had already visited Manchester, and Samaranch himself had
visited the city and had a very satisfactory meeting with the Prime
Minister in London. As President of the IOC Samaranch does not

vote, but he is generally believed to have considerable influence on the voting, and all bidding cities make exceptional efforts to earn his approval.

By this time Ladbroke's, the bookmakers, were offering 5 to 2 Manchester, and 4 to 9 Sydney, the eventual winner.

The vote

When it came to the vote, it may be that the new voting system, whereby the members of the IOC are not told between rounds of voting how many votes each city has won on the preceding round but only which city is to drop out, may have polarised the rivalry between Beijing and Sydney sooner than would have been the case under the old system. There seems also to have been a fear that Beijing might win in the first round, which probably caused those who were opposed to Beijing to amalgamate early on, and therefore to be less secretive about their voting intentions than is normal.

As the table shows, Beijing led for the first three rounds of voting, and the redistribution of Manchester's votes proved decisive. If we assume that none of Sydney's and Beijing's supporters switched allegiance after round three, then eight of Manchester's votes (probably including those of the two British members) went to Sydney, giving it the victory by a margin of two.

Round	1	2	3	4
Sydney	30	30	37	45
Beijing	32	37	40	43
Manchester	11	13	11	
Berlin	9	9	–	–
Istanbul	7	–	–	–

The IOC was widely congratulated on refraining from making a grand geo-political statement, and sticking, by however narrow a margin, to the sporting merits. Many commentators noted also that the IOC's Evaluation Commission had favoured Sydney's bid above all others, and saw the Commission as having been vindicated by the final vote. The Commission takes pains to make a technical assessment, rather than to present a verdict, partly because IOC members are jealous of their prerogative, and prefer the Commission not to rank the candidates. Nevertheless, its power within the Olympic movement will have been increased, over against that of the ordinary membership, by the fact that its opinion carried the day, and it will be more difficult in future for the IOC to make a decision which does not accord with that of the Evaluation Commission.

Manchester's team had certainly expected to win more votes than it in fact achieved, if only because until now a European city has always come first or second in the voting. But in 1993 there was no European solidarity, although there was solidarity among those Europeans who were opposed to Beijing.

The two British IOC members, the Princess Royal and Dame Mary Glen-Haig, may not, for their different reasons, have felt able to lobby with maximum force, but, however vibrant they had been, Manchester would not have won. As it is the city once again has much for which to be thankful. It is well placed to bid for the Commonwealth Games of 2002, an objective which may well be attainable; it has a new arena, a velodrome and a site cleared to take a new stadium, which might easily be built if the Commonwealth Games were in prospect; it has gained enormous experience in the rarified and esoteric atmosphere of bidding for international events, and has established itself nationally and internationally, so that now it has a claim to be seen as Britain's sport centre, just as Birmingham is its centre for exhibitions.

The secrets of political success

By comparison with its bid for 1996, Manchester was amazingly successful in gaining governmental support for its second attempt. The fact that the new Prime Minister was interested in sport and enjoyed it was of course a plus, but he had to be convinced that support for the bid was a proper use of public funds, and this the bidding committee triumphantly succeeded in doing.

There were three main reasons for this change. First, towards the end of the 1996 bid, Manchester City Council, which had initially been to some extent carried along in the wake of the bidding committee's enthusiasm, and greatly influenced by Bob Scott's personal charisma, began to assess what it had committed itself to, and to ask itself what Manchester ought to get out of the Games if they were awarded. In the original formulation Manchester itself had got little, because most of the new developments were destined for areas to its west. However, when the second bid came round the council, and particularly its deputy chief executive, Howard Bernstein, had been clearer that what they wanted was the creation of a new city, or at least a new eastern section. The bid's overall purpose then became to regenerate areas in the eastern part of the city which had been identified as in desperate need: thus the focus changed from green fields to the renewal of decayed urban areas. This new emphasis on regeneration gave Manchester a powerful route to Michael Heseltine, whose move to the Department of the Environment was an important factor in the city's attracting support from public funds, because Heseltine realised that the objective of winning the Olympic nomination fitted naturally with his overall brief to improve depressed areas.

The fact that Chris Patten, at that time Secretary of State for the Environment, had attended the Tokyo Session of the IOC, at which the 1996 Games had been awarded to Atlanta, was also important. He had readily agreed to go, but had been surprised that someone of his seniority should be required. The experience he gained was an eye-opener, because he saw at first hand the wealth of the Olympic movement and the size and cost of the Session and its attendant circus – not to mention the huge television coverage. He saw, too, that Manchester had been barely in contention, and that, if it decided to have another try, the government would have to back it in a much more sophisticated and thoroughgoing way, or not at all.

Another factor in the bidding team's success in winning governmental support was that it handled negotiations with civil servants and ministers with great skill, and had convinced them in the right order, so that when its members had their crucial meeting with the Prime Minister they already had a number of Permanent Secretaries friendly to their cause, as well as Heseltine and Patten.

An aspect of the team's skill was that it had secured Environment, and not Education (although the Minister for Sport was in Education), as the lead Department in government's dealings with Manchester. If the bid had been seen as a sports issue it would have been downgraded to fit into the scale of expenditure associated with sport: as it was, the £55m development aid (for that was what it was) received from the Department of the Environment was, of course, a sizeable sum, but not extraordinary in the context of the sponsoring Department's total budget. It was also fortunate, though probably not decisive, that Manchester was asking for money during the build-up to a general election.

Now that Birmingham and Manchester have failed three times, it may be that government will revert to the view that Britain should limit its aspirations in sport, as in so many other fields. In that case, Manchester may be well advised to concentrate on such events as the Commonwealth Games, and put its Olympic ambitions on one side for the time being.

Notes

1 Stephen Aris records a conversation with Lord Killanin in which the latter remembers a representative of Mexico City having tried to buy his vote by leaving behind him a valuable gold coin, which was discovered after he had left the house. *Sportsbiz: Inside the Sports Business*, London, 1990, p. 156.

2 Dr Kim Un-Yong, a prominent member of the IOC, gives these and other financial details, which are unfortunately incomplete and rather confusingly presented, in his *The Greatest Olympics: From Baden-Baden to Seoul*, Seoul, 1990, pp. 285–8.

3 D. Howell, *Made in Birmingham: the Memoirs of Denis Howell*, London, 1990, p. 314.

4 *Ibid.*, p. 318.

5 *Ibid.*, pp. 327–30.

6 *The Times*, 15 October 1986, David Miller, Lausanne.

7 *The Guardian*, 21 October 1986.

8 David Miller, *The Times*, 18 October 1986. Monique Berlioux wrote Chirac's speech, (*The Guardian*, 21 October 1986) but because of her unpopularity with some of the Olympic High Command she was kept out of the way. (*The Guardian* 17 October 1986).

9 *Running Magazine*, December 1986.

10 *The Guardian* 18 October 1986: John Rodda in Lausanne and Paul Hoyland in Birmingham.

11 Howell, pp. 337–40.

12 *The Times*, 8 May 1987, David Miller, Istanbul.

13 Howell, p. 342.

14 John Goodbody, *The Times*, 20 May 1988.

15 *Daily Mail*, 20 May 1988.

16 David Miller,*The Times*, 20 September 1988.

17 *Manchester Evening News*, 14 November 1988.

18 *Sunday Times*, 11 December 1988, Muriel Bowen.

19 *Manchester Evening News*, 21 February 1989.

20 *Manchester Evening News*, 10 July 1989.

21 *Daily Mail*, 11 July 1989. The *Manchester Evening News* diary of 19 July noted that Wooldridge's piece had been gleefully picked up by the *Melbourne Herald*.

22 *The Guardian*, 30 November 1990.

23 *The Times*, 7 December 1990, John Goodbody.

24 *The Times*, 19 December 1990.

25 *The Times*, 20 December 1990.

26 *The Times*, 19 April 1991.
27 *Manchester Evening News*, 5 February 1991.
28 *The Times*, 19 April 1991, John Goodbody.
29 *The Times*, 22 April 1991.
30 *The Times*, 23 April 1991, David Miller.
31 *The Times*, 25 April 1991, John Goodbody.
32 *Manchester Evening News*, 19 July and 6 August 1991.
33 *The Times*, 16 December 1991.
34 *The Financial Times*, 4 March 1992, Ian Hamilton Fazey.
35 Vyv Simson and Andrew Jennings, *The Lords of the Rings: Power, Money and Drugs in the Modern Olympics*, London, Simon and Schuster, 1992.

Postword

Since this chapter was written Manchester has been confirmed as host to the Commonwealth Games of 2002.

VI

The Moscow Games of 1980

Everything in our lives is governed by political decisions. We have varying degrees of freedom, but that freedom is obtained by political decision. What we in sport and the Olympic movement need is the interest and support of politicians, not their interference. – Lord Killanin[1]

Late in December 1979 the Soviet Union invaded Afghanistan, nominally on the invitation of its government. In January President Jimmy Carter warned that the United States would boycott the Moscow Olympic Games, due to begin at the end of July, as a retaliation for the Soviet action. Although not well informed on Olympic procedures, he did understand that only the United States Olympic Committee could decide not to send a team to the Games, and in February he informed USOC that he expected it to withdraw the United States team. After extreme pressure had been put upon it by the government USOC duly agreed to withdraw by a substantial majority. It did so, not only because of the pressure, but also because of the traditional respect in which Americans still held Presidential policy in international affairs, and because many delegates to the meeting at which the decision was taken agreed with the government that it would be improper to take part in the Games.

The American boycott (a word which was never officially used) was almost certainly the direct cause of the Soviet counter-boycott of the Los Angeles Games in 1984 (when 'boycott' was avoided in favour of 'non-participation'), and threatened to split the Olympic movement. The choice of Seoul as host for the 1988 Games made a split even more likely, and it was largely thanks to the skill and determination of Samaranch that the Soviets took part in the 1988 Games. Since then it has become customary to say that the age of boycotts is past.

How the Games were awarded to Moscow

It may seem surprising that the International Olympic Committee should have awarded the Games to Moscow in the first place, since the choice must have been seen as likely to provoke the anti-communist West, even if no boycott could have been foreseen. The best clues to this puzzle may be found in the explanations offered by Lord Killanin, who was President of the IOC at the time. He asserts that the voting for Moscow was purely on sporting grounds, in recognition of its facilities and professional ability. If, he says, the vote had been taken on political grounds it might well have gone differently, since the IOC is basically a conservative body. (At the same time he admits that the vote was at the height of East–West detente and that some IOC members may have cast their votes with that in mind.)[2]

The Games, he says elsewhere, 'surpass all political and ideological barriers' and 'To-day, thanks to the Olympic Movement, countries which have very different political, religious and social views are able to come together in peace to compete in sport . . . it is not the duty of the Olympic Movement to encourage revolution or effect changes in a government's policies.'[3] This assessment of the supra-political value of the Games deserves respect, although it is difficult to see it as having much connection with the real world. It may be true that Olympic competitors compete in peace, but since the murders in Munich in 1972 they do so only because the most extraordinary security precautions are taken, including United States warships at Seoul. Nor does the Olympic movement refrain from congratulating itself when it does bring about change in a country's political system, even if to promote such change is not part of its duty. Killanin himself passionately defends the Berlin Games of 1936 on the (dubious) ground that for every spectator who closed his or her eyes to events in Germany there was another who went home and disseminated the truth,[4] and Samaranch believed that the Seoul Olympics 'were a major factor behind the rapid democratization of the Republic of Korea'.[5]

Although Killanin's account has weaknesses it also contains the kernel of the truth. The Olympic movement sees itself as universal. To extend it is to be more successful; to cover the whole world is to be supremely so. If the IOC had not decided to give the Games to a socialist country it would have been open to the accusation of keeping them as the private plaything of the capitalist world. Even if the IOC's members do not vote with international political considerations in mind, the symbolism is inescapable. Tokyo was welcomed back into the family of nations by being given the Games of 1964; Moscow was welcomed in 1980.

Since the Olympic movement sees itself not only as universal but as a force for peace it is possible, even within its own 'non-political' terms, to justify the award of the Games to Moscow, especially if the IOC judged that détente was a reality and deserved to be encouraged. But the movement is open to the accusation that in taking such grandiose steps towards peace it was overestimating its own importance, and running risks which would better have been left to the professionals.

The award of the Games to Moscow in 1974 symbolised the USSR's complete integration into the Olympic movement. Tsarist Russia had taken part in the Games of 1908 and 1912, but after the revolution the USSR eschewed bourgeois competitive sport. However, in the post-war flush of victory the Soviets were ready to take on the world; they sent officials as observers to the 1948 Games, formed an NOC in 1951 and first took part in 1952.[6]

After the war Olympic officials feared that the Soviet Union would take the Olympic movement over and bring politics into what they saw as a hitherto politics-free club, and when they returned they did indeed bring the Cold War into the Games. The result was that for the athletes the Soviets became the enemy, the more so because they could not properly be described as amateurs, and, to the IOC's chagrin, the press began to keep a competitive medal score between the Soviets and the United States.[7] According to Guttmann the Soviets succeeded in ignoring the usual Olympic practice and insisted that they, rather than the IOC, should nominate the Soviet members of the IOC. Once their members had been elected they politicised the Games, in the sense that there were now disagreements along established political lines. In 1956 they proposed that the IOC be expanded to include representatives of all the NOCs and IFs, and by 1970 they had thoroughly politicised elections to the Executive Board.[8]

Killanin sees the decision to hold the IOC's 1962 Session in Moscow as a halfway house, after which the Soviets began to work towards being awarded the Games. Their first attempt was at Amsterdam in 1970, where they were bidding against Montreal and Los Angeles for the 1976 Games. Los Angeles had been over-flamboyant, and was eliminated on the first round, after which its 17 votes went to Montreal. At Vienna in 1974 Los Angeles bid again, this time for the

Games of 1980, but realised that Moscow was likely to be favourite, and gave a very low-key bid.

After Moscow had won, Killanin made the unprecedented ruling that the votes should not be made known but that the choice should be announced as having been unanimous, because he feared that if Los Angeles had realised how few votes it had got it would not have tried again. According to Killanin, only he and two tellers knew how many had voted for Los Angeles, and he was not at liberty to reveal the figures, but he does reveal that the IOC was nearly unanimous for Moscow.[9] According to Hazan, *Sovietski Sport* identified the tellers as the Marquess of Exeter and Prince Franz Josef II of Liechtenstein. He adds that the envelope containing the ballot papers was torn up and thrown in the Danube.[10] Tyler and Soar give a different picture of the voting (but without identifying a source) and assert that only 39 out of the 61 IOC members who voted chose Moscow.[11]

Genesis of the United States boycott

Several speakers in Congress and in the House of Commons made the same point, that there had been opposition to Moscow from the start, both outside and within the Soviet Union. Kanin, a CIA man rather surprisingly writing in the *Journal of Sport and Social Issues*, and who must have had some inside knowledge, although he used only unclassified sources for his article, records that Carter ruled out a boycott in relation to the treatment of dissidents in 1978 but that after Afghanistan 'Sport, that most peripheral and most publicized form of international relations, provided the perfect answer'. He thinks Carter was reluctant to boycott, perhaps because the President wanted to be consistent with his earlier decision, or perhaps because he thought most Americans would prefer the United States team to compete.[12] Be that as it may, the Soviet Union invaded Afghanistan on 27 December 1979, and in the first two weeks of January the boycott campaign began to roll. On 2 February 1980 Killanin received a visit from Lloyd Cutler, the President's Counsel, at his home.[13]

The meeting did not go well: indeed, there had been bad feeling between the IOC and Carter even before his boycott. One cause was, no doubt, a snub administered to Killanin by President Carter in 1978. On 20 October 1978 Tom Bradley, the Mayor of Los Angeles, had arranged that the ceremony of signing the contract between Los Angeles and the IOC for the 1984 Games should be held at the White

House, expecting Carter to attend – but he did not, because his wife
had been on television that morning, and he did not want to upstage
her. Carter was only a few yards away and Killanin, used to being
greeted by Presidents, was furious.[14] It is, therefore, hardly surprising that his hackles rose when he found that Cutler had come to
Dublin not merely to discuss the crisis but to demand that the IOC
should either postpone or cancel the Games. Killanin found Cutler
ignorant about the Olympic movement and, once he had read the
President's memoirs, passed the same verdict on Carter, whom he
describes as 'scrambling for his political life'.[15]

Later in the American campaign Howard Cutler came to London,
where he met a small group including Howell and Roger Bannister,
and seems, according to Howell's account, to have come off worst.
Among other *bon mots*, Howell told Cutler 'In this country Magna
Carta rules, not Jimmy Carter'.[16]

In January 1980, after the Americans had begun their moves
against the Moscow Games, the Greek President, Constantin
Karamanlis, took the opportunity to announce his intention to revive
the proposal that Athens should provide a permanent home for the
Games, and the *New York Times* supported the idea in a number of
editorials, in one of which it criticised President Carter for not supporting it himself.[17] Karamanlis presented the proposal to the IOC in
February. In April the IOC sent Louis Guirandou N'Diaye, the IOC's
member in the Ivory Coast and a member of the Executive Board, to
inspect sites at Olympia. Greece delivered detailed proposals in May,
and Maurice Dryon, head of the committee set up by the Council of
Europe to study the proposal, said it ought to be put into effect by
1984. Although the 1984 summer Games were booked for Los
Angeles, the Republican Presidential aspirant Ronald Reagan supported the idea, but it was discussed at the Congress of the Olympic
movement at Baden-Baden in 1981 and made so little headway that it
has since been dropped.'[18]

NBC and the television rights

The position of the media, especially television, was not easy. NBC
had paid $85m for the United States television rights to the Games,
and was in great uncertainty over whether to proceed with the
expensive and complicated preparations. They were covered at
Lloyds of London and elsewhere for 90 per cent of their expenditure,

but industry spokesmen estimated that the company stood to lose over $20m if there were a boycott and there was speculation in advertising circles that if there were no Games the advertisers who had been prepared to spend $170m with NBC might not be able to find alternative slots. NBC was still going ahead with the preparations at the end of March, in order to be sure of being able to collect the insurance, but finally NBC announced that it would not cover the Games. This cancellation would cost them at least $22m, and perhaps more than $40m, in lost advertising and expenses already incurred and not covered by insurance.[19] Later Cutler said that NBC would be allowed to cover the Games on a news basis, which it did in the same way as any other broadcaster, by buying clips.[20]

The battle with USOC

The American government also made life difficult for USOC, which alone could take the decision not to send a team to the Games. President Carter professed that his boycott was motivated partly by a concern for human rights, but his treatment of USOC suggests that he was not always interested in human rights in his own backyard.

USOC's President and Secretary-General, Robert J. Kane and Colonel Donald Miller, were shocked by Carter's attitude, but welcomed the opportunity to discuss the crisis with White House officials on 18 January 1980. After the meeting they were still brave enough to say that they would not necessarily comply with a decision by the US government to withdraw from the Games.[21]

The government recognised that under Olympic rules the decision would ultimately be made by USOC, but that the athletes, working through their federations, would have some influence. It therefore put great pressure on them to decide in the right way. Some brave athletes resisted, like the oarswoman Anita DeFrantz, who simply went ahead with her training and later, when USOC had decided to withdraw, sought, with eighteen other athletes, to overthrow the decision, contending that the Committee was blocking the athletes' constitutional right to take part in the Games.[22]

As well as pressure from the administration, there was enormous pressure from both political parties and both Houses of Congress. The House of Representatives approved by 386 to 12 a motion urging USOC to press for the Games' transfer or cancellation, and the Senate overwhelmingly approved the boycott, whether or not the Soviets withdrew from Afghanistan.[23] Such opposition as there was came from a coalition of dyed-in-the-wool Republicans and Democrats to the left of Carter.

By mid-January Carter was saying that if there were no Soviet withdrawal within a month he wanted USOC to vote to transfer or cancel the Games; if that failed he would suggest USOC formally withdraw the American athletes. Senator Kennedy, his main opponent for the Democratic nomination, reluctantly supported him. Killanin saw Carter's decision as a tragedy and reiterated that it would be legally and technically impossible to move the Games, but it is not surprising that Kane and Miller began to cave in, and agreed to try to obtain other nations' agreement to moving them.[24] At the same time Carter sent a personal letter to more than a hundred heads of government asking support for a boycott, but gained no immediate new support, as most countries were anxious to defer a final decision for as long as possible, and many were not at all anxious to be seen to exert pressure on their NOCs.[25]

According to evidence to a Congressional sub-committee, a public opinion poll carried out for the *San Francisco Chronicle* had shown that 75 per cent of respondents favoured the boycott.[26] These sub-committee hearings, under the chairmanship of a Mr Madigan, were unimportant in themselves, but interestingly demonstrate how the high purposes of politics may degenerate into time-wasting farce. This was particularly apparent in some contributions by the chairman, whose geo-political thinking and knowledge of African geography cannot have inspired confidence. He said that Nigeria was a principal supplier of light crude oil to the United States. The Soviet Union had surrogate forces in Angola and Ethiopia, which he stated were countries 'in close proximity' to Nigeria. He then posited a hostile move against Nigeria by these surrogate forces in 1984, when it would, he said, obviously be in the United States' national interest to send troops to Nigeria. He asked Colonel Miller whether, in this hypothetical set of circumstances, he thought the USA would have voluntarily to retire from hosting the 1984 Olympics. Miller no doubt drew a deep breath, but was able to answer that his first feeling was that Los Angeles should nevertheless go ahead and host the Games. He added, 'If the games are to be disrupted every time there are human rights violations or aggressions in the world, the games would never have been conducted for the last twenty-five or thirty years.'[27]

Another example of ignorant misjudgement can be found in a tour, apparently arranged by the State Department, undertaken by Muhammad Ali, formerly Cassius Clay, the Olympic boxer. He was asked to visit a number of African states to present the American position. When he arrived in Tanzania he stated that the USA was looking for an alternative place for the Olympics; the USA would support the alternative games financially and would not allow South Africa to take part. However, he was shaken to discover that his hosts were favourably inclined towards the USSR because it funded some African liberation movements, and was unable to answer when pressed to explain why the Africans should join the US boycott. A State Department unclassified telegram, containing the transcript of his press conference on arrival at Dar Es Salaam, shows that his briefing had been woefully inadequate. He was reduced to saying 'I can't answer the question of what America did or didn't do or what Africa did because I don't know. But I can box. I can tell you about boxing.' This naturally provoked the response 'But you think President Carter was correct then in sending you, a boxer, here rather than a diplomat to discuss this very sensitive issue?'.[28] Muhammad Ali went on to Kenya, where he said that his real object was to head off war between the US and the USSR. Then he visited Nigeria, where he got a cool reception, and finally Liberia. Despite the apparent chaos, the State Department had said during his tour that it was 'useful' and when he got home Muhammad Ali said he thought it had been a success.[29]

USOC's collapse

Meanwhile at USOC's headquarters in Colorado Springs its Executive Board unanimously agreed to ask the IOC to postpone, cancel or transfer the Games, which was exactly what the President had asked for. However, Julian K. Roosevelt, an American IOC member, remained loyal and attacked Carter's warning that he expected USOC to withdraw from the Games if the Soviet Union had made no significant move over Afghanistan by mid-February.[30]

The next big encounter was at the IOC's Session, just before the winter Games at Lake Placid, which was opened by the Secretary of State, Cyrus Vance. He considerably irritated Killanin by allowing the world press to see his speech, under embargo, before Killanin saw it. When he did, he found it grossly political, and bound to offend the Soviets. So he warned them that they had better stay away from the ceremony, at which Vance's speech was received in complete silence.

Yet, as Killanin emphasises, Vance's speech did have the good side-effect of drawing the IOC together; it was, after all, a conservative body of men (no women in those days), and it would have been surprising if none of them had been impressed by the American arguments. But their sense of propriety and dislike of being bullied were strong, and all seventy-three who were present at Lake Placid backed a document in Killanin's name, which stated that the Games must be held at Moscow as planned.[31] Killanin points out that twelve days after the IOC's decision at its Lake Placid Session America suffered the humiliation of the bungled attempt to rescue hostages from Iran, and thinks that disaster may have stiffened Carter's resolve to prevent American athletes going to Moscow.[32]

When the USA won a gold medal for ice hockey at the Lake Placid Games, having beaten the Soviet Union in the semi-final, Carter again displayed crass insensitivity by immediately inviting the team to a party at the White House, when he called them 'modern day American heroes.'[33] This move is said by Killanin to have antagonised the USOC and most of the athletes (though the latter did use the occasion to make one of several unsuccessful appeals to the President to change his position), and Killanin thinks the invitation added to the politicisation of an already highly-charged situation, and was a response to popular chauvinism rather than a party to celebrate a gold medal. However, this was not Carter's worst exhibition of insensitivity. That accolade must be reserved for the occasion in 1982, well after he had retired, when he was photographed jogging in an Olympic tracksuit, which had been designed for the sole use of Olympic athletes in the US team.[34]

In April the administration began a drive to ensure that USOC's House of Delegates' meeting would comply with its wishes. Vance, plus the chairman of the joint chiefs of staff, General David C. Jones, told USOC that the boycott was essential to national security. It was further reported that Carter was considering emergency economic powers to stop athletes going to Moscow and it was confirmed that there had been discussions with House Speaker Thomas P. O'Neill Jr and Senate Majority Leader Robert Byrd about stopping them with amendments to the Amateur Sports Act of 1978, which authorises USOC to field a team at Olympic events. USOC officials then had little choice but to say that the President's threats of legal actions seemed to have closed the door on American participation.[35]

At the meeting at Colorado Springs a vast congregation of

sportsmen and women and sports administrators was addressed by Vice-President Walter Mondale, after which the boycotters, by now including USOC's President, Robert Kane, won comfortably, by 1,604 to 797.[36] Neil Macfarlane, soon to become Britain's Minister for Sport, watched the meeting on television (as did Killanin) and wrote: 'It was almost embarrassing to watch the emotional nationalism that charged the meeting. It reminded me of an American political convention and there was no doubt about how a vote would go'.[37] As the months went by at least one former athlete changed his mind towards favouring the boycott for a bizarre reason: this was Bruce Jenner, a former decathlon gold medal winner, who received letters from members of the patriotic public, threatening not to eat Wheaties, which he promoted.[38]

Although the IOC had much to complain of in USOC's conduct, it is difficult not to agree with Ueberroth that USOC had no choice. Ueberroth's close associate Harry Usher had gone to the meeting on his behalf and reported that the government was considering not backing legislation whereby people would be able to give USOC $1 by ticking a box on their tax return (such a Bill came before the Senate in 1984, but made no progress). Furthermore the government had privately threatened to renegotiate the 'sweetheart lease' of USOC's headquarters and training ground in Colorado Springs, both of them government-owned.[39] The government was even ruthless enough to threaten Miller, who was a retired army colonel, with the loss of his pension.

Once USOC had decided for boycott, Killanin needed to talk to its officials and to Ueberroth and to gauge the feeling of the IFs and the European NOCs. In advance of Killanin's meeting with Kane and Miller, Carter sent a message reiterating that the United States' opposition to sending a team to Moscow rested solely on international law, human rights and the national security of the USA and many other free world nations. He added that this stand did not detract in any way from the United States' devotion to the Olympic movement. He continued to believe that sports should be run by private bodies and not by governments; the USA would continue to oppose the efforts of other governments to establish UNESCO Games, and would welcome athletes of all eligible nations at Los Angeles, as they had at Lake Placid.[40] The first part of this message may sound like claptrap, but the second was shrewd, since it appealed to the fear of interference by UNESCO which Killanin justifiably entertained, and pre-empted threats to remove the 1984 Games from Los Angeles.

Although the federal government had won its battle to prevent athletes from attending the Games, it took heed of the warnings it had had that, if representatives did not attend the various Congresses the USA would have no say in elections to the ruling bodies of the various federations. (The Soviets readily grasped the same point when they boycotted Los Angeles in 1984, but sent officials and judges.) Carter would not allow the United States' flag to be run up at the end of the Games, but Ueberroth managed to obtain a Los Angeles flag, which was used in its place.

The Soviet reaction

Once the prospect of a boycott became something to be reckoned with, the Soviet press began a counter-campaign. The Soviet campaign did not accept that the invasion of Afghanistan was the reason for the boycott. The 'real' reasons were that the USSR was a socialist country; that President Carter wished to undermine détente and that he needed to salvage his failing popularity. The campaign's main lines appeared in an article in *Sovietski Sport* on 20 January 1980:

We understand clearly why all real friends of sports and Olympism decisively oppose the provocative manoeuvres of supporters of cold war in the United States, England and some other imperialist states, who are striving to utilise sport as an instrument of their policy and hinder the forthcoming meeting of world youth on the arenas of the Moscow Olympic Games . . . The foreign policy of the USSR which is clear to the peoples of the world, corresponds with their basic interests . . . and serves as a reliable support of all forces struggling for peace and detente. Supporting the cause of preserving the unity of the Olympic movement, striving to prevent interference of politicians in sport and participating in Moscow's holiday of youth – despite threats, slanderous tricks and political pressure – this is the attitude of the sports world and the public of the countries participating in the Olympic movement toward the Olympiade in the first country of socialism.[41]

Kanin thinks that by the middle of March Moscow had probably decided that the Americans would definitely not take part in the Games, because from then on their reaction to the boycott included extremely harsh attacks on Carter and hints that a boycott could harm overall East/West relations.[42]

Hazan sees two stages in the campaign: up to 25 May the possible negative consequences were stressed; after that date had passed, and there was little prospect of further acceptances being received from

NOCs, the line was that nothing serious had happened. There were vague threats of boycotting Los Angeles, and the defeat of United States athletes by their own politicians was stressed. Afghanistan was seldom mentioned; when it was it was presented as Carter's excuse for something that he had long been planning.[43] As the Games approached, the Soviet authorities began to acknowledge that there would be fewer foreign visitors than had been expected (perhaps a blessing to the KGB) and lowered their guess from 300,000 or more to 70,000. As the final preparations for the Games began they closed Moscow to all Soviet citizens, except those who could prove that they lived and worked there.[44]

The Games and after

In the end 81 NOCs participated, compared with 88 at Montreal (1976), 122 at Munich (1972) and 113 at Mexico City (1968). The Games were attended by 5,326 competitors compared with 6,085 in 1972. The most important boycotters in terms of ability to win medals were the USA, West Germany and Japan. As Macfarlane puts it: 'In some ways the Games were devalued but, had the boycott succeeded, there would have been a real danger that the Olympic movement would have been destroyed.'[45]

For Killanin the Games were joyless. But he still believed that without the boycott, and with the presence of the three to four hundred thousand foreign visitors who had originally been expected, the Games might have played a part in breaking down the barriers between East and West, despite the difficulties of visitors meeting Soviet citizens. But so politicised had the Games become that the political journalists, according to Killanin, nearly outnumbered the sports writers, and many papers carried two accounts of the same events, though from two very different points of view.[46]

After the Games were over, Samaranch asserted that they had won the Olympic movement new strength and respect and that the Executive Board had been keenly aware that it could save the Games from fiasco only by collaborating closely with the Moscow organising committee.

The Executive Board asked the sixty-six Olympic Committees which had stayed away to explain why they had done so.[47] However, it seems that the enquiries were not very energetically pursued and that some quite feeble excuses were allowed to pass.

Looking ahead to Los Angeles

Peter Ueberroth, the organiser of the Los Angeles Games, was, to put it mildly, keenly interested in the boycott, though not himself at the eye of the storm. In the absence of any public money Ueberroth was running the first 'private enterprise Games' and the boycott immediately raised the possibility of all his sponsors defecting. However, although a boycott was very much against Ueberroth's interest, he seems to have understood at least part of the President's case for it. The season of primary elections was just beginning; Carter's nomination as the Democratic candidate was being contested and the negotiations over the Iran hostages were stalled. In Ueberroth's judgement Carter desperately needed a bold public relations stroke. Ueberroth himself was torn between supporting the government or supporting the athletes, and chose the latter (though he does not seem to have been his usual outspoken self). All his Board, save David Wolper, the film producer, voted for the government, and Ueberroth would have gone with Wolper, if he had had a vote.[48]

Just before the Moscow Games Ueberroth took a small LAOOC delegation to Moscow, in order to inform the IOC of LAOOC's progress with Los Angeles' preparations for the 1984 Games. Although he had been allowed to report to the IOC, he had not been permitted to stay for the Games themselves: 'Because of this farcical ruling the Los Angeles Organising Committee lost an opportunity to learn at first hand about the running of the games'.[49] So Ueberroth was back in the United States during the Moscow Games and went to a 'showcase meeting' of American swimmers, held to compare their times with those achieved in Moscow, and to meet Ronald Reagan. He briefed Reagan on how important the 1984 Games were to the USA and was disconcerted to find that he appeared to have taken nothing in. But a littler later Reagan played it all back in a speech to the crowd, as if the ideas had been his own.[50] It must be added that Reagan had chopped and changed over the boycott. He at first supported it, then said the decision should be left to the athletes, then supported participation in the Games, but finally returned to supporting the boycott, while denying that he had changed his position.[51]

As for the verdict of American history, Tip O'Neill, one-time Speaker of the House of Representatives, may be typical. He approved of Carter's stand: 'People criticized him for that decision, arguing that sport should not be confused with politics, but Carter knew that to the Soviets, the two were already deeply entangled. Our withdrawal from the Moscow games signified the true extent of our anger and came as a resounding thud to Soviet prestige.'[52] In his own memoirs Carter sounds less sure: 'I was determined to lead the rest of the world in making it as costly as possible. There was a balancing act to perform – America being the leader, but at the same time consulting and working closely with the other nations. To be effective, punitive action had to be broadly supported and clearly defined.' But he goes on: 'I knew the decision was controversial, but I had no idea at the time how difficult it would be for me to implement it or to convince other nations to join us', and 'we had a struggle all the way; the outcome was always in doubt. Most Olympic committees were wholly independent bodies, whose members deeply resented any government involvement in their decisions.'[53]

Perhaps if he had his time over again he would not have embarked on a crusade which was indeed costly in political credit and energy, and whose results were negligible.

International repercussions of the Moscow boycott

At its meeting in Lausanne on 23 April the Executive Board addressed the questions, which arouse so much passion, relating to the use of national flags. For example, the Italian government had made it clear that the Italian flag was its property, and that it could prevent its use outside Italy, though it would not seek to prevent athletes making their own decisions as to whether or not to attend the Games. It was agreed that they could use their NOCs' flags, or the Olympic flag, and that they could use the names of their NOCs rather than of their countries if necessary. This fitted with Killanin's long-term ambition to 'denationalise' the Games (an ambition which Samaranch has done nothing to promote). Nor did President Carter have his own way in every particular, for as the politburo filed in to the opening ceremony, performed by President Leonid Brezhnev, two Americans defied Carter's wishes, and unfurled the American flag in protest against their country's absence. But the IOC had to give way to Carter's pressure, and not raise the American flag or play its anthem at the closing ceremony.[54] In May Killanin called on both Brezhnev and Carter, and realised for the first time that Cutler was a strong man behind a weak President.[55]

Meanwhile the United States government was doing its best to persuade its allies to join the boycott. The western European response to Washington's pressure was marked by vacillation, because many countries (France was a notable exception) hoped to present a united front, and because governments' responses were linked to other issues in foreign and domestic politics. For instance, West Germany desired to preserve its good relationship with the United States, yet did not wish to jeopardise its Ostpolitik (at whose heart lay the intention to normalise relations with East Germany) by joining in the boycott. Nor were most western European governments willing to be seen to bring great pressure to bear upon their NOCs. West Germany was an exception, but the Italian government (to take an example) did not have any hard feelings when the NOC decided to participate, although the government had been in favour of the boycott. Among governments of developed nations the most important to follow the American were those of West Germany, Japan and Great Britain, the last a special case, in that the British Olympic Association decided to defy it, and to send its team to Moscow.

In the Third World the satellite or 'client' states of both super-powers followed their leaders: for example in Africa (where the American cause had not been helped by Muhammad Ali's tour) Zaire, Libya and Kenya embraced the boycott, whereas Nigeria did not, while in the Muslim world Pakistan and Saudi Arabia boycotted and Iran did not. Smaller states which had no particular relation of clientship with either party were divided, and most of Latin America took part in the Games.[56]

The British response

Britain would no doubt not relish being described as a client state, but its government, under the enthusiastic guidance of the then Prime Minister, Mrs Margaret Thatcher, made a major effort to follow American policy, although in the end without success. The issue sharply divided Parliament, the country and the media. Outside Parliament great pressure was put on the British Olympic Association, though to nothing like the American extent, and in the House of Commons the longest debate that the House had ever held on a sporting subject amply reflected the divisions in the country at large.

In Parliament responsibility for the Games, about which a number of questions were put to ministers, was constantly shunted from Department to Department, but when it came to the main debate on

17 March 1980 the unfortunate Minister for Sport, Hector Monro, was not even allowed to take part, partly because he was known to be opposed to the government's line, and partly because the Olympic affair attracted so much public attention that it had to be dealt with by senior ministers.

The motion before the House was proposed by Sir Ian Gilmour, the Lord Privy Seal. It read: 'I beg to move that this House condemns the Soviet invasion of Afghanistan and believes that Great Britain should not take part in the Olympic Games in Moscow.' As Gilmour rightly said, the first part of the motion was relatively uncontroversial, although there were a few members, of whom the most notable was Tam Dalyell, who, while not exactly congratulating the Soviet Union on the invasion, nevertheless wanted the Commons to understand why it had judged the invasion to be necessary.[57]

The not especially strong amendment moved by the opposition Labour Party called upon the Soviet Union to withdraw from Afghanistan; it asserted that an effective response on the Olympics, as in the economic, trading and political fields, could be achieved only by securing substantial agreement among the governments of western Europe, the USA and elsewhere; regretted the government's failure to consult properly with the sporting bodies in Britain, and asserted 'the right of individual citizens at the end of the day to make their own decisions'. Thus the House was not being invited to make a clear-cut decision for or against participation in the Olympic Games.

The debate was both lively and reflective. It was wound up for the government by Michael Heseltine, Secretary of State for the Environment, under whom sport normally fell, although much of the activity had been undertaken by the Foreign Office. He admitted that much was being asked of the athletes, but in the circumstances of the 'unique contrast of the Olympic Games and Afghanistan' the role was one that only they could be asked to accept. Nor would he agree that there had been inadequate consultation with sporting interests. But he did assure the House that reprisals would not be taken against public servants who asked for unpaid leave to attend the Games; ordinary citizens wishing to go as spectators would not be interfered with, and the government would not interfere with decisions over coverage of the Games taken by the BBC and IBA.[58]

It was necessarily rather a weak speech, but the House broke on more or less predictable lines, defeating the Labour amendment by 305 to 188 votes. However, as Macfarlane points out, thirty

Conservatives abstained, despite the three line whip on attendance, by which the government ensured a good turn-out.[59]

Killanin comments on the messiness of argument and extent of misinformation in the House of Commons debate of 17 March 1980, but he exaggerates its poor quality. The impression one gets from reading it today is that of course few of the members who spoke knew much about the minutiae of the Olympic movement (though a few, like Terence Higgins, had direct experience) but many of them did have a perfectly sound understanding of the political issues and deployed the arguments for and against taking part in the Games in a reasonably competent manner.

The Olympics divided the press no less than they divided the country and Parliament. Killanin tells the story, later retold by Denis Howell, of the Duke of Edinburgh, who appeared at Lausanne as President of the International Equestrian Federation. The redoubtable Ian Wooldridge of the London *Daily Mail* had spoken to Prince Philip and obtained his confirmation that he had taken a hand in wording a statement that all the IFs would be present at Moscow. There followed what Killanin (himself a journalist) understandably calls 'one of the most appalling instances of news manipulation I have known'. The story was replaced with a denial from Buckingham Palace, after appearing only in the first edition, and Wooldridge's follow-up, reconfirming what he had written, was not printed at all. Killanin does not believe that the Prince was a party to all this, but does imply that, since the story was against the *Daily Mail*'s editorial line, it may not have been difficult for the Palace to have it suppressed.[60] It must, however, be added that Wooldridge himself, who might well have told this story in his retrospective collection of articles, instead pays tribute to the *Daily Mail*'s willingness to print his stories, although he disagreed with its editorial policy. The paper believed that this was an example of the freedom which was not allowed in the Soviet bloc and which America and its allies were seeking to defend.[61]

The British government did not display the same mixture of ruthlessness and stupidity as the American, but what turned public opinion against it was its insistence that the athletes would be behaving irresponsibly if they went to the Games, while it allowed trade and other official links to continue undiminished.

The whole affair may have marked a turning point in thinking in

British sports circles about the relationship between sport and politics. According to Macfarlane, Dickie Jeeps, the Chairman of the Sports Council, thought British sport would never again have an existence independent of politics. Dick Palmer, Secretary-General of the BOA, strongly differed and thought the moral was that sport must form itself into an effective political pressure group, in order to protect itself against undue political pressure.[62] In either case, British sport could never again be politically innocent.

So far as the IOC was concerned, the hatchet was buried in March 1993, when Samaranch went to see President Carter. They had not, Samaranch said afterwards, discussed the Moscow boycott, 'but I think my visit closes the subject. We consider President Carter a great man who defends poor countries and human rights all over the world.'[63]

Notes

1 Lord Killanin, *My Olympic Years*, London, 1983, p. 3.

2 *Ibid.*, pp. 166–9.

3 Lord Killanin and John Rodda (eds), *The Olympic Games 1984*, London, 1983, p. 13.

4 Killanin, p. 3.

5 Kim Un-yong, *The Greatest Olympics: from Baden-Baden to Seoul*, Seoul, 1990, p. 14.

6 James Riordan, 'Elite Sport Policy in East and West', in Lincoln Allison (ed.), *The Politics of Sport*, Manchester, 1986, pp. 70–3.

7 Richard Espy, *The Politics of the Olympic Games*, Berkeley, 1979, pp. 26, 28, 34 and 38.

8 Allen Guttmann, *The Games Must Go On: Avery Brundage and the Olympic Movement*, New York, 1984, pp. 139, 171–3.

9 Killanin, *My Olympic Years*, pp. 164–8.

10 Baruch A. Hazan, *Olympic Sports and Propaganda Games: Moscow 1980*, London, 1982, p. 3.

11 Martin Tyler and Phil Soar (eds), *The History of the Olympic Games*, London, revised ed., 1980, p. 161.

12 David B. Kanin, 'The Olympic Boycott in Diplomatic Context', in *Journal of Sport and Social Issues*, 4, 1, spring/summer 1980, pp. 5 and 6.

13 Killanin, p. 172.

14 Kenneth Reich, *Making it Happen: Peter Ueberroth and the 1984 Olympics*, Santa Barbara, 1986, pp. 210–11 and Killanin, pp. 105–6.

15 Killanin, p. 174. (However, Carter's memoirs say little about the Games!)

16 Denis Howell, *Made in Birmingham: the Memoirs of Denis Howell*, London, 1990, p. 304. His remark is also quoted with admiration by Neil Macfarlane, Conservative Minister for Sport from 1981 to 1985. *Sport and*

Politics: a World Divided, London, 1986, p. 225.
   17   *New York Times*, 17 January 1980.
   18   Killanin, p. 231.
   19   *New York Times*, 29, 30 January, 29 March, 7 May 1980. Neil Wilson, *The Sports Business: the Men and the Money*, London, 1988, p. 18, puts NBC's uninsured loss at $34m.
   20   Killanin, p. 214 and David A. Klatell and Norman Marcus, *Sports for Sale: Television, Money and the Fans*, New York, 1988, p. 170.
   21   *New York Times*, 8, 16, 17 and 19 January 1980.
   22   *New York Times*, 24 April 1980. Although the suit made no progress, DeFrantz has subsequently had a notable career in the Olympic movement. She was active in LAOOC, and played a leading part in trying to persuade African NOCs, save Ethiopia's, not to follow the Soviet Union into boycotting the Los Angeles Games. In 1986 she was elected to the IOC, of which she is an atypical member, being female, black and not especially rich. At the IOC's Istanbul Session in 1987 she spoke passionately for the Games being open to all, amateur or professional, and in 1988 and 1989 respectively she became a member of the IOC's Athletes' Commission and Programme Commission.
   23   *New York Times*, 20, 24, 25, 29, 30 January 1980.
   24   *Ibid.*, 9 February 1980.
   25   *Ibid.*, 22 January 1980. This appears to be the communication, a list of whose addressees Peter Ueberroth was to see in mid-February, and which included South Africa: *Made in America*, London, 1986, p. 66.
   26   Evidence before Sub-Committee on Transportation and Commerce of the House of Representatives' Committee on Interstate and Foreign Commerce, pp. 48–9.
   27   Sub-Committee proceedings, p. 47.
   28   *Ibid*. The telegram is at p. 27.
   29   There were daily references to the Ali story in the *New York Times*, 3–11 February 1980. For a more sympathetic account of Ali's expedition see Stephen R. Wenn and Jeffrey P. Wenn, 'Muhammad Ali and the Convergence of Olympic Sport and U.S. Diplomacy in 1980: a Reassessment from Behind the Scenes at the U.S. State Department', *Olympika*, II, 1993, pp. 45–66. They add that Carter, as well as Ali, thought he had done well.
   30   *New York Times*, 7 February 1980.
   31   Killanin, pp. 177–86.
   32   *Ibid.*, p. 192.
   33   *New York Times*, 20 February 1980.
   34   Killanin and Rodda (eds), p. 48.
   35   *New York Times*, 9, 10, 12 April 1980.
   36   *Ibid.*, 12 and 13 April 1980.
   37   Macfarlane, p. 221 and Killanin, p. 192.
   38   *New York Times*, 28 May 1980.
   39   Ueberroth, p. 69.
   40   Killanin, pp. 193–4.
   41   Quoted by Hazan, p. 129.
   42   Kanin, p. 7.
   43   Hazan, pp. 131–45.

44 *New York Times*, 3 and 10 July 1980.
45 Macfarlane, p. 228.
46 Killanin, pp. 217–18.
47 *The Times*, 1 November 1980.
48 Ueberroth, pp. 65–6.
49 Killanin, p. 4.
50 Ueberroth, pp. 75–6.
51 *New York Times*, 1, 6 and 11 April 1980.
52 Tip O'Neill, with William Novak, *Man of the House; the Life and Political Memoirs of Speaker Tip O'Neill*, London, 1987, p. 298.
53 Jimmy Carter, *Keeping Faith: Memoirs of a President*, New York, 1982, pp. 472, 482, 526. Sir Nicholas Henderson, who was British Ambassador in Washington, says very little about the Olympics in his memoirs. He records that President Richard Nixon derided Carter's action; he makes the fair point that Carter wanted to make a conspicuous gesture, his earlier and quiet signals having failed to deter the USSR, and he notes that Mrs Thatcher's failure to persuade the British Olympic Association to boycott Moscow contributed to her government's reputation in Washington of being unable to 'deliver'. Nicholas Henderson, *Mandarin: the Diaries of an Ambassador 1969–1982*, London, 1994, pp. 324, 327, 342.
54 *New York Times*, 1 August 1980.
55 Killanin, pp. 210–13.
56 Kanin, *passim*.
57 The debate is at 981 *H.C.* Deb., cols 31–160, 17 March 1980.
58 *Ibid.*, cols 149–60. The quotation is at col. 154.
59 Macfarlane, p. 229.
60 Killanin., pp. 196–7.
61 Ian Wooldridge, *Sport in the 80s: a Personal View*, London, 1989, p. 9.
62 MacFarlane, p. 228.
63 *Olympic Review*, 306, April 1993, p. 130.

VII

The Los Angeles Games of 1984

The Los Angeles Games of 1984 will no doubt be remembered largely as an exercise in super-power politics, but they were also significant for domestic Olympic reasons. They marked a shift in power (which has proved temporary) from the IOC to the host city. Because there was no competition to host the Games the IOC could not have its own way to anything like the normal extent, and once Los Angeles had been awarded the Games it was able to ignore established practice in a manner which would not have been tolerated if any alternative city had been available.

Thus, the Games were sharply political, both for these internal reasons and because of the Soviet boycott. They were also sharply commercial, because the taxpayers of California refused to fund them. The organising committee (LAOOC – the Los Angeles Olympic Organising Committee) responded to the taxpayers by creating the first private enterprise Games, and therein gave a lead to the whole future development of the Olympic movement.

Harry Edwards claims that 'Most commonly, sportspolitics becomes manifest in the tendency of a society's established political authority to characterize athletic achievement as demonstrable proof of the adequacy, if not superiority, of prevailing ideological sentiments.' In other words, American governments see athletic prowess as proof that capitalism and the American way of life are better than any other system. Very similar notions may be found in Soviet writings: for example, Riordan quotes a publication dating from 1951: 'Each new victory is a victory for the Soviet form of society and the socialist sports system; it provides irrefutable proof of the superiority of socialist culture over the decaying culture of the capitalist states'.[1]

Edwards's remark contains an element of truth, since it is true that ever since the Soviet Union rejoined the Olympic movement in 1952 American governments have been willing to use the Games as an instrument of political competition. However, in the case of Los Angeles it was not the 'established political authority' that asserted the peculiar value of capitalism, but the businessmen who ran the Games as a commercial enterprise. Nor was it the government that revelled in chauvinism, but the people. Had there been no boycott the Games would have been nothing like as popular as they turned out to be under the stimulus of anti-Soviet sentiment.

Los Angeles had held the games in 1932 and had developed the revolutionary and cost-cutting innovation of housing all the athletes in a single Olympic village. The city had bid again in 1970 (for 1976) when, according to Killanin, 'their representatives appeared short on experience' and were defeated by Montreal. At their next attempt, in 1974, Killanin thought them 'resigned to a Soviet victory'.[2] Geoffrey Miller puts a rather different gloss on the 1974 attempt. He records that at that time the city's standing could not have been higher; the bid was sensibly cheap (for example, the athletes were to be accommo-dated in universities, so that no Olympic village would have to be built), and Mayor Tom Bradley made a good impression on the IOC. Nevertheless, despite Los Angeles's good showing, the Committee felt that it had no alternative but to give the Games to Moscow, although Killanin praised Los Angeles's bid and encouraged the city to try again.[3]

Local antagonism was enough to ensure that State and local govern-ments refused to contribute to the cost of bidding or, once the bid had been successful, to that of holding the Games.

Public expenditure in California had been much reduced under the Governorship of Ronald Reagan and the taxpayers were worried about damage to the environment, which they believed would result from holding the Games at Los Angeles; the financial costs (especially in view of the losses incurred by Montreal in 1976); and the prospect of disruption to their daily lives. Nor would the federal government risk unpopularity by giving any subsidy, although in fact some cost fell on federal security agencies, and a great deal of governmental time was spent trying (half-heartedly and ineffectually, according to Peter Ueberroth, the President of LAOOC), to fend off the Soviet boycott.

The voters' attitude rested on an overwhelming popular referendum of 1978, which resulted in what is known as the Jarvis

Amendment, limiting statewide property tax increases to 1 per cent and thereby severely constraining the State's spending power. Nor was it possible for the Games to benefit from a State lottery, since these were illegal in California. LAOOC also decided not to seek donations from the public because it would have been competing against many good causes, including the United States Olympic Committee (USOC).[4] The result of this complete absence of public funds was that in May 1978, when it was the only candidate for the 1984 Games (Tehran having withdrawn), the Los Angeles team was truculent, stated its own terms, and in a dozen places on the application form said 'no' where 'yes' would have been expected. The most glaring example was in respect of television, where the IOC has to approve every contract and, since it owns the proceeds, divides them between the various parties entitled to a share. However, Los Angeles said it would retain the entire proceeds, but would agree only as an act of grace to remit an appropriate portion of the net revenue to the IOC.

John Rodda, the London *Guardian*'s distinguished sports correspondent, was, according to Geoffrey Miller, the first journalist to discover what was happening, because he acquired a copy of the completed questionnaire. At that point the dozen or so IOC members to whom Miller had talked privately wanted to reject the Los Angeles bid out of hand, knowing that Mexico, Munich or even Montreal would have been able to step into the breach at short notice. Normally, Killanin records, 'there would have been a polite rejection and the show business people behind the application would have been turned aside', but he preferred a flexible response, in the hope of persuading Los Angeles to enter into suitable contracts. So long drawn out were the negotiations that in January 1979 Killanin began to look for other possible host cities. In due course Los Angeles changed most of the offending replies, although the contracts were not ready until March 1979, the biggest delay having been caused by the difficulty of finding a formula which would release USOC from financial responsibility if the Los Angeles organising committee failed.

The IOC found an acceptable formula for funding the Games, although it did not accord with the letter of its own Charter; that is, the Games were to be awarded to Los Angeles, which would hand them over to an independent organising committee. This body would accept final responsibility jointly with the United States Olympic Committee, and its officials, Robert Kane (President) and Colonel

Don F. Miller (General Secretary), would seek guarantees from industry to cover losses. Thus, the solution was a form of sponsorship, and Los Angeles had won the battle with the IOC.[5] In all but the most legalistic interpretation the language of the contract under which the Games were formally awarded by the IOC represented a clear violation of IOC rules by absolving the city of Los Angeles of all financial liability for them. Another blunder was made, according to Kenneth Reich (a journalist who had long specialised in Olympic news, and was to write a book about the 1984 Games), by Madame Berlioux and Lord Killanin. They had committed themselves to allow all the profits of the 1984 Games to stay in the USA, without, of course, having any idea of how great the profits would turn out to be. Reich states that when Ueberroth, after the Games, began to reveal the real figures, Samaranch, according to Berlioux, 'briefly considered trying to abrogate the 1978 agreement but bowed to advice not to do so. Actually, there might have been legal grounds for a challenge. In the view of IOC lawyers the 1978 verbal [sic] agreement on the profits had never been legally formalized'.[6] This extraordinary assertion would be quite unacceptable from a less respected reporter than Reich. As it is, one can only marvel that Madame Berlioux, normally a tigress in support of the IOC's rights, can have allowed Ueberroth to make a fool of her by permitting an oral agreement to govern the destination of the Games' profits.

Private enterprise Games

This, then, was the origin of the 'private enterprise' Games, from which the Olympic movement drew so much of its inspiration for the Games' wholehearted commercialisation under Samaranch. The grandees may not particularly like Peter Ueberroth, and his memoirs show that he did not become excessively attached to them, but they owe him a great deal.

It was possible to organise the Games on a private basis at Los Angeles because they were spread out over a very large geographical area, 250 miles long by 50 miles wide, in order to use existing facilities and so to avoid great capital expenditure. It was necessary to have all twenty-three venues arranged by the time of the Olympic movement's Congress at Baden-Baden in 1981 in order to prove to the Olympic world that it had not been a mistake to award the Games to Los Angeles. As Ueberroth put it 'We weren't going to be the whipping people for the Carter boycott.'[7] This great geographical spread was not, of course, ideal from the spectators' point of view, but it makes little difference how far the events are physically separated from one another if the Olympics are regarded primarily as a television spectacle, on which the medium imposes an illusory sense of place.

Once Ueberroth had taken on the presidency of LAOOC he had to start more or less from scratch. Although the city had hosted the Games in 1932 all he received by way of guidance from City Hall when he started work was one cardboard box, marked 'All the records of the Los Angeles Olympic Games'. There were other difficulties too. For example,the owner of LAOOC's first offices reneged on the lease, and had the locks changed, as he disapproved of Los Angeles holding the Games.[8] Despite these inconveniences Ueberroth swiftly built up a powerful organisation. He was not, however, unequivocally admired. Reich suggests that his management style was authoritarian, erratic and unpredictable. His public utterances were often misleading and contradictory, so that it was not always possible to tell, even in retrospect, when he had been telling the truth. At the end of his long book Reich remains ambivalent about Ueberroth, yet he is able to say 'To me the organizing committee . . . became a kind of totalitarian Utopia.'[9]

Forecasting the profits

Ueberroth persistently said that the Games were going to make only a small profit, although he must have known some time ahead that the profit was going to be very large. Indeed, he admits as much when he says 'We made a conscious decision to underestimate projected revenues as this was our only protection against unknown cost factors and an unstable international political environment'.[10] So dedicated was Ueberroth to secrecy that, according to Reich, he kept the real position even from people whom one would think would have had the right to be informed. For example, when he visited the IOC ten days after the USSR had declared its boycott on 8 May 1984 he angrily refused to discuss LAOOC's financial state.[11] His reference to political uncertainties suggests that the possibility of a Soviet boycott was in his mind from very early on. He apparently believed that LAOOC needed a secret cushion, or reserve, in case the Soviets should not take part. If they pulled out and if ABC's viewing figures fell unacceptably (both conditions had to be satisfied), then the television company would have had the right to renegotiate its payment.[12]

Ueberroth insisted that the winner of the contest for the North American television rights must agree at the same time to act as host broadcaster, which would cost $75m. ABC paid $225m, so that from Ueberroth's point of view the deal was worth $300m, although the figure generally used is $225m. Ueberroth rightly forecast that, in view of the IOC's precarious finances (about which he had received private information), Madame Berlioux was hardly likely to use her power to veto the contract. He is, however, scathing about the IOC's business acumen in those days and recounts that the IOC counsel carried the first cheque, of $25m, about with him for twenty days, losing bank interest all the while. Again, the assertion seems fantastic, but there is no reason to doubt the accuracy of Ueberroth's memory.

Ueberroth had to make it clear that he intended to be master in his own house. Thus, ABC was left in no doubt that, although it had paid heavily for the Games, it was not going to be allowed to run them, as it had done at Lake Placid.[13] Similarly, Ueberroth had to stand up to the overweening egos of the grandees of the Olympic movement and his frankness about them must surely have made him enemies: perhaps that is why he was not even invited to the Seoul Games.

Relations with the IOC and international federations

Ueberroth shows his talent for settling old scores when he discusses Monique Berlioux. He recalls that he had been warned that she was a stickler for detail and would demonstrate her superiority by testing his knowledge of the Charter and the Olympic movement. Ueberroth had managed to deflect her from her original insistence that the IOC must approve all contracts made by LAOOC (a right that the IOC has retained with subsequent organising committees) but she had insisted on approving the television contract for United States rights, and paid what sounds like a state visit to Los Angeles for the purpose. Ueberroth remembers that her demands were encyclopaedic.

We had to make sure that a swimming pool was available, that Evian water was supplied, that there were exquisite flower arrangements, that the room service met her French tastes, that restaurant arrangements were made for the finest eateries, that appointments were not scheduled either early in the morning or late at night, and that her travelling staff received equally impeccable treatment.[14]

Likewise the IF presidents, Ueberroth writes, are 'accustomed to pomp and circumstance and are extremely status conscious'.[15] In searching for venues LAOOC had particularly difficult dealings with FIFA, the football federation, and with Tom Keller of rowing. FIFA did succeed in having new stadia built, but when Adriaan Paulen, then President of IAAF, threatened to withdraw from the Games if they did not build him a new stadium, LAOOC called his bluff.[16] Both Reich and Ueberroth have stories to tell about Primo Nebiolo, who succeeded Paulen as President of IAAF. Reich says that at the Los Angeles Games Nebiolo asked for the positions of the IAAF and the Olympic flags to be reversed from what had been intended, so that he could look up from his seat at his own flag. LAOOC did as he asked. For his part, Ueberroth recalls that Nebiolo had been daily pressurising Samaranch for special treatment and extra accreditations at Los Angeles, and that Samaranch asked Ueberroth to help. Although the latter had always vowed to give no special treatment to anyone, he knew that he would have to relent in this case and agreed that Nebiolo could have what he wanted, but not until nearer the Games, in order to prevent all the other IFs from making similar demands. As he ruefully puts it: 'Not all sports federations, or NOCs for that matter, – so it turns out – are created equal.'[17]

Although Los Angeles had been able to make its own terms, the IOC continued to keep its usual close eye on the preparations for the Games. Ueberroth had also to retain the United States government's support, and for this reason he was pleased that Samaranch, who had been pressing for a meeting with President Reagan, achieved it on 28 January 1982 and obtained a stronger version of the letter of support that President Carter had signed when Los Angeles was first awarded the Games. 'More important', Ueberroth writes, 'it meant support for the Games had passed from one administration to the next.'[18]

The sponsors

Ueberroth's originality lay in limiting his sponsors (whose contributions came to $126.7m) to relatively few, though not as few as became the IOC's practice in its TOP programme (see Chapter IV). Ueberroth decided that there should be no more than thirty, with a minimum subscription of $4m and an 'exclusivity program': that is, not more than one company from any product category was to be included in the list of sponsors. Perhaps not surprisingly, in view of its long association with the Olympic movement, the first company to subscribe was Coca-Cola, which gave $30m to LAOOC, as well as sponsoring, according to Ueberroth, more than thirty countries' teams. Madame Berlioux, the guardian of Olympic propriety, was displeased by the early announcement of the Coca-Cola and ABC deals, which she saw as stealing Moscow's thunder.

Ueberroth displayed his well-known determination in dealing with another sponsor, Kodak, and the story has passed into Olympic folklore. The company was dragging its feet over signing a contract, which irritated Ueberroth into making alternative arrangements with Kodak's Japanese competitors, Fuji. This strange dilatoriness caused heads to roll at Kodak, as Ueberroth recalls. Another close observer adds that Fuji increased its penetration of the American market from 3 per cent to 9 per cent, while Kodak had to undertake extremely expensive 'ambush advertising' and, as a second best, sponsored the American track and field team at the Games.[19]

The torch relay

One of Ueberroth's most striking innovations, which had connections with international politics which, though serious, also bordered on the farcical, was the torch relay which brought the Olympic flame from Greece to Los Angeles.

The Olympic torch is a modern invention, dating only from 1936. Samaranch and Madame Berlioux were at first worried about Ueberroth's intention to commercialise it by selling off kilometres at $3,000 each as it was carried across America, but withdrew their objections on learning that the proceeds were to go to youth charities. Meanwhile Ueberroth had a willing sponsor in the communications company AT&T, which became even more anxious to back the relay when it needed to reconstruct a national image after a federal judge had ruled that it must deregulate. However the Greek IOC members Nikos Filaretos and Nikolaos Nissiotis, backed by Angelo Lembessis, the President of the Greek NOC, objected to the commercialisation of the flame, which was already heavily commercialised by the Greeks, as it played a significant part in the economy of Olympia, and refused to let it leave Olympia. The problem was how to abstract the flame from under the eyes of the recalcitrant Mayor of Olympia, who was making considerable political capital from the affair, and Samaranch solved it in a dramatic manner. Suddenly he telephoned Los Angeles to say that the flame was safely in Lausanne. Two Swiss students working in Greece on an Olympic project had been to Olympia and, armed with an instruction manual, had lit the flame by the sun's rays. The whole operation had been filmed to avoid any possibility of the Mayor claiming that the flame was not truly Olympian.

Now that the ground was cut from under the Mayor's feet Ueberroth made one last request for an official lighting of the flame at Olympia, accompanied by a threat that otherwise he would not only make public the manner of its removal but also oblige the Greek team to march in its alphabetical position at the opening ceremony of the Games, instead of in its customary place of honour at the head of the procession. Filaretos swiftly caved in (though it is not clear how he overcame the Mayor's objections), but despite Filaretos's assurance Ueberroth also made arrangements for the flame to be brought clandestinely from Lausanne to the United States.[20]

At this point it appears that Samaranch saw a need to be magnanimous, for he let it be known that the IOC might seek a compromise between LAOOC and the Greek Olympic authorities, and might weaken its hitherto strong endorsement of the scheme to sell kilometres.[21] Indeed, it sounds, from an astringent, even horrified, article written at the time by Ian Wooldridge, as if the Olympic authorities would have done well to act according to their first doubts and that if they had wished the flame to retain any vestige of its mystical dignity they should never have endorsed the event at all.[22]

Security

Security became a major preoccupation at Los Angeles: indeed it is a feature of all Games since Munich in 1972 that the conditions are akin to those of an armed camp, though the athletes, preoccupied as they are with winning, may not particularly notice the precautions taken on their behalf. By late June Samaranch was getting edgy about rumours that the Soviets might try to create an incident. Later Samaranch said that the Israeli secret service, Mossad, had told him that their great mistake at Munich had been to have two agencies involved. This led Samaranch to ask which agency would be in ultimate charge at Los Angeles, as well he might, given the proliferation of police and security services in the USA. According to George Schultz, the Secretary of State, to whom the question was referred, the ultimate authority was the FBI. However, rivalry between the FBI and the police threatened security planning, and the Los Angeles police commander would not agree that the FBI was ultimately responsible.

Ueberroth did not simply leave security to government agencies. As LAOOC's head of security he head-hunted Ed Best, 'the FBI's special agent in charge of Los Angeles' and eventually there were no fewer than eighteen sub-committees for different aspects of security. Ueberroth evidently had no difficulty in obtaining co-operation from government intelligence agencies. In addition the Security Planning Committee received federal funds amounting to $50m for equipment. This subvention raised the question of taxpayers' money being spent after all and caused Ueberroth to issue a very strong press statement insisting, perhaps disingenuously, that 'Any government services we request, we will pay for, but we will not pay for any services we do not order'.[23]

There were differences with the police, who wanted enhanced security and Bill Rathburn (Commander of the Los Angeles Police Department, and now an adviser on security to the Atlanta Organising Committee) went so far as to say of LAOOC 'I don't think I would ever describe their attitude as being co-operative.' Rathburn believed that LAOOC was trying to save money, which was true up to a point, but their main concern was to preserve an unoppressive appearance. For example, Ueberroth and Harry Usher were adamant that barbed wire must not be used to repel intruders and the police agreed to use the much less effective smooth taut wire. In the end a compromise was reached, although Ueberroth admits that Rathburn would have been entitled to use his professional judgement and oblige the committee to pay for whatever level of protection he considered essential. Yet the precautions sound thorough. Ueberroth and Usher had bodyguard drivers; they took special precautions at home and in their cars and there was tight security at the committee building, partly, Reich thinks, because Usher had a mania about the security of documents. Police precautions were at their most intense at the Olympic villages, where they required two perimeter fences and had specially trained counter-assault teams, and special protection for such teams as the Turks and the Israelis.[24]

Ueberroth, not surprisingly, shared Samaranch's worry about the great number of police forces in the Los Angeles area. 'Since athletes would be transported through more than forty separate law enforcement jurisdictions during the Games, we needed a system that would work and lessen the prospects of disaster.' The various agencies 'needed a compatible communications system just to talk to one another'. Ueberroth perceived that some forces hoped to make money out of the Games and it became necessary to prevent new equipment being charged to LAOOC, which a force had been unable to obtain by conventional means. But he was firm in scotching such try-ons and successful in promoting co-ordination between rival forces, thanks in large measure to the expertise of Ed Best.[25]

The Soviet boycott of Los Angeles

On 8 May 1984 the USSR announced its intention 'not to participate' in the Los Angeles games which were due to begin on 28 July. The factors involved in the decision were many and complex, but the simple explanation for the boycott is probably the right one – tit for tat.

Had relations between the two governments been happier it would have been possible to overcome the various grievances offered by the USSR as explanations for its action. Many political actors were involved: in the USA the State Department; the CIA; LAOOC; and public opinion manifesting itself through such fringe groups as the 'Ban the Soviets' organisation, which gave great offence to the USSR. In the Soviet Union the main actors were the government and the not even nominally independent NOC, and holding the ring between the super-powers stood the IOC and the various other organisations within the Olympic movement.

The lead-up to the boycott

Although the USSR did not announce its intention to boycott the 1984 Games until very shortly before the deadline for acceptance of invitations, there had been doubt about whether they would attend ever since 1980.

On the United States' side of the diplomatic battle, the government and LAOOC did not always agree. Ueberroth, who throughout the crisis over the Soviet boycott seems to have had an exaggerated idea of the importance of the Games to the United States government (he even at one point expressed the opinion that the outcome of the Games could have a profound effect on the Presidential election), records that the boycott forced LAOOC to 'establish our own foreign policy and repair the international damage that the L.A. Games had suffered. At the same time we had to work with our government and make sure it respected and upheld the Olympic Charter.' So convinced was he of his own ability to influence events that he always regretted that he had not been allowed to meet President Konstantin Chernenko and to try to talk him out of the boycott.[26]

The shooting down by the Soviets of a Korean airliner at the end of August 1983 immediately made Ueberroth think the possibility of a boycott more likely, and he turned out to be right, because the incident provoked reactions in the USA which in turn provided one of the excuses for Soviet non-participation. As a result of the attack the California State Legislature passed a resolution condemning the USSR and recommending that the Soviet athletes be banned from Los Angeles. A more significant result was the formation of the 'Ban the Soviets' Coalition, an unimportant body in itself, but one to whose activities the Soviets were able to point as evidence of the United States' hostility.[27]

The Soviet demands

Having sent one reasonably successful delegation in December 1983, the USSR sent another to the Executive Board's meeting in Los Angeles in January 1984. This time the portents were less good. At the last moment the fourteen-man delegation was reduced to seven and Sergei Pavlov, at that time President of the Soviet NOC, was replaced as its leader by Victor Ivonin. Samaranch was not surprised, and said that Pavlov's influence had been steadily diminishing since Yuri Andropov had come to power a year earlier. At his press conference Ivonin raised four issues: the cost of the athletes' stay in the Olympic villages; the United States government's recognition of Olympic identity cards instead of visas; permission for Aeroflot to take athletes to Los Angeles; and for a Soviet ship to dock in Los Angeles harbour. A few weeks later came the notification that Marat Gramov, 'a veteran Soviet propagandist from the Ministry of Information', had replaced Pavlov as President of the Soviet NOC. He said that the decision whether or not to participate would not be taken until 24 April 1984.

The Olympic attaché

Ueberroth asked for an Olympic attaché to be sent to Los Angeles as soon as possible and made it clear that, if he were appointed some months in advance, his application would have to be processed in the normal way. (Usually NOCs appoint someone who lives permanently in the host city, so that the question of entry does not arise.) So began one of the more famous rows of the Los Angeles Olympics.

The affair moved forward when Gramov sent a list of twelve people who would accompany him on his forthcoming visit to Los Angeles. It included a certain Oleg Yermishkin, and within two hours Best, LAOOC'S head of security, was able to say that Yermishkin was a 'known KGB operative', who had served at the Soviet embassy in Washington for several years. (History does not relate whether Best thought it necessary to obtain this information, or whether it was forced upon him.) Despite Yermishkin's KGB membership the State Department allowed him a visa and at their first meeting in Los Angeles Gramov told Ueberroth that Yermishkin was to be their Olympic attaché. An agreement was signed whereby the attaché would take up residence in Los Angeles not later than 1 March 1984, LAOOC would process the Soviet requests for landing rights and docking privileges and the USSR would notify its participation by the new deadline of 2 June 1984.[28]

It seems perfectly clear to the observer, though evidently it was not to Ueberroth, that he had begun to overplay his hand in conducting his own foreign policy, and to promise more than he could deliver. After the meeting with Gramov he tempted fate by telling the White House that the Soviet requests were in accordance with the Olympic Charter, and should be seen as a test of the Reagan administration's willingness to abide by it. It would hardly be surprising if professional diplomats, faced with such self-importance, had formed the opinion that Ueberroth needed taking down a peg. Certainly the diplomats took little notice of him; the State Department failed to follow up the agreement that had been made to establish Olympic liaison officers at every American embassy and consulate, and when the officers were appointed they rarely took the job seriously.

By early in January Gramov was demanding answers and saying that the United States government was blocking various Soviet requests: for their attaché to be appointed; for charter flights, and for their transport ship, the *Grazia*, to be allowed to dock in Los Angeles. Gramov, who must have realised that Ueberroth was playing out of his league, asked whether he should go directly to the State Department, instead of working through Ueberroth. To this Ueberroth naturally replied that Gramov should abide by the Olympic Charter and work through LAOOC. He then went to Washington to complain about bureaucratic foot-dragging, but was told by Michael Deaver, the responsible official, that there was nothing to worry about: 'the Russians will be here'. Once back in Los Angeles he learned from his representative in Washington that the Soviet requests had been sitting on another official's desk for a month, and that no one in the State Department had even seen them. On 19 January Gramov publicly complained that the State Department did not recognise LAOOC's authority.[29]

Meanwhile the Yermishkin affair lingered on. According to Best, the Soviets were genuinely worried about defections and wanted Yermishkin as a professional shepherd. Best also understood that the appointment of a KGB officer as Olympic attaché would have been popular in the FBI, which would have enjoyed playing at spies with the KGB. Nothing had been heard about Yermishkin's visa, and it was not until 1 March, the very day on which he had been due to arrive, that the State Department refused to issue it. The timing suggests either that the State Department enjoyed the childish non-sense of playing cat and mouse until the last moment, or that an inter-departmental wrangle between FBI men and diplomats had gone on so long that it could be brought to an end only by using as its cut-off point a deadline which there was no real need to respect, since it had been set by LAOOC (which had agreed Yermishkin's arrival date) and not by the government. (The timing may be coincidental, but on 2 March, the day after Yermishkin's visa had been refused, Ueberroth agreed to become United States Commissioner of Baseball once the Games were over.)[30]

The Soviet decision

Whatever private games the governments of the United States and the USSR were playing, it was plain that for the Olympic Games the crisis was approaching. On 24 April Samaranch called what he probably saw as a last ditch meeting at Lausanne, at the Soviets' request, attended by the three Vice-Presidents of the IOC, Madame Berlioux and delegations from LAOOC and the Soviet NOC. The press release after the meeting noted the firm Soviet intention to take part in the Games, provided the Charter were respected. It affirmed that the Soviet NOC and any other NOC would have free scope to solve problems relevant to the Olympic Games through the sole agency of LAOOC, particularly with regard to the Olympic identity cards and the list of participants. All members of the Olympic family and accredited journalists would have free access and the rules governing the ships anchored in the port of Los Angeles would strictly conform to international regulations and the hospitality usually granted to Games participants. (This rather obscure formulation means that the United States authorities would have the normal right to inspect the *Grazia*, but that the IOC hoped the right would be exercised with restraint.)[31]

This communiqué showed that the IOC and the USSR were doing their best to talk to each other, but of course it was no more than a statement of Olympic hopes, whose intentions could be achieved only with the active agreement of the United States Government. Nevertheless, perhaps because Samaranch knew full well that the Soviet NOC was not autonomous, he seems to have seen the meeting as a crucial demonstration of Soviet willingness to solve the problems that they and the United States government had created, and to have felt correspondingly let down when the decision to boycott was announced a fortnight later.

On 5 May Gramov broadened the arena by informing Mario Vásquez-Raña, the president of ANOC, that he was not sure that LAOOC was capable of organising the Games according to the Charter, and inviting him to Moscow to discuss the role of the NOCs in future Games. This shift to a concern for the power of the NOCs was a new complication (though not a new concern of the NOCs), and one with which much play was to be made later. It was a subtle move, both because Raña, whatever his personal views, could not be seen to avoid taking seriously any wish to give power to the NOCs, and because it was a clear signal that the USSR intended to retain influence in the Olympic movement, whatever happened over Los Angeles.

The new development worried Samaranch, who had already arranged to meet President Reagan after attending the opening of the torch relay in New York on 8 May. He now thought that it would be helpful to have a firmer letter of support from the President than the one already given, but it was too late. Just before Samaranch and Ueberroth took off from New York for their meeting with the President in Washington a first report was received that the Soviets were to boycott and on arrival in Washington Samaranch's party received an agency message written by Victor Louis (whom Samaranch identified as a journalist often used by the Soviets to break news stories in the West), confirming the report.[32]

Reactions to the Soviet boycott

The full text of the Soviet communiqué focused most of the Soviet attack on the United States government, since the USSR plainly did not want to create an irretrievable breach within the Olympic movement. Thus the attack emphasised the government's connivance with the anti-Soviet campaign by reactionary forces in the USA, and the authorities' continuing interference with LAOOC's business. The Soviet NOC emphasised that it had no wish to influence American public opinion, nor to spoil the good relations between their sports people, and would support the IOC and other Olympic institutions.[33] Once Tass had announced the Soviet 'non-participation' the Soviet bloc, with the exception of Romania, fell into line quite quickly, but it appears that no advance warning had been given, either to the satellites or to sports bodies within the USSR.

As we have seen, the news reached Samaranch just before his meeting with President Reagan, who readily agreed to write to President Chernenko, in the hope of changing his mind. However, during the meeting Samaranch decided that Olympic protocol would be better served if Reagan were to address his letter to him, Samaranch. The idea that Reagan might invite Chernenko to the Games was mooted, but vetoed by the Secretary of State, George Schultz, as such an invitation would 'complicate other existing issues'.[34] In the United States the 'Ban the Soviets' organisation, the body of Soviet émigrés whose activities had so enraged the Soviets, naturally saw the Soviet withdrawal as a personal victory. Reagan, as well as expressing disappointment, said he wished the modern world were as civilised as the Greeks, referring to their so-called 'sacred truce'.[35] Meanwhile, it appeared that the Soviet decision was not intended to cover all sporting events, or perhaps there had merely been a failure of communication, for it was reported on 9 May that the French basketball federation had received a telex confirming Soviet participation in the men's qualifying Olympic tournament.[36]

Reactions to the boycott

The boycott naturally attracted considerable coverage in the press and from politicians. Reagan's letter to Samaranch, published the day after he received it, was supportive but it was made clear that the United States government intended to make no further concessions, nor would it beg the Soviet Union to reconsider. Ueberroth himself did not think Reagan would give any more help, as the boycott would help him electorally.[37] The USSR was correspondingly firm. Its Ambassador in Washington swiftly announced that the decision was irreversible,[38] and the fact that Samaranch had received a supportive letter from Reagan would not, specialists thought, make any difference. The decision had been taken at the highest level, and should be seen as part of a general hardening of Soviet policy towards the West.[39]

The Soviet decision inspired worldwide comment by major figures, many of whom must have seen some political advantage in taking a view, or political disadvantage in not doing so. But, rather surprisingly, it was reported that there was no real crisis atmosphere at LAOOC, and not much interest among the citizenry, in the stifling 34 degrees in the shade then prevailing.[40] Nor were the sponsoring companies thought to be dismayed. ABC, the company with potentially the most to lose, was said not to be worried about the television audience declining. Indeed, some people, one of them Roone Arledge, head of news and sport at ABC, thought it would be bigger because the United States would have a better chance of winning gold medals in the absence of some of the major sporting countries.[41] Nevertheless, the possibility was floated that ABC might pay LAOOC $40–70m less than the $225m agreed. Harry Usher did not think the Soviets' absence would make much financial difference[42] and of course he was right, not only because, as we have seen, Ueberroth took a firm line with the television company, but also because the powerful Arledge was prepared to argue to his board (correctly, as it turned out) that ratings would not suffer.

The courageous and self-interested Romanians broke the Soviet boycott, and Ueberroth draws attention to the decision's immense symbolic importance. It also brought Romania sporting success. It had been ninth in the medal table at Montreal and seventh at Moscow, but at Los Angeles Romania's 127-person team came third, behind the USA and West Germany. LAOOC contributed $60,000 of the $180,000 cost of bringing the Romanian team to the Games, and the IOC another $60,000.[43] In due course Ceaușescu received the Olympic Order from Samaranch. He plainly saw it as an honour, and accepted with humility and gratitude.[44]

The State Department seems not to have been taken by surprise by the boycott, since it reacted very promptly. The spokesman, John Hughes, stated that the United States government had 'gone the last mile' to accommodate Soviet requests; the only question unresolved was Yerminshkin's appointment and the government would be willing to accept another official, but not Yermishkin, who was believed to be a high-ranking KGB officer. He added that the government had given no encouragement to the Soviet émigré groups which had protested against Soviet attendance and vowed to encourage Soviet defectors, but, although it must be difficult for the Soviets to understand, the USA was a free country. The difference between the two boycotts was 'the extraordinary brutality shown by the Soviets in Afghanistan. There is no comparable action by the United States here.'[45]

The salvage operation

Ueberroth complains that he was given little help by the IOC or the United States government in his efforts to salvage Soviet participation. This is probably a fair judgement so far as the government is concerned, since, although it was happy enough to use the Olympics if any advantage could be squeezed from them, it naturally did not attach the same value to them as did Ueberroth or Samaranch. However, it would be unjust to claim that the IOC was inactive, though its priorities may have been rather different from Ueberroth's. His concern was to do his best for Los Angeles, whereas Samaranch had to look to the future and ensure that the Olympic movement did not suffer permanent damage, even if the Soviets could not be persuaded to change their minds.

The Soviet NOC members, and the NOC President, Marat Gramov, protested their loyalty to the Olympic movement and insisted, in the face of all reproaches, that the responsibility for their *volte face* since the meeting at Lausanne on 24 April lay with the American administration. The specific cause, they claimed, had been a bad meeting at the State Department (to which Ueberroth was furious not to have been invited), presided over by Edward J. Derwinski, at which no progress had been made with the Soviet demands. Derwinski was to profess himself puzzled by the Soviet account of the meeting, since in his recollection 'There were no demands on their part, and therefore no rejections'.

The last meeting of any significance was with the sports ministers of the socialist countries in Prague on 24 May, which Samaranch attended, flanked by Raña and Nebiolo. Samaranch said that the IOC had to act as a bridge between two great political systems; Rana, who had been touring socialist countries 'in order to consolidate relations with them' had no choice, as President of ANOC, but to accept the socialist NOCs' decision gracefully, whereas Nebiolo was free to urge them to reconsider. Again the various sports ministers took the opportunity to rehearse the usual grievances, but the meeting was notable because they also inflamed an open sore by making much of the need for NOCs to play a greater part in the Olympic movement, and in particular in the choice of the Olympic city. They were especially incensed by the choice of Seoul, which many of them thought virtually an American colony, to host the 1988 Games. The meeting was also unusual in its overt acrimony, and because no agreed communiqué was issued: instead there were two, one put out by the IOC and the other by the delegates.[46]

While the IOC did its best to limit the damage, LAOOC was not idle. Intensive persuasion by telephone coupled with visits to key countries like Romania, China, East Germany and Cuba, brought the record number of 140 'countries' to the Games (the previous record had been 122 at Munich, against 81 at Moscow and 88 at Montreal).[47] Good inducements were offered. For example, LAOOC paid for air charter for African athletes, and many of the Romanian costs, and the number of athletes was kept up by such strong Olympic countries as Britain, France, West Germany and Australia being invited to increase their teams. The number of countries taking part was inflated by allowing some territories to participate which were not properly qualified according to Olympic rules. For example Tonga was admitted, although it had insufficient affiliations to international federations, yet after the Games Tonga was told that it was ineligible for that very reason! (However, the situation was saved by Samaranch, who visited Tonga in March 1987 and promised to facilitate the necessary extra affiliations.)[48]

In Cuba, where Raña and Ueberroth travelled together, they were well received, but Castro would not break the boycott because during the United States' boycott of Cuba in the 1960s Cubans had been able to find no sporting opponents except teams from the Soviet bloc, and now he felt a debt of loyalty. However, he did agree not to disrupt the games and to make a public commitment to this effort, Ueberroth having flattered him by referring to his many troops in Africa and the great respect in which he was held there. He also agreed that security at Los Angeles was not a problem and allowed the point to be made for him at a press conference, after which the Soviets never again used the security excuse. Samaranch had cautioned against the meeting with Castro, but in Ueberroth's opinion he had done so only because he considered it his own prerogative to deal with heads of state.[49]

Samaranch's first thought had been that he must go to Moscow, although he was determined that he must be received at a level appropriate to his own high office, which meant Chernenko or some other very senior politican. His request for such a meeting was telexed to Gramov on 10 May and thereafter he was warned on various occasions that the President would be unlikely to receive him. Eventually, despite the warnings, he went to Moscow on 31 May, and saw only Gramov and Nikolai Talysin, one of fourteen deputy Prime Ministers. After the meeting he admitted that no hope remained of saving Soviet participation in the Games. Despite this failure, which he must have realised was inevitable, Samaranch started work on the major task of salvaging the long-term unity of the movement by asserting that the IOC's links with Moscow were not severed. Soviet officials agreed and promised to 'struggle to maintain the Olympic movement's unity and purity'.[50] Back in Los Angeles Samaranch was in tougher mood and said that no excuses would be accepted for non-participation in future Games and that the IOC was to hold an extraordinary meeting in Lausanne in December to decide how to deal with non-participants.[51]

Verdicts on Los Angeles

The boycott definitely had an adverse effect on the athletic quality of the Olympics because the seventeen boycotting states included six of the top ten medal winners at Montreal: the USSR, East Germany, Poland, Bulgaria, Cuba and Hungary. On the other hand the boycott helped to make the Games a success in that the American people became more interested in them than would otherwise have been the case.[52] As Ian Wooldridge tartly put it: 'The corporate sporting knowledge around here is that the filthy, cheating Russians are too scared to turn up.'[53] There were also many protests about the crude bias of ABC's concentration on American exploits, which led

Samaranch to issue a stern warning to Roone Arledge.[54]

Though the Games may not have been of the first quality, they had many good points; indeed David Miller generously summed up the Games as having been memorable, and Samaranch went so far as to say that they had given the Olympic movement a shot in the arm, with half a dozen candidates already in the field for the summer and winter Games of 1992.[55]

That, of course, is the crux. The Games had necessarily become a commercial operation on a scale hitherto unknown, although Harry Usher had claimed that their great achievement would be to return the Games to the athletes.[56] But their greatest achievement was to make a huge profit, which emboldened other candidate cities, and assured the IOC that it would never again be placed in the position of having to give way to a city's excessive demands, simply because no other was available.

Notes

1 Harry Edwards, 'Sportpolitics: Los Angeles 1984 – the Olympic Tradition Continues', in *Sociology of Sport Journal*, 1, 1984, p. 172 and James Riordan, *Sport in Soviet Society*, Cambridge, 1977, p. 364.

2 Lord Killanin, *My Olympic Years*, London, 1983, p. 104. For the background to the 1932 Games, see Al Stump, '1932, the "Hopeless" Dream of William May Garland', *Olympic Review*, 274, August 1990, pp. 381–7.

3 Geoffrey Miller, *Behind the Olympic Rings*, Lynn, Massachusetts, 1979, p. 136. I have drawn heavily on Miller's work in this section, especially on his pp. 136–48.

4 Peter Ueberroth, *Made in America*, London 1986, pp. 13, 14 and 46 and Kenneth Reich, *Making it Happen: Peter Ueberroth and the 1984 Olympics*, Santa Barbara, 1986.

5 Killanin, pp. 104–7; Miller, pp. 138–48.

6 Reich, p. 245.

7 Ueberroth, p. 91.

8 *Ibid.*, pp. 11–13, 21, 37.

9 Reich, p. 246.

10 Ueberroth, p. 60.

11 Reich, p. 101.

12 *Ibid.*, pp. 88–9.

13 Ueberroth, pp. 53 and 55; Reich, p. 15.

14 Ueberroth, p. 54.

15 *Ibid.*, p. 118.

16 Reich, p. 130. However, Miller, pp. 73–4, makes the related point that, if the IOC ever tried to reduce the importance of track and field events in the Games, the IAAF would simply drop out of them.

17   Reich, p. 242; Ueberroth, p. 197.
18   Ueberroth, p. 104.
19   *Ibid.*, pp. 47–52 and 57–8.
20   *Ibid.*, pp. 158–66, 174 and 191–2. According to Thomas Alkemeyer and Alfred Richartz, 'The Olympic Games: from Ceremony to Show', *Olympika*, II, 1993, pp. 79–89, the idea of a torch relay at the Berlin Games of 1936 originated in Joseph Goebbels's Reichspropaganda Ministry.
21   *The Times*, 23 February 1984.
22   'The Great Olympic Hype', Ian Wooldridge, *Sport in the 80s: a Personal View*, London, 1989, pp. 78–9.
23   Reich, p. 204; Ueberroth, pp. 108, 111–12.
24   Reich, pp. 196–8 and 200–3. The quotation is at p. 196.
25   Ueberroth, pp. 97, 98.
26   Ueberroth, pp. 168 and 77.
27   *Ibid.*, pp. 127–30 and Reich, pp. 213–14.
28   Veberroth, pp. 148–54. The quotation is at p. 150.
29   *Ibid.*, pp. 166–7 and 171. The quotation is at p. 167.
30   *Ibid.*, pp. 183–4.
31   *Ibid.*, p. 206 and IOC press release, 24 April 1984.
32   *Ibid.*, pp. 213 and 218–21.
33   *Le Monde*, 10 May 1984.
34   Ueberroth, p. 221.
35   *AFP*, Washington, 9 May 1984.
36   *UPI*, Paris, 9 May 1984.
37   Ueberroth, p. 225.
38   *Le Monde*, 10 May 1984.
39   *AFP*, Moscow, 10 May 1984.
40   Gerald Marcout, *AFP*, Los Angeles, 9 May 1984.
41   Ueberroth, p. 224. Interesting light is thrown on Arledge's swashbuckling methods in David A. Klatell and Norman Marcus, *Sports for Sale: Television, Money, and the Fans*, New York, 1988, Chapter 8.
42   *AFP*, Los Angeles, 10 May 1984.
43   Reich, pp. 229–30.
44   *The Times*, 6 August, 1985, David Miller, Sofia.
45   *UPI*, 8 May 1984.
46   Ueberroth, *passim*; Reich, Chapter 12; IOC Press Release, 24 April 1984; *The Times* (Richard Owen) and *International Herald Tribune*, both 15 May 1984, reporting from Moscow, and *Guardian*, 19 May 1984, John Rodda, Lausanne. Vitaly Smirnov (one of the two Soviet members of the IOC) has since said that he thought the decisions to boycott Moscow and Los Angeles were both bad and that he did all he could to show that they were mistaken. See his interview with Marie-Hélène Roukhadze in *Olympic Review*, March–April 1991, p. 132.
47   Reich, p. 229.
48   David Miller, *The Times*, 5 March 1987.
49   Ueberroth, pp. 248–54.
50   *The Times*, 1 and 2 June 1984, Richard Owen, Moscow.
51   *Ibid.*, 30 July 1984.

52   Reich, pp. 227 and 232.
53   Wooldridge, p. 78.
54   *The Times*, 6 August 1984.
55   *The Times*, 14 and 13 August 1984.
56   Harry Usher, 'The Games in Los Angeles: a New Approach to the
Organisational Tasks', *Olympic Review*, May 1982, p. 257.

VIII

The Seoul Games of 1988

The Seoul Games of 1988 were a political exercise for the South Korean government from the beginning, and swiftly became a major political preoccupation internationally. In this respect they certainly achieved the Korean objective of putting the country on the map.

Once the decision had been taken to bid for the Games the campaign to gain the IOC's votes was seen as a means to extend Korea's relations with countries which hitherto had tried to ignore its existence, because they saw it as a neo-colonial invention of the Americans; to improve its standing in Asia and worldwide, and generally to increase national prestige and raise the nation's profile from that of a rather backward newly developing country to that of a fully-fledged member of the advanced industrial world, which could reasonably hope soon to be admitted to membership of the OECD. In its pursuit of the Games Korea enjoyed the advantage of a ruthlessly authoritarian government, which was, however, hampered in its dealings with dissenters by the need not to be too obviously indifferent to human rights in the run-up to the Games.

Korea had been divided between North and South since the end of the 1939–45 war, following decisions taken at the Potsdam and Yalta conferences. In August 1945 the United States army, which occupied the southern zone, drew the line as far north as it was thought the USSR would accept, on the 38th parallel some thirty miles north of Seoul. That border remains in place, although the North nearly succeeded in destroying it in the Korean War of 1950 to 1953.

In August 1948 the US handed the South over to President Syngman Rhee and in September the People's Democratic Republic of North Korea was established under Soviet auspices, with Kim Il-sung as President. He remained President until his death in July

1994, when he was succeeded by his son, who had been proclaimed his sole heir in 1984.

In the South President Syngman Rhee and his successors continued the tradition of authoritarian rule. In 1972 Major-General Park Chung-lee, who had been President since 1963, introduced the Yushin (Revitalising) constitution, which effectively made him President for life. He was assassinated in October 1979 and a period of chaos ensued, from which Major-General Chun Doo-hwan emerged as President, and was confirmed in office under a new constitution in February 1981. He governed with a mixture of firmness and reluctant conciliation and after its first direct presidential elections at the end of 1987 the country experienced its first peaceful transfer of power in February 1988. But although it was peaceful it was traumatic, and the run-up to the Olympics was conducted against the background of a continuing political battle.

In the spring of 1987 many middle-class Koreans had joined in active dissent. President Chun reduced his unpopularity by dismissing ministers who might be rivals to his expected successor, Roh Tae-woo. The ruling Democratic Justice Party planned a national convention on 10 June 1987 to choose its presidential candidate, and Chun's views were crucial to their choice. These events took place against the background of public anger over the cover-up of a police inquiry into the death in custody in January of a student who had been tortured, and over a financial scandal. The anger was fuelled by Chun's 'grave decision' in April to call off, until after the Games, talks with the opposition parties about constitutional reform, on the plea that the nation could not afford the risk of instability that continuing political argument could cause.[1] At the convention he duly nominated Roh and, although Roh committed himself to a more democratic approach to government, anti-government rallies turned to violence and thousands of students were detained.[2]

Brian Bridges comments that the nationwide protest that followed the suspension of talks about constitutional change and the nomination of Roh as his successor rested on a broader social base than hitherto, which convinced Roh, and ultimately Chun, that there must be reform. American influence, including a message from President Reagan urging Chun not to use troops against the protesters, played some part in this realisation, but the main factor was the strength of the domestic opposition. In normal circumstances martial law might have been an option, but the times were not normal, because all eyes were fixed on the Games and to have introduced martial law might well have caused the Games to be moved to another city.[3]

Kim Young-sam, president of the opposition Reunification Democratic Party was one of the politicians who saw that the Olympics could be used against the government. 'Now is the time', he said, 'when President Chun must take either democracy or the Olympics. According to the current situation in Korea, it looks almost impossible to have the Olympics unless we have a democratic government.' The government had persuaded ten universities to close early for the summer holidays, hoping that things would calm down once the students had gone home, but this may have been wishful thinking, since 25 per cent of the country's population lived in Seoul.[4]

The Sunday Times reported that Roh had resolved the crisis with a short, emotional speech, and saved the 1988 Games from disaster. Roh, a retired four-star General, had blood-stained hands, and had been hated as much as Chun, but now he had become a national hero, because he had said that Chun must either accept all the opposition's demands, including direct presidential elections (which had not been held since 1971), or Roh would resign. Chun accepted all this in a statesmanlike speech.[5]

During the election campaign Roh promised to carry on democratic reforms, eliminate corruption, release political prisoners and similar measures. He was determined to win the elections by fair means and, although there were almost certainly irregularities, he won for acceptable reasons. The opposition was in disarray; his Democratic Justice Party's machine was more effective than those of its opponents, and it had become possible for him to represent himself as a statesman of international stature following a visit in September to the USA and Japan. He won with 37 per cent of the vote against 28 per cent, 27 per cent and 8 per cent for the three opposition parties, but need not have won at all if the two main opposition parties had been able to suspend their differences and decide upon a single presidential candidate to oppose him. However, in the April 1988 Assembly elections the DJP won only 125 seats, the first time a ruling party had failed to gain a majority over the combined opposition, so that the 'opposition can now provide a real balancing force to the presidency'.[6]

The two Koreas and the IOC

The division of Korea posed problems for the IOC no less difficult than those presented by the two Germanies, but the Korean question, in its sporting context, attracted less public attention and took up less of the IOC's time. Before the Korean War a single Korean NOC had been recognised, with its seat in Seoul, but the North naturally was not satisfied with this lack of representation and made repeated requests for a separate NOC to be recognised. These were rejected, on the ground that there could not be more than one recognised NOC in any one country.

At the 1957 Session the Soviet member, Andrianov, proposed provisional recognition for North Korea similar to that accorded East Germany, whereby the two Koreas would be obliged to form a unified team if they were to compete in the Olympics. In 1958 and 1959 Andrianov, aided by the Bulgarian member, Stoytchev, 'demanded full recognition for North Korea because of the South Korean refusal to consider a unified team'. In 1959 the IOC decided that it would not be practicable to expect the two Koreas to select a single team on the basis of joint competition, but instead asked them to do so by arranging for the international federations to select athletes on the basis of times achieved in separate competitions. The unity of the resulting team would be demonstrated by its having a joint flag, emblem and uniform at the Olympics. South Korea agreed to this proposal, but negotiations broke down, and North Korea did not take part in the 1960 Games.[7]

At the 58th Session of the IOC, held in Athens in June 1961, the Romanian member, Alexandru Siperco, spoke in favour of recognising the northern NOC. The northern representatives asked for the matter to be deferred until the following year because of the recent changes in their government, and the Session duly agreed to postpone further discussion until 1962.[8] In 1962 the IOC went a step further and granted the North Korean NOC provisional recognition on the same lines as that of East Germany, namely that a unified team should be formed as a result of joint competition. This time North Korea agreed, but the South refused. The IOC then began to lose patience and ruled that either the South must form a joint team, or North Korea would be allowed to compete independently. The South persisted, and the IOC kept its word, so that North Korea participated in the Games for the first time at Tokyo in 1964.

The run-up to the Games

The account of Seoul's successful bid given by Dr Kim Un-yong, who played a leading part in it, is in many ways similar to that given by Denis Howell of Birmingham's abortive bid to host the Games of 1992; indeed, it would be surprising if it were not, since all bidding cities share the objective of gathering as many IOC votes as possible, and there are only a limited number of ways in which lobbying can be conducted. The great difference between the two was that Birmingham was bidding on a low budget and with little help from the government, whereas Seoul's bid was a truly Korean effort and not only supported by the government (albeit after much procrastination by the President, who remained lukewarm right up to the Baden-Baden Congress of 1981), but actually led by it in all but name.[9]

Kim was so highly valued by Samaranch that when he was elected to membership of the IOC at the 91st Session at Lausanne on 17 October 1986 the IOC dispensed with the usual gap of a year between election and swearing-in because Samaranch wanted him in Korea as a fully-fledged member during the two crucial years before the Games. Only two years later, in October 1988 at Seoul, he was elected to the Executive Board, when he and Gunnar Ericsson were chosen from seven candidates.[10]

Korea's sporting ambitions are not new. It put in a bid to hold the Asian Games of 1966, but withdrew it when the government decided that the cost of the Games could better be spent on economic development.[11] It was the success of the World Shooting Championship of 1978 which gave the Korean sports administrators the momentum to consider trying for the Olympics and in March 1979 Park Chong-kyu, President of the Korean Shooting Federation and later of the Korean Amateur Sports Association (KASA) recommended to the Ministry of Education that they make a bid, having already obtained a feasibility study. A high-level committee was set up, and in September 1979 decided to bid both for the 1986 Asian Games and for the 1988 Olympics. Once President Park Chung-hee's approval had been obtained the leaders of the government and the ruling party decided to throw their weight behind the effort. The Mayor of Seoul announced the bid on 8 October. However the President was assassinated on 26 October and the NOC president Park Chong-kyu had to resign 'for political reasons'.

In the subsequent confusion there was a great reshuffle of political jobs. A new President of the Korean Olympic Committee was appointed, who was also President of KASA, and a new Mayor of Seoul. The KOC, after a good deal of doubt, made a provisional decision to bid, (though it would not have gone ahead without governmental backing). The new President, Chun Doo-hwan, who had taken office on 1 Steptember 1980, and who was asked for a fresh ruling on the Olympics, pronounced in favour of a bid, despite reservations by the city of Seoul, having been persuaded by Roh Tae-woo (at that time Minister for Political Affairs), whereupon the Ministry of Education instructed the KOC to apply. The IOC announced on 15 December 1980 that Seoul was the fourth candidate city, after Melbourne, Nagoya and Athens.[12]

In fact, however, no firm decision was to be made until May 1981. The result of this vacillation was that when Seoul was invited to make a presentation in Lausanne it did not even reply, leaving the field open to Nagoya, its only remaining rival, which had been campaigning for two years. (Melbourne had withdrawn in February, as had Athens, whose bid was apparently linked to the idea that Athens would provide a permanent home for the Games.) Seoul might easily have been ignored after this failure to respond, but Samaranch saved its candidacy by sending an evaluation mission to both cities, because he thought it better to have two cities bidding for the Games than one.[13]

Opposition to the Games continued, because of their cost, but the President remained in favour, albeit not enthusiastic, and in May 1981 Ministers decided that they could not back down without substantial damage being done to Korea's international credibility, and that a campaign must be launched, largely through Korea's overseas missions, in order at least to win enough votes to save face. The overwhelming view among sports experts was that Nagoya stood a much better chance than Seoul, because Korea lacked experience, was the capital of a divided country and could expect fierce opposition from North Korea and its communist allies. On the other hand, the Education Minister thought they could enlist support from other developing countries.

Despite the Presidential instruction to go ahead, indifferent officials, initially lukewarm support from Korea's overseas missions and lack of budgetary support meant that Seoul's promotional activities were not vigorous – perhaps, indeed, because the President was still seen to be hesitating. According to Park Seh-jik, Mario Vázquez-Raña owed his position as first, and so far only, chairman of

ANOC to Korean influence. In return he gave the Korean bid every encouragement, and urged the Brazilians to defer their planned bid, in order to make way for Seoul.[14]

The first serious arena in which the Korean bidding team performed was a meeting of the Pan-American Sports Organisation in Caracas in July 1981, where Seoul had the good fortune to find that there was no team present from Nagoya. In the same month Kim Un-yong (who, as well as being a leading member of the bidding team, was President of the International Taekwondo Federation) set off on a tour of Europe and North America, during which he had the dedicated help of overseas Taekwondo instructors, and met thirteen IOC members. IOC officials, who until then had thought Korea's bid virtually withdrawn, advised Kim to launch extensive activities immediately.[15]

By early August 1981 sixty IOC members had been met, and an evaluation by the Education Ministry suggested that sixteen were for Korea; sixteen would consider its bid favourably and eighteen were uncommitted. America and Oceania seemed to favour Seoul, and the Middle East and Europe to be more inclined towards Nagoya. The general feeling was interpreted to be that Seoul was the better equipped candidate, but Korea's lack of diplomatic relations with the communist states was a disadvantage, and there was a lingering fear of war with North Korea. Furthermore, Nagoya had begun to invite IOC members to visit it in September 1979, whereas Seoul's late start had made people wonder whether it was serious.

The evaluation led economic ministers to take a more co-operative attitude and to decide on thorough preparation for Baden-Baden, where the Games were to be awarded at the IOC's Session in September 1981, immediately after the Congress of the Olympic movement. The President now committed himself, with an instruction that 'the country should do absolutely everything to obtain the Olympic hostship'.

Just before Baden-Baden Seoul's count of the 82 IOC members expected to vote (*sic*: these figures total 84!) was 26 for Seoul; 6 friendly; 36 uncommitted and 16 against. Seoul's targets for lobbying at Baden-Baden were, therefore, the undecided from Latin America and Africa, as well as NOC and IF Presidents and 'those figures who exercised background influence in the international sporting community'. The press were cool and IOC leaders seemed to think Nagoya had as good as won, but 'the atmosphere changed overnight with the opening of the Korean exhibition hall'.

So successful was the lobbying that in the early hours of 30 September, the day of the vote, the team was confident enough to be able to cable home that they stood to win with 45 votes. In fact they did even better and won by 52 to 27, after a voting session which lasted one and three-quarter hours, although there were only two candidates.[16]

Why was Seoul chosen?

There is of course a problem. Why should so unlikely a candidate as Seoul have won the coveted accolade of the IOC, and why, once the all too obvious difficulties of sticking to that choice became clear, should the IOC not have changed its mind?

The simple explanation of why Seoul should have been preferred to Nagoya is probably the best, namely that the IOC had to award the Games somewhere, and that at the last minute there was no other plausible candidate. Nagoya had shot itself in the foot, or rather its environmentalist protesters had done so (although some IOC members still speculate that the protesters may have been acting at the behest of Seoul or its sympathisers), and Melbourne and Athens had withdrawn: all the IOC could do was accept Seoul, whose bid was at least whole-hearted, and fully in tune with the commercial spirit of the age. There seems also to have been a general feeling in Lausanne that it was time to award the games to an eastern city, as they had been held in the Americas or Europe ever since the Tokyo games of 1964.

Peter Ueberroth, the organiser of the Los Angeles Games and so an experienced, if jaundiced, observer, adds a down-to-earth assertion of corruption. As well as trinkets and brochures, 'Seoul also gave away, quietly, two first-class roundtrip tickets to each IOC member. The tickets were easily redeemed for cash; many were.'

After the demonstration against the Games by citizens of Nagoya, 'Masaji Kiokawa, Japan's IOC member and an IOC Executive Board member, criticized Seoul in a vitriolic outburst that alienated many IOC members from the Arab–Asian bloc.' In Ueberroth's judgement, Masaji's bad manners, the demonstration and the new-found strength of the Arab–Asian bloc all contributed, 'But the free tickets had already turned the trick'.[17]

These factors may have been present, but it is possible that the IOC, or at least the Executive Board, also had in mind the incalculable political and economic benefits to which siting the Games in Korea could contribute, such as the eventual reunification of the Korean peninsula, the healing of old wounds between Korea and Japan (dating from the Japanese colonisation), and the opening up of relations between South Korea and other Asian countries. It would, however, be disappointing to find that this had in fact been the IOC's calculation, because it could so easily have turned out to be a disastrous mistake. The Games could have led to exacerbation of the already tense relations between the two Koreas, perhaps even to war, and if the Soviet bloc had boycotted the Games nothing would have been done to improve Korea's relations with the wider world, and irreparable damage could have been done to the Olympic movement.

Other explanations for the choice of Seoul can be found. There were observers, like Neil Macfarlane, and for a time David Miller, who believed that the power of Adidas had turned the IOC away from Nagoya, and, if Park Seh-jik is to be believed, Horst Dassler favoured Seoul. (The role of Adidas in the Olympic movement has been discussed in Chapter IV.) Those inclined to flights of fancy may even say that it was some kind of reward given by the USA to a faithful neo-colonial servant.

At the political level the choice of Seoul can be argued in two different directions. Either it showed a courageous devotion to the universality of the Olympic movement and a determination to assert the values of sport over those of politics, or it showed overweening pride and a complete misunderstanding of what sport is about and of the movement's proper status. Few in the sports business would nowadays assert that it is possible to keep politics out of sport, but Samaranch himself constantly says that the resolution of political questions must be left to politicians: yet to award the Games to such a country as Korea looks more like an irresponsible importation of politics into sport.

Once, *faute de mieux*, Seoul had been chosen, its disadvantages became only too obvious, even to those who had not been aware of them in advance. At that point simple pride and the need to save the IOC's face came into play. It was unthinkable that the Games should be cancelled, and in any case the movement, by now accustomed to spending very large sums of money, could not afford it. The alternative was to stick through thick and thin with the sitting candidate, arguing throughout that to support Seoul was to assert the supra-political values of sport.

No doubt in a real crisis the IOC would have been able to find some experienced city that had already held the Games to take them over at short notice, and it does seem that Korea's leaders believed that this could happen if they allowed opposition by students and others to become so out of hand that it had to be quelled by unacceptably harsh measures. On the other hand, the IOC has in the past beeen tolerant of harsh measures – one has only to remember Mexico City or, indeed, Berlin. The timing of internal repression in any host city also presents problems for those in the IOC who might be inclined to protest. If it occurs well ahead of the Games it can be argued that it forms part of domestic policy with which it is not the IOC's business to interfere. If firmness becomes necessary in the weeks immediately preceding the festival it may be too late to do more than turn a blind eye.

The diplomatic task

Once Seoul had won it was time to begin worrying about whether the communist bloc and some non-aligned nations would participate in the Games.

Like Peter Ueberroth's LAOOC at Los Angeles, the Seoul Olympic Organising Committee (SLOOC) had to develop foreign relations of its own, although for different reasons. In Los Angeles's case the United States' government's lack of co-operation (at least as it was perceived by Ueberroth) had forced Los Angeles to act independently: in Seoul there was of course no question of the Korean government failing to co-operate, although not all officials were enthusiastic, but Korea had no diplomatic relations with countries in the socialist bloc, and had to use Olympic channels instead. SLOOC was helped by the fact that some sports leaders in eastern Europe were government ministers as well as Olympic officials. Gradually a number of countries in the Soviet bloc followed the Soviet lead in realising that it would be useful to have consular relations with Korea on a temporary basis for the period of the games, and these proved to be the prelude to full diplomatic relations with Hungary, Poland, Yugoslavia, Bulgaria, Czechoslovakia, Romania and Mongolia and, in October 1990, with the USSR.[18]

Boycott threats started as soon as Seoul had been chosen at Baden-Baden in September 1981 and calls for the site to be changed began soon after and continued for a considerable time. Soviet bloc opposition to Seoul continued after the Games were awarded, and the situation worsened with the boycott of Los Angeles. However, during the Los Angeles Games Horst Dassler of Adidas again demonstrated his considerable influence by arranging the first official meeting between the two sides: Valery Syssoev (Vice-Minister of Sports of the USSR) participated and his sympathy was engaged, although he could not, of course, commit his government. Manfred Ewald, the President of the East German NOC, who was later to take the lead in pressing the Soviets to attend, was also supportive, not surprisingly when one remembers how reluctant the East German leader Erich Honecker had been to boycott in 1980, especially as he had been given little or no notice of the Soviet intention.

Some of the USSR's concerns over Seoul were very similar to those which had bedevilled Los Angeles, but they seem to have been handled more effectively on the Korean side than they had been by LAOOC, and the Soviets also were probably more intent on achieving a satisfactory outcome than they had been in 1984.

One of the chief Soviet worries was about whether they would be permitted to dock a ship at Inchon. Kim himself considered the request reasonable, but knew that his government would oppose it. The Soviets were also anxious, again as at Los Angeles, to obtain landing rights for Aeroflot. One further difficulty was that assurances were sought (it seems not only by the USSR) that Korea would not offer political asylum to defectors. Kim could have given the assurances without contravening Korean policy, which was to refuse asylum, but this could not be admitted without risking accusations of offending against international law and practice. In December 1987, after talking to the President, Kim was able to give an unofficial assurance that a ship could be moored. Very shortly thereafter the Soviet bloc countries, led by East Germany, began to accept their invitations to the Games.

Kim puts it down mainly to personal contact and good human relations that all but six of the 166 NOCs competed, but there is, of course, more to the story than that.[19] Part of the difficulty for the USSR was that it needed to be seen to have given reasonable support to its North Korean ally in its demand to co-host the Games, yet did not wish to carry that support to the point where it would have to boycott. To have done so would have relegated the USSR to the second rank of sporting powers and perhaps provoked overt discontent, or even outright disobedience, among athletes and their governments in satellite countries.[20]

North Korea's demands

North Korea had made its demand to share the Games in the summer of 1985. President Fidel Castro of Cuba promised to help, and Moscow let it be known that some movement by Seoul towards sharing would help the Soviet bloc to participate. Seoul was at first opposed to any such gesture, but Samaranch went ahead with arranging talks between the two Korean NOCs, the first session of which was held at Lausanne on 8–9 October 1985. North Korea insisted on co-hosting what it would have liked to call the 'Pyongyang-Seoul Games' and on a single team for the two countries, but with two organising committees and two opening and closing ceremonies. However, the IOC drew the line at co-hosting and ruled that the (by no means new) issue of a single team was for the two Koreas to settle, but it did not exclude sharing the games, in the sense that some sports, or some events within sports, might be held in the North. At the second meeting, in January 1986, North Korea persisted in its demand for co-hosting and the IOC continued to say no, but suggested sharing a few more sports with the north than the South had hitherto agreed. South Korea then proposed that four sports, and some events in others, be held in the North. Much the same positions were adopted at the third meeting, held in June 1986.

At the IOC Session at Istanbul in May 1987, shortly before the final North/South meeting, North Korea demanded eight sports. Kim, who replied at Samaranch's request, said that the door was still open to negotiations, and the IOC delegated the next steps to its Executive Board, which sent a mission to Pyongyang later in May. The mission (headed by the influential Romanian member, Alexandru Siperco, who was seen in Seoul as too sympathetic to the northern point of view) sought permission to return to the South via the border post at Panmunjom, but visas were refused by the North. The request was widely seen as a test by Samaranch of how far the North would go, and the refusal of visas as a further portent of failure. The fourth and final talks were held in Lausanne on 14–15 July 1987. Seoul was by now ready to give up six sports and Samaranch advised an opening offer of five. North Korea continued to insist on eight sports with their associated television rights and the IOC at last decided that there was no point in further negotiations, although it never closed the door to the North Koreans' changing their minds, and deciding to attend the Games.[21] However, the socialist countries had been impressed by the efforts that the IOC had made, although experienced observers con-tinued to doubt whether the games would be held at Seoul at all. In November 1987 the North blew up a South Korean aircraft, with 115 people, on its way from Baghdad to Seoul, and in the following January it finally announced that it would not participate in the Games, giving as its reason its disappointment with the progress of the talks.[22]

It is clear that Samaranch conducted the negotiations with extra-ordinary skill. Richard Pound, a Vice-President of the IOC, has given a detailed account of them from the point of view of an insider with full access to the IOC's documents. He may exaggerate the extent to which Samaranch always knew that the negotiations must fail in the end, but he is certainly right that without them it would have been very difficult for North Korea's allies to attend. The negotiations were presented as a search for conditions in which North Korea would feel able to send its team to the Games, but their broader purpose was to save the Seoul Games, not so much for the sake of Seoul as of the whole Olympic movement.

Pound may also over-estimate the extent to which Samaranch gained the trust of the two Korean NOCs, and through them of their governments, but he does realise that the governments of the USSR, the USA, Japan, and no doubt other countries, were using the Games as a peg on which to hang far more important developments in international politics. Sometimes, however, it seems as if Samaranch himself did not appreciate the limits to the importance of the Olympic movement. For example, he twice asked the President of South Korea to delay elections, and even advised him to put off the military exercises, Team Spirit, held annually with the Americans. Such advice was resisted, but the most interesting point is that Samaranch felt able to give it.[23]

Television

Kim correctly states that 'the development of television has made TV no more a spectator, but one of the main organizers of the Games'. The IOC thought SLOOC would be doing well to get $400m for the American television rights, whereas SLOOC hoped to sell them for $500 or $600m, despite the fourteen-hour difference between Korean and American east coast time, which made it difficult to schedule events for prime time on United States television (8 p.m. to midnight). Indeed, although there is a growing awareness that commercial sport must adapt to the needs of its sponsors, some of the adjustments that were made to the timing of events at Seoul are still remembered with regret.[24]

The negotiations with the television companies were not easy, perhaps partly because of the relative weakness of ABC, which had had the contract, 1980 apart, ever since 1968, but whose declining viewers had forced the company to lay off 10 per cent of its staff.[25] CBS, ABC and NBC all made disappointing offers, though Kim claims to have understood that $500m was not a realistic target. 'I was caught between Korea's national pride and the cold reality of a maximum market price.'[26] In the end, after NBC had discovered that it was now the only serious bidder, Kim had to accept only $300m, with an additional, face-saving, $200m on a risk-sharing basis. The Japanese rights attracted great public attention. SLOOC and the Korean government thought they could fetch $80m; the IOC thought about $30m and in the end $52m was achieved. One argument used by SLOOC was that the Games were in the right time zone for the Japanese, to which the latter were able tellingly to reply that they were not, because the events had already been scheduled to fit United States prime time.

Once the North American and Japanese markets had been settled and the European rights sold to the European Broadcasting Union, the sale of other rights was a political more than a financial question: in Korean eyes the only important point was to get more than Calgary or Los Angeles. The East bloc rights were also important politically, and SLOOC had to be careful not to announce too much of what had already been achieved until the bloc had decided to participate. The domestic rights were almost given away to the Korean Broadcasting System for $3.25m, a figure which Kim wryly contrasts with the $25m paid to the Barcelona organising committee for the Spanish rights. Seoul's final worldwide total, according to Kim, was $408m, against Calgary's $324m and Los Angeles's $288m.

The Games

The security operation was massive: 'Security was not only needed on the ground but also on the water, in the air and under the sea' and the USA, apart from its 40,000 troops along the border and manning the Panmunjom check point, stationed two aircraft carriers off Seoul as a warning to the North.[27] According to Park, all the shopkeepers at the airports were recruited as surveillance agents, and he quotes with apparent approval the Director of Security who thought that 'all dangers could be lessened if the whole population turned into security agents'.

As part of the operation 'The background of 122,043 participants in the Games was examined to eliminate those with criminal records, alcoholic records, mental disorder, etc.', and 81,630 military and police guarded 264 facilities.[28] But despite all the precautions, which many observers have said gave the Olympic areas the feeling of armed encampments, radical students (whose riotous behaviour Kim often attributes to Korea's rapid democratisation) were able to interfere with some of the arrangements.   There were the usual trivial-seeming disputes which, if not dealt with, could have led to disaster. For example, an Israeli gymnast wished to compete at 8.30 a.m. for religious reasons, and was urged by the Games' authorities to compete at 11.00 or abstain altogether. This disregard of the gymnast's religious needs caused the Israeli NOC to threaten to withdraw its entire team. Numerous national teams, like those of Iran and Iraq, had to be kept apart: the Taiwanese national flag could not be used, for fear of offending the Chinese, although there was no objection to the use of the Taiwanese NOC's flag. Even the electronic scoreboard was an unexpected source of difficulty because it showed Jerusalem, not Tel Aviv, as the capital of Israel. Kim also records an embarrassment of a perhaps novel kind: 'Some media people wanted complete hotel-type services, but some maid personnel, for example, were volunteers from good families and any misconduct was intolerable.'

Another event which upset Kim occurred when Korean coaches protested against a Bulgarian beating a Korean at boxing and NBC gave the ensuing fracas live coverage for an hour. It would be naive to expect any news organisation to have done otherwise, but the worldwide unfavourable publicity caused anti-American feeling, which was not dampened down by some American swimmers being caught shop-lifting, NBC crews ordering T shirts with symbols depicting the boxing incident and disorderly behaviour by the Americans at the opening ceremony. The trouble also provoked renewal of the perennial debate about whether so dangerous a sport as boxing should be included in the Olympic programme. Kim was relieved that there was not much anti-American feeling, though he does revive the accusation that the judging at Los Angeles had not been fair. 'Such anti-Americanism as there had been among Koreans had been largely inspired by NBC's inquisitorial televison coverage of boxing, a sore point in light of the blatant American bias in judging in 1984.'[29]

The home front

While Kim and his allies were active on the diplomatic front much was also happening at home. The bidding campaign had been run as a truly national effort and once the bid had been won the preparations for the Games were tackled in a similarly whole-hearted way, although the lukewarm attitude of some officials had to be overcome. In June 1985 the first sponsorship agreements were signed with Coca-Cola and Kodak: the latter had obviously had been quick off the mark, in order not to repeat the fiasco of 1984 when its dilatoriness had caused it to lose the Olympic sponsorship to Fuji.

A variety of nationwide activities was undertaken. Sports support officers or sections were established in each city and provincial government and the Ministry of Government Administration 'formulated a program called "Orderly Life and Mentality Education", for government employees and their families'. One of the more bizarre programmes, which is recorded in the *Report* without any indication that it was considered in any way odd, was undertaken by the Office of Monopoly, which 'put on sale 200 million packs of Olympic commemorative cigarettes and 90,000 sets of specially wrapped cigarettes to support public relations and revenue-generating projects; the office also marketed red ginseng as an Olympic product'.

Local committees for environmental beautification and consciousness-raising were set up, but tended to be weak, and it became necessary to create a central Council in March 1985. This body organised support committees throughout South Korea and abroad. The purpose was to build on the momentum of the Asian Games for order, cleanliness and kindness and to 'instil civic pride among the people so as to project a good image as modern and cultured people in connection with the Olympic games'. The Council introduced all sorts of activities, of which the most enjoyable sounds a cheerleading contest, which 'contributed to the development of new styles and techniques of cheerleading'.

Minute attention was paid to the improvement of shops, taxis, lodging houses and restaurants. There were campaigns to promote 'the development of a general atmosphere of reliable commercial transactions, eliminating outmoded commercial practices' and 'to serve customers kindly and to avoid altercations'. A major campaign was undertaken to depollute the Han river, which flows through the central part of Seoul. Streets were extensively improved and disorderly street stalls and unauthorised roadside heaps dealt with. No fewer than 224,975 stalls were removed or relocated in 1988 and even the bland language of the *Official Report* suggests that the process may not have been altogether benign 'when their removal was deemed inevitable, stall vendors were ordered to move their stalls to back alleys out of public sight.' Owners of stalls near Olympic sites 'were advised to pull down their stalls and stands on their own accord so as not to deal a crippling blow to their daily living'. There were even lavatories reserved exclusively for foreigners.[30]

Journalists with an eye to human rights naturally did not care for this. One commented that along the route that the Olympic torch was to travel a hundred miles of walls had been built to hide the slums and poor quality houses and there were understandably disapproving references to the large number of poor people who had lost their homes during the extensive facelift given to Seoul in preparation for the games.[31]

A successful Games?

The city of Seoul obviously benefited greatly from its refurbishment, which created numerous parks and required architects of buildings to spend one per cent of the construction cost on decorative artwork. Tremendous efforts were made to reduce air pollution and to keep the areas liable to be seen by visitors clean and to decontaminate the yacht-racing course in Suyong Bay. There was a strong emphasis on public health, especially on AIDS control, 'to protect local people against infection with AIDS through incoming foreigners' though in the context of public health it does seem odd that the Olympic family should have been exempt from normal vaccination requirements. Runways were extended; more foreign airlines ran flights to Seoul and the national airline extended its fleet.[32] Kim naturally sees the Games as having been a success, both as a sporting occasion, and as the beginning of a new phase in Korea's existence as a nation, at last free from the inferiority of having been a colony of Japan. 'Korea emerged from its Japan complex in Baden-Baden,' he says. 'Baden-Baden was a start. The Olympic Games were a turning point for Korea to move into the ranks of the world's advanced nations.'[33]

Proud as he is of the Games and their results for his country, Kim does not take kindly to the idea that Seoul may stick in the popular mind largely because a positive dope test caused Ben Johnson to be deprived of his gold medal for the 100 metres, which he had run in the world record time of 9.79 seconds. He points out that out of 1,598 dope tests only ten were positive, compared with twelve at Los Angeles: two were in the modern pentathlon, five in weightlifting, one (Johnson) in athletics, one in wrestling, and one in judo.

The public sector investment was immense at $1.7bn and SLOOC invested $1.5bn 'in direct and private-sector investment and in operation of the Games'. The eventual profit at Seoul was $497m, and handsomely achieved the organisers' ambition to outdo Calgary and Los Angeles. However the profit figure was not arrived at in an orthodox manner, since most of it did not represent a surplus on operations: instead it included donations and premiums on the sale of apartments amounting to $347m.

Seoul was able to make a good deal with the IOC, which normally set aside 20 per cent of television income for the local organising committee as a TV installation fund before dividing the remainder between the organising committee (two-thirds) the IOC itself, and IFs and the NOCs, via Olympic Solidarity, (one-ninth each). However, Seoul argued that 20 per cent would have amounted to only $80m, and Samaranch agreed to Roh's request that they should instead receive $125m. In total, $320m stayed with SLOOC, and the IOC, the IFs and the NOCs (via Olympic Solidarity) shared the remaining $92m. A further concession was made. It appears from Kim's figures that the IOC would normally have received $4.5m for its share of the profit from marketing the Olympic symbol, yet it consented to receive only $1.75m. This was possible because, although for reasons of pride Seoul was allowed to declare a surplus which included income from donations and from the sale of flats, when it came to dividing the proceeds it was allowed to work on a much lower profit figure, which excluded those items. The Olympic movement as a whole cannot therefore be said to have done as well as it might have done out of the 1988 Games, but Seoul got the best of both worlds.[34]

It is impossible to quantify the effect of holding the Olympics on

Korea's political system. Samaranch was certainly optimistic, though he may have exaggerated when he said at the beginning of the Games: 'Today I can assure you that South Korea is really a democracy where they have the liberty to film and write what they want.'[35] Just after the Games fifty-two political prisoners were released 'to set a tone of post-Olympic reconciliation'.[36] A few days later the Pope spent a weekend in China and added his voice to those urging Korean reunification, warning the South's rulers that he was keeping an eye on their justice and human rights record.[37]

The internal picture was further improved by former President Chun's return to Seoul at the end of December 1990 from two years of internal exile at a remote mountain temple. Plans to demonstrate did not materialise, partly because most of the student activist leaders had been arrested over the past few days, and partly because nearly three thousand riot police were mobilised.[38]

In his preface to Kim's book Samaranch sums up the political value of the games: 'Apart from being a tremendous success for the whole Olympic family, one could perhaps even say that the Olympic Games in Seoul were a major factor behind the rapid democratization of the Republic of Korea and the development of an element of international goodwill, cooperation and fraternity, a new hope for peace'.[39]

Notes

1   *Financial Times*, 'Man in the News: Roh Tae Woo: an Heir apparent but not certain', 30 May 1987, Maggie Ford, Seoul.

2   *The Times*, 11 June 1987, David Watts, Seoul.

3   Brian Bridges, 'East Asia in Transition: South Korea in the Limelight', *International Affairs*, 64, 3, summer 1988, pp. 381–92.

4   *The Times*, 18 June 1987, David Watts, Seoul.

5   *The Sunday Times*, 5 July 1987, Jon Swain, Seoul.

6   Bridges, p. 384. The historical data in this section are taken from Bridges's article and from his book *Korea and the West*, 1986. Chapter 2: 'Political Culture in the Two Koreas', London, pp. 5–20.

7   Richard Espy, *The Politics of the Olympic Games*, Berkeley, 1979, pp. 66–7.

8   58th Session, Athens, June 1961, *Minutes*.

9   I have drawn freely on the *Official Report* of the 1988 Games and on *The Greatest Olympics: from Baden-Baden to Seoul*, by Kim Un-yong, Seoul, 1990. For a further account of the Seoul Games see Park Seh-jik's *The Seoul Olympics: the Inside Story*, London, 1991. Park was a soldier, academic and politician, who became President of the Seoul Organising Committee. The work is selective, and sometimes rather eccentric in the choice of material.

For Denis Howell's account of Birmingham's bid see his *Made in Birmingham: the Memoirs of Denis Howell*, London, 1990, Chapter 14.

10   Kim, pp. 26–7. Elsewhere he states that there were originally seven candidates, but that Robert Helmick had withdrawn.

11   *Ibid.*, p. 53.

12   *Report*, pp. 33–4.

13   Kim, p. 54.

14   Park, pp. 1–4.

15   Vyv Simson and Andrew Jennings claim that the overseas Taekwondo clubs were used by the Korean CIA. *The Lords of the Rings*, London, 1992, pp. 139–40.

16   *Report*, pp. 35–9, 42.

17   Peter Ueberroth, *Made in America*, London, 1986, pp. 92–3.

18   Kim, p. 32.

19   *Ibid.*, pp. 48, 116–17, 121–7.

20   J. Horne and others, *The 1988 Seoul Olympics*, North Staffordshire Polytechnic, 1988, p. 18.

21   Kim, pp. 133–40.

22   *The Guardian*, 13 January 1988, John Rodda.

23   For a detailed account of the negotiations preceding the Seoul Games see Richard W. Pound, *Five Rings over Korea*, Boston, 1994.

24   Kim, pp. 88, 173 and 177. In David Miller's view, the only sports in which starting times might present problems for US television were athletics, gymnastics and swimming. *The Times*, 9 October 1984, David Miller, Delhi.

25   *The Times*, 14 September 1985, David Miller, Lausanne.

26   Kim, p. 89.

27   *Ibid.*, p. 261 and *The Times*, 17 November 1987, David Miller.

28   Kim, pp. 261 and 260. Park, pp. 123 and 119. At p. 118 he puts the number of security personnel at 112,000, of whom half were soldiers.

29   Kim, pp. 175, 271, 155, 230–1.

30   *Report*, pp. 234–9.

31   *The Guardian*, 30 August 1988, Mike Green.

32   *Report*, p. 241 and Kim, p. 35.

33   Kim, p. 60.

34   *Ibid.*, pp. 291, 282–3, 286–8.

35   *The Observer*, 18 September 1988, Christopher Brasher, Seoul.

36   *The Guardian*, 3 October 1988. His figures are inconsistent, since he also refers to donations of $80m and apartment sales premiums of $300m.

37   *The Times*, 9 October 1989.

38   *The Times*, 31 December 1990, Simon Warner, Seoul.

39   Kim, p. 14.

IX

The Barcelona Games of 1992

The history of Barcelona's bid for the Games of 1992 and of its subsequent preparations for them well illustrates the many difficulties that face an Olympic host. First, support must be gathered not only within the city itself, but throughout the country as a whole, for if a country's government and people are not seen to be behind a bid the IOC is unlikely to take it seriously.

Once the bid has been won there is an interval of six years (seven from 1993) before the Games are held. During that long period a multitude of problems arise and it becomes an important task of the organising committee to maintain the support which was gathered earlier and to see that internal rivalries and political disagreements do not prejudice the momentum of preparation for the great event. In Barcelona's case such rivalries were only too apparent.

The genesis of Barcelona's bid

Barcelona naturally makes much of its pertinacity in seeking to host the Olympic Games. It bid for 1924, but lost to Paris, because Coubertin had asked for the Games as his swan song; it tried again for 1936, and even built the Montjuic stadium in anticipation, but was defeated by Berlin on a confused postal vote. Its third attempt was for the Games of 1972, when it again lost to a German city, this time Munich.

Another important point in Barcelona's favour was its long sporting tradition. The Barcelona Football Club was founded in 1897 and the Barcelona Swimming Club in 1907; the Spanish National Olympic Committee (Comité Olímpico Español – COE) was established in Barcelona, as were numerous Spanish sports federations, and there is a flourishing sporting press. In recent years numerous international contests have been held in Barcelona, so that the city can truthfully say that it has had practice in organising major events.

When it came to bidding for the 1992 Games (against Amsterdam, Belgrade, Birmingham, Brisbane and Paris) the Spanish case was rather different from the British. In Britain the British Olympic Association had had to decide between rival candidates: in Spain there is a traditional rivalry between Barcelona and Madrid, but once Barcelona had announced its candidacy Madrid did not oppose it. Instead, as one observer put it, Madrid's politicians 'played the politics of generosity, though with knives in their pockets'.

The idea of holding the Olympics in Barcelona was the brainchild of, among others, Narcis Serra, a socialist Mayor of Barcelona who later became Minister of Defence, and was succeeded by the present Mayor, Pasqual Maragall. Serra seems first to have thought of Barcelona as a site for the Games as long ago as 1978, perhaps with some prompting from Samaranch himself, and then to have looked into the practicalities with great discretion, in order not to alert Madrid. Serra saw both the Olympics and the International Exhibition to be held at Seville in 1992 as means to give Spain a new focus after the abortive attempt of 23 February 1981 to reimpose dictatorship on the country, and had realised that the best way for a city to promote itself as of worldwide importance was for it to host the Olympics, better even than the old route of holding an international exhibition.

When Maragall became Mayor and took over the prospect of bidding for the Games he had to make sure that the objective of winning the bid become a national, not merely a local, ambition, which would involve the central government without sacrificing Barcelona's control, and, by being above or outside party politics, become a worthy object for the King's support. To contrive such an image for the bid required considerable political skill, since the next tier of government above the socialist municipality of Barcelona has a distinctly conservative and Catalonian nationalist tinge. The central government in Madrid is again socialist, but the political affinity that one might expect it to have with Barcelona seems often to be strained by the rivalry between the two cities, as well as by the different traditions from which the national and local socialist parties spring.

Gathering support for the bid

Once Barcelona's intention to bid had been formally announced by Serra at a dinner in honour of the best exporters of 1980 on 30 January 1981, the public campaign was under way. It lasted nearly six years until its successful conclusion at Lausanne in October 1986. After the announcement events moved swiftly. In May Serra asked King Carlos for his approval and patronage; at the end of June the Barcelona City Council unanimously approved the initiative and encouraged a first study, and the world's sporting press was briefed on Barcelona's aspirations at the football World Cup of 1982. Barcelona had, of course, been chosen some years ahead to host the World Cup, but once the city had bid for the Olympics the football festival became an obvious promotional vehicle.

In December 1982 Serra became Minister of Defence in the Madrid government and was succeeded as Mayor by his deputy, Pasqual Maragall, who became Mayor in his own right when he won the municipal elections of April 1983. Also in December the Prime Minister, Felipe González, informed Maragall of his cabinet's total support for Barcelona's candidature. In the following month the President of the Generalitat (provincial government) of Catalonia, Jordi Pujol, and Maragall signed articles of association of the organising committee. This body in turn created an Olympic office to take charge of the candidature, which was approved by a resolution of Spain's Council of Ministers in March 1984.

The Catalan Parliament was concerned about the place that would be accorded in the Olympic Games to the Catalan language and national anthem, to which Maragall could only reply that they would be favourably treated within the framework of the Catalan Statute of Autonomy of December 1979 and the laws of Spain.[1] The Catalan question (regarding the degree of autonomy, or even full independence, which Catalonia ought to enjoy) has naturally grumbled on, but was apparently not regarded as a major security problem in the context of the Olympic Games. Most Catalans are to some extent nationalists, but there are few who seriously expect complete independence. Conservatives concentrate on the need for a more favourable interpretation of the Statute, whereas socialists focus more on the objective of a truly federal Spain.

There is, it is true, a small fringe of Catalan separatists, known as Terra Lliure, but they, like the Basque terrorist organisation, ETA

(Euskadi ta Askatsuna), were seen as controllable: indeed, a number of leading ETA activists were rounded up shortly before the Games. What the organisers feared more than violence were such demonstrations as Catalan separatists jumping into the swimming pool during the events. Measures of this kind had been threatened by the Esquerra Republicana de Catalyuna, led by a member of the Catalonian Parliament named Ángel Colom, unless a separate Catalonian Olympic Committee were recognised by the IOC in time for the games. However, any such recognition was out of the question, and the fears turned out to be groundless. Meanwhile, Jordi Pujol did his best to claim, for himself and Catalonia, all the credit for attracting the Games to Barcelona.[2]

There continued to be points of dissension between the various levels of government, but on the whole a very convincing unity was maintained for most of the time. February 1985 was a particularly active season of goodwill. For instance, the Generalitat promised Samaranch that it would do all it could to help the city administration; the Barcelona Diputación (a local government body, of which Samaranch was once president) unanimously backed the candidature; the city, the Generalitat and the Diputación agreed to spend ptas 140m ($0.825m) equally divided, on getting the sports hall ready for the 1988 World Basketball Championships; Ramon Trias Fargas said that the Olympics were above politics and Don Alfonso de Bourbon (President of COE) said that all must work together for Barcelona.[3] Javier Solana, the Minister of Culture, called the Games 'A compromise for the whole of Spain'[4] and Jordi Pujol, the President of the Generalitat (who often refers to himself as President of Catalonia) was anxious to strengthen Catalonian relations with Italy and used a visit to the Milan fair to push Barcelona's candidature. Later he was to use the prospect of the Games to strengthen relations between Catalonia and the Rhône–Alpes region of France.[5]

Problems in the Spanish sports establishment

The COE (Spanish NOC) did not come officially into the picture until June 1983, when its plenary session supported the candidature, and there was another long delay before the Spanish Committee of Olympic federations ratified the decision in March 1984.

There was a continuing crisis within the COE, revolving round its chairman Alfonso de Bourbon, Duke of Cádiz. When he had been elected President of the COE in 1984 he had received a minority of the votes, 29 against 28 and 25 for the other candidates, and thereafter always claimed to have been the first democratically elected president.[6] Another source of trouble in the COE lay in the relations between the Olympic and non-Olympic federations, with the former thinking themselves under-represented. The relations between the COE and the interim organising committee of the Games were never good, not, it seems for any institutional reason but because of Don Alfonso's unusual character and history. He had bid for the monarchy in the 1960s and was closely linked to the Franco regime, and it was even whispered that, as Pretender to the French throne, he had really favoured the French bid for the Games, although he declared that he had played his part in Barcelona's victory. He was credited with some odd notions, having even been thought to have toyed with the idea of posthumously giving Franco the COE's gold medal.[7] Nevertheless, Olympic protocol continued to be observed to the extent that it was Don Alfonso who officially presented the candidature document at Lausanne on 16 May 1985.

The relations between the COE and Maragall's organising committee took a turn for the worse when the COE let it be known that it was ready to sue the committee for unauthorised use of the Olympic logo, probably because of its poverty following a cut-back in its funding from the state.[8] The relationship between the two bodies was clarified on paper in January 1987 when Don Alfonso and Maragall, with visible coldness, signed a document to create the joint committee, which would in turn spawn the permanent organising committee, COOB '92. The purpose of both Maragall and central government in creating this joint committee was thought to be to relegate the COE to second place until its internal affairs were sorted out and the question of the presidency resolved. The Duke's resignation was predicted daily, but he was determined not to go before the end of his mandate in 1988.

The Duke complained, not without reason, that the Mayor of Barcelona had grabbed all the campaign funds raised from private sponsors, leaving nothing for the NOC.[9] However Miguel Abad, Chief Executive of the interim organising committee, asserted that the internal crisis of the Spanish NOC would not inhibit the founding of the permanent organising committee. (The latter was to be known as COOB – Comité Organizador Olímpico de Barcelona – '92, usually abbreviated to COOB'92, the natural acronym, COJO (Comité

Organizador de los Juegos Olímpicos) having had to be rejected because in Spanish it means lame man or cripple, hardly a suitable name for an Olympic Games organising committee.)[10]

In May 1987 elections for the presidency of the COE were held, and Carlos Ferrer Salat emerged victorious. Ferrer Salat, normally known simply as Ferrer, was a prominent businessman who had made his fortune in banking, chemicals and pharmaceuticals and had been elected to the IOC in 1985. Once he had been elected President of the COE he became a Vice-President of COOB and relations between the two bodies improved greatly. Don Alfonso died in an accident on 30 January 1989 and *The Times*'s obituary summed up well in recalling that he had been attacked for opposing revision of the COE's rules and that it had seemed to many that he was being used by leftovers from the Franco era to resist a democratisation of Spanish sport, which would make Spain more prepared for hosting the 1992 Games.[11]

The interim committee was succeeded in December 1986 by COOB, which had a complicated structure, reflecting the complexity of the political state of affairs. It consisted of a General Assembly, containing representatives of the Catalan and Spanish sports federations, and the economic, social and cultural worlds, as well as of the four consortium members – the COE and the three tiers of government. (The COE was in a special position, in that its lack of funds rendered it unable to accept any of the financial responsibility.) The Assembly delegated responsibility to an Executive Board and a Standing Committee which dealt with the day-to-day work. These bodies were led by Maragall as President, and four Vice-Presidents, Carlos Ferrer, Javier Gómez Navarro (Secretary of State for Sport in the Madrid government), Josep María Vilaseca and the Chief Executive Officer, Josep Miguel Abad (formerly of the interim committee). Beneath this superstructure spread a rash of companies and directorates, but the principle of political control of COOB, upon which Maragall always insisted, was preserved.

COOB itself was not always a happy ship. The press described it as a battlefield where problems quite unrelated to the Olympics were fought out.[12] In December *Euroletter* summed up the four elements of the crisis in COOB. First, Seoul's success had made COOB realise how much work it had to do; secondly Samaranch's constant involvement in Barcelona's affairs created complications, largely because the organisers did not always fall in with his ideas, especially in the matter of the sale of television rights; thirdly, the central government was displeased by Maragall's bad relations with its Secretary of State for Sport, Gómez Navarro. Finally it was still necessary to delimit the areas of competence of Abad and the new Director-General of COOB, José María Vilá and to give some teeth to the consultative committee of businessmen which had been set up by Maragall, but which had practically never met. *Euroletter* added that another of Maragall's projects had also never got off the ground, namely the creation of an effective committee of representatives of the city, the Generalitat and the central government to oversee the financing of the Olympics.[13]

Even at official level things did not go smoothly. The unpopularity of the organising committee's first director, Jaume Clavell, led to his dismissal in November 1988 and his replacement by Miguel Abad. The complaint against him was 'insubordination' at an Executive Board meeting, where he had complained of the limitations placed upon his powers.[14] Another view is that he was dismissed for not being enough of a socialist, or perhaps for not being faithful enough to Maragall.

This crisis within COOB was soon followed by a second, arising from an attack on Abad. It was suggested that in socialist circles this former communist municipal councillor was not considered to have a good socialist pedigree and there were fears that he might be toppled if the crisis were not resolved.[15] Be that as it may, he was saved by Maragall's total support, and the successful sale of the television rights in the games consolidated both their positions and put an end to the crisis.

The international task

Despite Barcelona's rivalry with Paris, which turned out to be the city's most dangerous adversary, Maragall's main energies until mid 1984 had been spent on creating unity of purpose between the three tiers of government in Spain, so much so that when he returned from a trip to Madrid, where he had been selling the Games, all the questions at his press conference were about politics, rather than sport.[16] However, once the decision was announced to send a delegation to promote Barcelona's case at the Los Angeles Games the campaign entered its international phase, although there was still political rivalry to be handled at home and periodic faction fighting within the organising committee.

Maragall clearly did well in Los Angeles. Samaranch could of course not give open support, but said that all the candidates were good, and that Barcelona's bid would be strong if the city maintained its sporting, political and social unity. His heart, he said, was in Barcelona, but there were five other candidates. Maragall made a big presentation at the Biltmore Hotel, and got Julio Iglesias and Plácido Domingo to sing at a reception given by Barcelona's team. He showed his capacity for saying the right thing by stating that 'Olympic votes are not bought or sold, but won'.

The first major figure in the sporting world from outside Spain publicly to announce his support for Barcelona was Dr Primo Nebiolo, President of the International Amateur Athletic Federation, who was followed by João Havelange, the powerful President of FIFA, and close associate of Samaranch. Nebiolo said that as a Latin he would prefer Barcelona to other cities, and that, after the problems of Moscow, Los Angeles and Seoul, Barcelona would be ideally quiet. Nebiolo and Joan Mas Conti, the Olympic Commissioner for Barcelona, rejected the idea floated by Nelson Paillou, President of the French NOC, that the 1988 Games might be taken away from Seoul and given to Barcelona, leaving the field free for Paris in 1992.[17]

In November 1984 Barcelona made a big impression with its presentation to the Association of National Olympic Committees (ANOC) in Mexico. The delegation was led by Joan Mas Conti, and merely accompanied by the embarrassing Don Alfonso. This was the first time Barcelona had met ANOC, and the Mexican press did the delegation proud, which is not surprising when one remembers that much of it belongs to Mario Vásquez-Raña, the President of ANOC, who was probably supporting Barcelona even at this early stage. Later he was to call the 1992 Olympics 'my Games' because he had helped to get them for Barcelona.[18]

The slow process of gathering international support continued, on the whole, to go well. José Beracassa, Honorary President of the Pan-American Olympic Committee, said Barcelona could count on all the countries of Central and South America.[19] Despite his international efforts, Maragall did not make the mistake sometimes made by bidding committees and forget the need to raise Olympic consciousness at home. On 29 September 1985 Pujol told the Catalan Parliament how essential it was that Barcelona should get the Games; the Barcelona Diputación voted ptas 1,000m ($6m)* for

* Pesetas are converted to dollars at the average rates for 1985 and January 1989.

infrastructural development and an opinion poll showed that 64 per cent of Spaniards, especially those living in big cities, believed that the Games in Barcelona would benefit the whole of Spain. By early November a correspondent of *Le Martin* in Lausanne was tipping Barcelona as favourite, as were the Barcelona papers *El Mundo Deportivo* and *Sport*.

Getting the IOC's votes

Ambassador Ignacio Masferrer was seconded from the Spanish diplomatic service in 1985 to help with the international side of the bid, and in particular to sell it to IOC members, since it was thought that he would have a higher standing with them than would a firm of public relations agents. The international operation, known as the Commission for External Relations, was run by Leopoldo Rodés and Carlos Ferrer. The third member of the Commission, which was given complete independence and discretion by the municipality, was Andreu Mercé Varela, a journalist and another old friend of Samaranch.

Barcelona's bid seems to have cost well above the average, as did that of Paris. Ferrer was asked by Maragall to raise industrial money to assist in financing the bid. He and Rodés set up a Foundation and were able to recruit over ninety other businessmen, each of whose companies contributed at least ptas 10m ($60,000) to Barcelona's fighting fund.

As with all bids, it was necessary to persuade as many IOC members as possible to visit Barcelona. All of them were invited and more than half accepted. As with other visits, they had their fares and hotels paid, some brought their wives or another family member, and they would be invited to stay with the industrialists who had contributed to the fund. Their programme for visiting IOC members would include meeting Maragall and Pujol and seeing Barcelona from the air. They would also receive gifts, of a personal rather than a luxurious nature (the most valuable was a lithograph, signed by the artist, of Salvador Dali's 1968 oil painting *The Cosmic Athlete*) though there were, it is said, also favours rendered which it might have been difficult to justify had the details been publicly known. It must be added that there was considerable talk, though never of a specific nature, about other gifts which were alleged to have been given, and there lurked in the background, as no less a sports journalist than David Miller pointed out, the shadow of Adidas.[20]

To many of the members money was not important: what mattered was to study the personal psychology of each of them when deciding what programme would be most suitable. Perhaps the master stroke of the exceedingly well-run campaign was that, shortly before the crucial vote at Lausanne, each member of the IOC received a personal letter from King Carlos, worth little in itself, yet a flattering mark of attention.

In addition to making as good an impression as possible, it was important, as it is in any such campaign, to form an assessment of the degree of independence an IOC member would enjoy from his government. Of course, all IOC members are appointed by the IOC (in practice largely by its President) as independent individuals, but some are more independent than others. Governmental influence may be reduced by the fact that even those members who are willing, or obliged, to listen to their governments would not have time to consult between the rounds of voting. On the other hand, those who are open to influence are probably aware in advance of their governments' second and even third preferences.

Voting day

Although it is often denied that blocs of voters exist, Barcelona felt sure of the Latin American vote, thanks to Spain's historical links. Its relationship with those countries is regarded by Spaniards as similar to that between the United Kingdom and the rest of the Commonwealth, without the structure, but with more affection.

On the day of the vote (17 October 1986) David Miller wrote in *The Times* that Barcelona's strength lay not so much in its promotional budget as in solid support from the King, and in not having had to sell itself on sentiment, as Paris had done. He could not see Barcelona failing, although the IOC had many members who were only interested in making friends. He did, however, think Barcelona's projected income from radio and television rather high at $293 million, unless, as he acidly put it, they decided to start the 100 metres at two in the morning for the benefit of American prime time viewers.[21] Another article in the same day's *Times* commented that no one could forecast the effect on IOC members of the bombings in Barcelona earlier in the week, but that William Hill, the British bookmakers, had Barcelona as favourite at 3–1 on, with Birmingham at 2–1 against.

As we have seen in the section on Birmingham's bid, Barcelona's footwork was impressively swift and decisive. When it became clear how great an impression the speech by the French Prime Minister, Jacques Chirac, had made, Barcelona was able to divert those IOC members who would have given the winter Games to Falun (Sweden) to voting for the French candidate, Albertville, instead. This extraordinary manipulation ensured that Albertville had a very good chance of being awarded the winter games and rendered it virtually inconceivable that Paris would win the summer competition as well.[22] Reporting Barcelona's decisive win, Miller said that the pattern of voting showed that Samaranch's influence had not been a factor, since Barcelona had got a minority in the first two rounds of voting.[23] John Rodda presciently concluded that, once the euphoria was over, Samaranch might find it difficult to be strict enough with his native city in relation to the actual organisation of the Games.[24] Meanwhile Barcelona celebrated. Many of its citizens had never believed that they could possibly fail and when the result was announced the city erupted in fireworks.

Thereafter development accelerated: new hotels were built; much of Barcelona's seafront, which had previously been obscured by a railway, was opened up by diverting the railway to allow space for the Olympic village, and the flats which were to be built in the village were already for sale two years ahead of the Games. A new ring road was constructed and insalubrious parts of the city were cleaned up: in short, the prospect of the Games forced the three tiers of government to co-operate on projects which might otherwise have been indefinitely delayed by in-fighting.

Problems of 1992

Winning the bid does not guarantee a stress-free life thereafter and Samaranch was frequently, and justifiably, worried about the failure of some of Barcelona's plans to materialise. For example, an early hope, subsequently abandoned, was to extend the city's metro system up to the Montjuic stadium. The report of ANOC's Commission on the Olympic Games, presented to the ANOC meeting at Barcelona in June 1990, was also not altogether sanguine. One particular worry was about the capacity of the Olympic village. Seoul had had fewer events, and fewer participating NOCs than Barcelona. It had provided for more than 9,000 competitors, plus 3,900 officials and 1,500 extra officials who stayed outside the Olympic village. Barcelona was banking on 10,000 competitors and 5,200 officials, which was an increased projection necessitated by the larger programme and the larger number of NOCs, but it was not clear to the Commission where the extra officials were to be accommodated. Nor was it pleased to learn that competitors in the finals of demonstration sports (not full Olympic sports, but allowed on the fringe of the Games) were to be housed in the main village, contrary to what had previously been agreed.

The Commission summed up that the preparations for the Olympics had shown reasonable progress since its visit in July 1989. But it added that there was much concern about the capacity of the Olympic stadium for the Opening Ceremony. Its current capacity was 55,000 and consideration was being given to the feasibility of increasing this to 70,000. The report added, without comment, that there was a plan for the athletes to be sent to the Palau Sant Jordi (capacity 17,000) sports hall after their parade, when they could watch 'the cultural program of the opening ceremony' on a giant television screen.

At the plenary meetings of ANOC some of the complaints were less politely phrased than in the Commission's report. COOB was strongly criticised for planning to relegate the athletes to the sports hall and there was bitter talk, particularly by some African NOCs, of meanness on the part of Barcelona. Their complaint was that the athletes alone were to be accommodated free of charge in the Olympic village, and not their entourages, and even the athletes would only be accommodated free on the days on which they were actually competing, plus six further days. Faced with this barrage of complaint Abad remained firm: he regretted the annoyance caused to some NOCs, but insisted that the position had been made perfectly clear in Barcelona's bidding documents. No less a personage than Mario Vázquez Raña, ANOC's President, remained dissatisfied, and referred darkly to the 'humility with which some people speak when they are presenting their candidature and the pride that they show once they have been successful.'[25]

The remarks made in the ANOC Commission's report and at the meeting itself raised the question of why the Opening and Closing Ceremonies could not have been held in the Barcelona football club's stadium, which, although old and nothing like as magnificent as

Montjuic, is larger and more easily accessible. The answer appears to be entirely a matter of politics and 'face'. The Club has always been a centre of Catalonian nationalism, and therefore politically opposed to the socialist administration of Barcelona; consequently Maragall was firmly opposed to its being used. It was one thing to hold some of the football matches in the stadium: it would have been quite another to give the Club worldwide publicity by holding the main Olympic ceremonies there, and so giving the world the impression that the city fathers were not capable of providing an adequate stadium of their own.

Worries within the 'Olympic family'

Samaranch, who tended to be worried and satisfied by turns about Barcelona's preparations for the Olympics, was perceived in COOB as continually interfering in the preparations for the Games. His visits to the Prime Minister and even to the King to complain about slow progress naturally annoyed COOB, although the public attitude was one of indulgent tolerance. He has extraordinary access, which he would never be granted in, for example, London, to these high personages, and on the whole his interventions bear fruit.

Others of the multifarious Olympic bodies expressed worries. For example, the Liaison Commission of the IOC which visited Barcelona in October 1987 was favourably impressed in general, but unhappy with COOB's failure to designate a site for the yachting events. Palma de Mallorca would have been happy to oblige, but the IOC was known to favour Barcelona, where no satisfactory facilities existed.[26] In the end it proved possible to build a yacht basin at Barcelona, which pleased Samaranch, who naturally believed that the events should not be held anywhere except at the Olympic city[27] (though it must be added that the pollution of the Mediterranean can hardly have been agreeable for the yachtsmen).

There were also great difficulties over the equestrian events, which it was feared might have to be moved to a site outside Spain because of outbreaks of African horse sickness. Again, Barcelona would have suffered loss of face if the events had been held elsewhere, and the income from television rights would have been seriously affected. The issue was finally decided in Barcelona's favour by the International Equestrian Federation (of which Britain's Princess Royal was President) in November 1990.

There was also some doubt, which only became noticeable in 1990, about whether the Games would make a profit. Fortunately a modest surplus (of $3.27m) was achieved: if there had been a loss the central government would have met 20 per cent of it, which it would have seen as compensation for increased tax revenue generated by the Games, and the remaining 80 per cent would have been shared by the three tiers of government in the proportions 40 per cent central government; 30 per cent Barcelona municipal government: 30 per cent Generalitat.

The financial dangers may have seemed less significant to the principal actors than did the political and personal. Maragall's position was not altogether comfortable until the 1991 municipal elections, because he ran a real risk of losing office if trends in the national elections of October 1989 were reproduced. The prospect of the games being held in Barcelona strengthened his position, but they had to be sold to the people of Barcelona as a whole, and he was much criticised for the disruption to daily life caused by the preparations. In fact he returned safely to office: had he not, the Olympic Games would, of course, still have gone ahead, but it would have been exceedingly galling for Maragall not to play the leading part given to the Mayor of the host city, and to feel that the great efforts he had made to bring the Games to Barcelona had, in a personal sense, been wasted.

He may have been reassured by a poll conducted for *La Vanguardia* in May 1990, which showed that 70 per cent of Spaniards believed the Games would be a success, and only 9 per cent thought they would be a disaster. Of the people of Barcelona 80 per cent thought the Games would be beneficial for the city, and about the same percentage of Sevillians thought they would benefit from the 1992 exhibition there. Taking the two events together, 72 per cent of Spaniards thought they would be beneficial. Yet 16 per cent of Barcelonans thought the Games would be bad for the city (compared with 10 per cent who believed the exhibition would be bad for Seville). The pessimistic minority was to be found most strongly in the United Right (Izquierda Unida), followed by the nationalist parties, and they were more pessimistic about the Games than about the exhibition.[28]

Samaranch had more to lose than anyone if the Barcelona Games turned out a fiasco. He had not lobbied for his home city in any overt way, but he made no secret of his hope that Barcelona would be chosen, and once it had been he took a close interest in the preparations – sometimes too close for COOB. To have the Games in his home town was the culmination of his career, and made him a popular figure there. He has nothing to lose financially, but a less than perfect Games would have caused him incalculable distress and loss of face.

Conclusion

Olympic records were set at Barcelona. The United States television rights fetched $401m, 169 NOCs took part, and no fewer than 129,185 people were accredited. Of these, only 10,253 were athletes, as may be seen from the table showing the principal categories of accreditation.[29]

It is difficult to quantify at all accurately the economic effect on Barcelona of having held the Games, although Professor Ferran Brunet has made a first attempt. In reviewing Brunet's work, not altogether favourably, Professor C. Frank Zarnowski agreed that 'There is no doubt that the legacy of the 1992 Barcelona Olympics is a better quality of life for its residents, more employment opportunities and greater accrued capital. The question is, how much better?, how much more?, how much greater?'[30]

Even if accurate figures are difficult, perhaps impossible, to produce, Barcelona has been put on the map as a city of world

Athletes		10,253
Judges		2,387
Officials	4,845	
Extra officials	1,966	6,811
IOC, NOCs and IFs: members and staff, and their guests		3,465
Other guests		2,340
Journalists, written word and photographers	4,880	
Radio and television	7,951	12,831
Personnel of COOB '92 (of whom the great majority were volunteers)		41,650
Personnel seconded by sub-contractors		23,474
Security services		21,116

The security services numbered over six thousand more than had originally been envisaged.

importance; more hotels have been built, and the city attracts more visitors and conferences than ever.[31] In any case, as Josep Miguel Abad, the Chief Executive Officer of the Games, has said, 'people are only the anecdotes of history. Only events really count. And they have to be seen in the context of the time. The last chapter of the Olympic Movement has yet to be written.'[32]

Notes

1 El Periódico, 23 November 1984.
2 El País, 22 October 1989. For Pujol's manoeuvres, see The Times, 20 July 1992, Edward Owen, Madrid.
3 El Periódico, 18 February 1985.
4 El Mundo Deportivo, 22 May 1985.
5 Le Dauphine Libéré, 9 January 1987.
6 La Vanguardia, 25 January 1989.
7 Libération, 30 January 1987, Bernard Cohen.
8 Diario, Madrid, 16 September 1985.
9 Libération, Bernard Cohen, 30 January 1987.
10 EFE, 20 January 1987.
11 The Times,1 February 1989.
12 For example, Tribuna, 21 November 1988.
13 Euroletter, 2 December 1988.
14 El Mundo Deportivo, 18 January 1989; see also El Periódico, 25 January 1989.
15 El País, 18 November 1988.
16 El Mundo Deportivo, 11 July 1984.
17 Ibid., 7 June 1984. Richard Pound corroborates the story of Paillou seeking to remove the Games from Seoul, and adds that Maragall supported the initiative. See Five Rings Over Korea, Boston, 1994.
18 Barcelona Olímpica, 6, Dec./Jan. 1989, p. 21, Antonio H. Filloy.
19 El País, 28 August 1985.
20 The Times, 18 October 1986, David Miller, Lausanne.
21 The Times, 17 October 1986.
22 John Rodda in Running Magazine, December 1986. Rodda makes the additional point that the voice was Chirac's, but the speech had been written by Monique Berlioux, the former Executive Director of the IOC whom Samaranch had sacked.
23 The Times, 18 October 1986.
24 John Rodda, Running Magazine, December 1986.
25 La Vanguardia, 8 June 1990.
26 AP, 26 October 1987.
27 EFE, 2 December 1987.
28 La Vanguardia, 4 June 1990.
29 The table is derived from COOB'92's Official Report on the Games, vol. III.

30 Ferran Brunet, *Economy of the 1992 Olympic Games*, Barcelona, Centro de Estudos Olímpicos, 1993; reviewed by C. Frank Zarnowski, *ISOH Journal*, 3, 1, winter 1995, pp. 37–9.

31 See, e.g., *Barcelona Bulletin*, 70, 15 February 1994.

32 'Games of a New World: Robert Parienté Interviews Josep Miguel Abad', *Olympic Review*, 299, September 1992, p. 437.

X

South Africa and the Olympic Games

The isolation of South African sport is an exceptionally stark example of the use of sport for political ends, and the Olympic movement was naturally involved from the earliest days. Dennis Brutus, the founder of the campaign to exclude South Africa from world sport, and his friends at first thought it necessary to say that their protests were not political but directed to strictly sporting issues. This response became less necessary as time went by and it became ever more widely understood that South African sport could not be separated from its broader social context.

This is not to say that the concern with sport was a pretence, but it did have the further purposes of raising consciousness about South Africa internationally and of keeping up the morale of those engaged in the struggle in exile, most of whom were powerless to agitate directly at home. Some of the campaigners were sports people, who used what they knew best to advance the general struggle for black emancipation. Others valued the sports boycott as another weapon in the fight against apartheid, even if they were not themselves particularly interested in sport.

The success of the campaign is difficult to evaluate, because it is not clear what counted as 'success', but even if it had achieved no definite result in the shape of internal change in South Africa, it would still have had a value if it succeeded in sustaining activists' morale and, in the same way as the fruit or wine boycotts, in raising public awareness of the South African problem outside the Republic.

The brilliantly conducted campaign attacked on various fronts. At the level of the individual, the purpose was to persuade sports people that apartheid was a uniquely evil system, and that to play games against the South Africans was to condone it, or even strengthen it.

Some of the targets agreed, but others thought that sport was something outside politics, and that sports people should be allowed to get on with their own lives and to leave politics to the politicians. Others went further, and said that playing against South Africa might liberalise the system, by bringing South Africans into contact with the outside world. (Much the same was said by people who favoured western participation in the Moscow Olympics of 1980.) Some sports people believed that it would be wrong to cut off contact with South Africa, because they believed that they could do good on the sports front by, for example, coaching underprivileged young people.

Dennis Brutus and the early days of the boycott

At the level of institutions, SASA, the South African Sports Association, founded by Brutus in Port Elizabeth in 1958, sought to persuade international federations to withdraw recognition from their South African affiliates, on the grounds that they were for whites only (albeit with non-white affiliated organisations), even if their rule books did not explicitly exclude non-whites. In other words, SASA was objecting to a policy of multi-racialism, and seeking to put in its place a non-racial system. (In a multi-racial system the different racial groups are identified as such, and an effort may then be made to treat them equitably, whereas a non-racial system seeks not to distinguish between the groups.) Table tennis had already provided one strikimg example of recognition being withdrawn, and SASA's objective was to persuade all the other IFs to follow suit. Unfortunately many defenders of South African practice, in South Africa and outside, had great difficulty in understanding the difference between multi-racialism and non-racialism, and in some cases honestly thought that SASA had no cause for complaint.

The ultimate purpose was to push the International Olympic Committee into cancelling its recognition of the South African National Olympic Committee, SANOC. To this end SASA spawned SANROC, the South African Non-Racial Olympic Committee, in 1962. The new body saw itself as SANOC's rival for recognition by the IOC, although Avery Brundage (President of the IOC, 1952–72) objected to its use of the Olympic label and said at the IOC's Tehran Session in 1967 that the IOC would have no further dealings with it unless it changed its name. It therefore substituted 'Open' for 'Olympic', a change that was never taken very seriously.

In the strictly sporting context 'non-whites', as they were called in the 1950s, had two major complaints. (Much later Africans, Indians and Coloureds (people of mixed descent) defined themselves as 'black', and became conventionally known as such.) First, although there were no laws specific to sport, the notion of people of different population groups taking part in mixed sport was anathema to white politicians and to many of the white rank and file, whether the mixing occurred in a mixed team or in competition against racially different teams or individuals. Secondly, in the government's mind there was no room for federations which contained no colour bar: the approved model of sports federations was that they should be controlled by whites, and that black federations could only be affiliated to them. Some black organisations accepted what was offered, and enjoyed a good deal of autonomy, provided they accepted the basic power structure, but their acceptance was seen by SASA as connivance.

Brutus has been eased out of South African sports politics in recent years and his name is seldom mentioned, but he is the father of the whole movement to exclude South Africa from international sport. On 4 May 1959, writing as president of SASA, for which he claimed the support of some seventy thousand South African sportsmen, he despatched a seminal memorandum to the IOC. The IOC's concern with issues of racial discrimination was in its infancy. The first serious mention of it by Avery Brundage comes as an aside to his report to the IOC's 55th Session, held in Paris in June 1955, on a meeting with IFs, followed by joint meetings with IFs and NOCs. He took the occasion to discuss discrimination against persons of colour in certain countries. But it is only a sentence, in which he says discrimination is against the Olympic spirit, before he goes on to something else.

In his memorandum Brutus set out the then current position. SAONGA (South African Olympic and National Games Association, later SANOC, South African National Olympic Committee), founded in 1912, had about twenty affiliates; because it was restrictive in constitution and practice, a number of new sports bodies had been founded and were vociferously demanding national and international recognition. These new bodies were determined to be non-racial, and it was naturally important to Brutus to show that, even if in practice they were limited to non-whites, the blame lay with the whites.

It must be made clear at this stage that most of the non-white sporting organizations are in fact, *non-racial* organizations. They are non-white by accident, and not design . . . On the other hand, many of the recognised bodies' constitutions contain a clause limiting membership to amateurs 'of European descent'.

Brutus thought that there had recently been a very considerable modification in white bodies' attitudes, particularly since the beginning of 1959, presumably as a result of criticism in South Africa and overseas. SAONGA had only that year announced that it had no colour bar, but this had not yet had any practical effect; nor had it any real meaning, since SAONGA admitted that its components, the affiliated federations, did have a colour bar. It had not even considered sending non-whites to the Olympics. Some had passed as white in the South African Olympic team (boxing and weightlifting) in 1956, but when found out they had been asked to 'retire'. The dispute, Brutus wrote, was about status. It was not disputed that some white bodies helped their non-white counterparts, particularly in cycling, athletics, soccer and weightlifting. Affiliation was offered by white bodies, but the blacks were given no more voting power by the national bodies than they gave to a white province, and the representatives, who voted on behalf of a non-white group, had to be white.

Another point that Brutus needed to make, particularly in the early years of the campaign, was that he was not furthering his objectives by illegitimately introducing politics into sport. Thus he said of non-white protest: 'If anything, their stand is anti-political. Yet it is precisely this stand which is described as "political agitation" by politicians and sportsmen who have brought racist politics into sport.' He went on:

Any attempt to alter the sporting set-up in South Africa is almost certain to have some effect on the social structure, but this is surely not the concern of the sportsmen . . . What has happened is that there has been an unwarranted intrusion of political ideas into the field of sport: their resolve to see this foreign influence expelled from the field of sport is surely not politics, but no more than a desire to play the game according to rules which are universally accepted.

Brutus had to assume that the IOC knew little about the recent history of sport in South Africa and set down the story of the international recognition of the non-racial table tennis body, and corresponding withdrawal of recognition from the white body, which had been achieved as early as 1956. The next battle had been in football, between the white Football Association of South Africa and the non-racial South African Soccer Federation. The Federation had presented the facts to a commission of FIFA (the International Football Federation) which had pronounced the Association non-representative, and had seen no justification for the colour bar. Recognition of the Association was withdrawn in September 1961, after FIFA had adopted a statute against racial, religious or political discrimination.

Brutus's memorandum continued that the most significant of all the efforts to lift the colour bar had been made by weightlifting. It had split on racial lines and in 1956 the non-racial body had written to the IOC asking to compete in the 1960 Olympics. This move had been intended to force the IOC to make a decision, which of course had been easy to evade by passing the application on to the proper authorities, the International Weightlifting Federation, to SAWLU (South African Weightlifting Union, for whites only) and to SAONGA. The British Empire and Commonwealth Games Federation had taken the same route when faced with similar enquiries. Apart from trying to advance non-racialism in their own federation, the weightlifters had also been the fathers of SASA. They had held two conferences. The first, in 1955, had been poorly attended, but the second, in 1958, had led to the foundation of SASA.

Brutus's memorandum, which set the scene for many future years of struggle, concluded with an appeal to SAONGA to cease its discrimination against non-whites or to ask the IFs to look into the activities of their South African affiliates, failing which the IOC should find South Africa ineligible to compete in the Olympics.[1]

The politics of apartheid

The policy which Brutus and his friends were opposing had always been part of the conventional thinking of white South Africans, but, like every other aspect of South African life, it was influenced by the advance of 'grand apartheid', or 'separate development'. Dr Hendrik Vervoerd, Prime Minister from 1958 until his assassination in Parliament in Cape Town on 6 September 1966, when he was succeeded by Johannes Balthazar Vorster,[2] was the great architect of apartheid (separateness), one of whose central ideas was that different races (we would usually refer to 'ethnic groups') are bound to be antagonistic, to the point where the only solution is to keep them apart.

The core idea of 'grand', as opposed to 'petty', apartheid was that the different groups should not only be kept apart in daily life, but that the European and African groups (not the Indian and Coloured, but Zulu, Xhosa, Tswana, etc.) should be given separate geographical areas, to be known as 'homelands', which would eventually be given independence and be internationally recognised as states. Every black South African would be made a citizen of one of these homelands, so that there would no longer be any black South Africans. The problem of whites being heavily outnumbered by blacks would thus be defined out of existence and the old South Africa would be replaced with a new white heartland (occupying about 87 per cent of the original territory) and a circle of new black nations.[3]

This excursion into the thinking behind apartheid makes it possible to understand Vorster's sports policy. In 1963 policy had shifted to allow South African teams, which had to be all of one racial group, to compete against the 'wrong' groups, but only outside South Africa. In April 1967 Vorster, who had come to power only in the previous September, announced in Parliament that foreign teams visiting South Africa might include non-white members, and that South African white teams might play against them. This 'multi-national' principle justified the South African Games of 1973 and the more radical changes introduced in September 1976, the year of the New Zealand rugby tour, the Soweto riots and the Montreal boycott, when Vorster allowed the extension of multi-national competition to club level. This concession meant, in the context of the governing ideology, that the various 'nations' within South Africa could engage in sport against each other. In plain language, black teams could play against white. The reasoning was that if mixed sport was acceptable in contests with real foreigners, why not also in those with blacks who had been designated foreigners?[4]

The IOC, reasonably enough, referred Brutus's representations to the South African NOC, which was the only South African Olympic body that it recognised. It was assured by Reginald Honey, the IOC member in South Africa, that if in a trial an amateur non-white performed at international standard there should be no objection to participation abroad, and that the government of South Africa would issue a passport. Thus, non-whites would not be barred from the Olympics. The IOC was satisfied enough with this assurance for Brundage to sign a circular to IOC members, IFs and NOCs on 5 July 1960, saying that the IOC had entire confidence in SANOC.

However, the representations continued. The Reverend Michael Scott appeared before the Executive Board at Rome on 24 August

1960 (the day before the opening of the Games), 'accompanied by a gentleman of South Africa' and in the presence of Reginald Honey and Frank H. Braun, the President of SANOC. On this occasion Scott did not make progress. The IOC representatives felt that the South African Olympic Association had made every reasonable effort to implement Mr Honey's undertaking that no competitor of requisite calibre was excluded from the South African team. The minutes record that:

It was considered also that . . . there need not be from the viewpoint of South African sport and despite the admittedly difficult political position, any reason why such misunderstandings as had led Mr Scott and his friend to ask for the present meeting should occur in the future.[5]

South African sportsmen seem to have hoped to go to the Perth Empire Games of 1962, although South Africa had left the Commonwealth in 1961. But by June 1962 Otto Mayer, the Chancellor of the International Olympic Committee, was already very pessimistic, as was Honey.

The IOC's Executive Board, meeting at Lausanne on 2–3 March 1962 had to note that there had been no progress, despite Honey's promises at Rome. The Board decided to ask SANOC for explanations and for reconfirmation of its intentions, and the Session in Moscow in June 1962 warned South Africa that it would be suspended in 1963 if the government did not change its policy of racial discrimination in sport by the time of the October 1963 Session, which was to be held at Nairobi. This resolution was passed by what Mayer described as a 'great majority' as an amendment to a Soviet proposal for immediate suspension.[6]

After the Moscow Session, which had received a report from 'our esteemed South African member Mr Reg Honey', Mayer wrote to SANOC, referring back to the discussion in Rome, at the 1960 Session, when

we were assured that your Government would permit the inclusion of coloured [presumably meaning 'non-white', rather than 'of mixed race', which was the South African meaning of 'coloured'] athletes in your team for the Olympic Games. Now we understand the situation has changed and that your Government has forbidden such a mixed team. In this event, of course, you cannot fulfill your obligations as a National Olympic Committee recognised by the IOC.[7]

The pessimism spread to the South African press. For example, *The Argus* said, 'if the government is not prepared to countenance sending a mixed team to the 1964 Games in Tokyo there will in all probability be no South African team: and if the government does yield it will surely prove a significant crack in the granite edifice of Verwoerdian apartheid'.[8] However, Senator J. de Klerk, Minister of the Interior, made it clear that the government would not budge from its insistence that black and white should not be in the same team. On the other hand the normally timid SANOC realised that the government must give an absolute assurance that any non-whites that SANOC might choose would be given passports. Otherwise South Africa would be out of the Games.[9]

The South African Non-Racial Olympic Committee (SANROC) was launched at Durban on 7 October 1962, sponsored by SASA, and on 12 October Dennis Brutus, as president, officially reported its formation to Mayer. He went on to record the terms that he had offered Honey: 'We have assured him that if his Association will arrange to see that all South Africans are allowed equal and full membership of the national bodies affiliated to his association, then we will not proceed with the development of SANROC'. As always, Brutus did not miss a trick, but put Mayer on the spot by innocently implying that the new body was operating in partnership with the IOC.

The meeting gratefully acknowledged the material supplied by the IOC which will be used as the basis for the constitution of SANROC. I trust you will allow us to consult you if there are any difficulties, as we are anxious to comply with the requirements of your International Olympic Committee on all matters.[10]

On the same day, in a separate letter, SANROC asked permission to use the five Olympic rings on its stationery. Meyer of course was embarrassed, and had to write to SANOC to explain that the IOC had not corresponded with SANROC, but had only sent the rules as printed matter, which it would have done to anyone. Suspension, not expulsion, was being considered.[11]

South Africa's apologists

The next important development was a report by Braun to the IOC at Baden Baden in October 1962. He recognised that South Africa would have to conform with Olympic statutes by the Nairobi Session of October 1963, or be suspended. Yet he insisted that there was no basis for the accusation against the South African government that it did not allow amateurs of all nations in fair and equal competition. He reaffirmed that athletes were selected on merit and that those who were properly affiliated would be included in South Africa's team for Tokyo. (He was completely missing the point at issue, which was that the official South African notion of 'properly affiliated' was unacceptable to SANROC, and became unacceptable to the IOC.) South African white and non-white competitors had, Braun said, taken part in a number of international events, for example, Mr Universe in London, 1963, and had had no difficulty in obtaining passports.

Braun asserted that a great deal was being done in South Africa for the benefit of non-white sportsmen, a contention which Brutus would have accepted, but would have thought irrelevant since he was determined never to agree to any form of parallel affiliation. Braun listed all the national bodies (athletics etc.) which were affiliated to international federations, and insisted that 'Affiliation to all these national governing bodies is open to respective non-white associations as and when they may be constituted'. So far only weightlifting, athletics, cycling, boxing, football and swimming had been constituted, but 'Any non-white who is a member of an affiliated body is eligible on merit to nomination and selection for participation in the Olympic Games'.[12] It is clear from all this that there was no meeting of minds and that Honey and Braun simply did not understand what the fuss was all about.

The failure of minds to meet was not confined to the IOC and its South African interlocutors. Another good example comes in a report by a certain Rudolf Balsiger in *Der Neue Tip*, a magazine published in Basle. The report took the form of an open letter to the Olympic Chancellor, Mayer, on Balsiger's researches in South Africa, in which he cited as evidence of the non-political nature of sport in South Africa the fact that Field-Marshall Jan Smuts's son-in-law was a member of the South African Olympic Committee!

He went on to recount a meeting, arranged by Braun, with 'some malcontents', who had included Brutus. This was the first he had heard of 'the dissident South African Olympic Committee'. Braun had asked Brutus if, as a 'listed person', he was allowed to participate in this ten-man meeting. Brutus replied that he was not participating, but wished only to meet Balsiger and to introduce his friends. At this point two plain clothes police arrived. They took Brutus away and he was released on R400 bail a few days later.

Balsiger was dumbfounded by their demands, which he thought

were already met by the excellent facilities that he had seen. 'The SAN-ROC people behaved like politicians who do not want what they plead for, but just want everything.' He was convinced 'they had not the interest of sport at heart but abused sport to further their political intrigues'.[13]

The greatly admired Sir Stanley Rous fell into much the same way of thinking. He visited South Africa with Mr J. P. Maguire in 1963 to investigate the Football Association of South Africa (FASA), and came to the conclusion that it did not practise racial discrimination. Non-white groups were all affiliated to it, and the non-whites had good stadia. FASA was recognised by national and local government as the sole governing body of football, and there were arrangements for joint committees, etc., between it and the South African Bantu FA.

The Baden-Baden Session, 1963

The next IOC Session was to have been held at Nairobi, but in August 1963 doubts surfaced about whether Kenya would admit South Africans. It was quickly confirmed that the venue of the Session might move and Brundage went further than he might have done by threatening the expulsion of Kenya from the Olympic movement. The crisis then moved to ministerial level: Tom Mboya (Minister of Justice) and his deputy, Joe Murumbi, met President Jomo Kenyatta in search of a solution and Murumbi said that he thought only a multi-racial South African delegation would be welcome. To agree to admit a South African delegation at all was a concession, made because the Kenyans were anxious not to lose the Session, but by then arrangements had been made to switch to Baden-Baden, and it was too late to change them again. The upshot was that the Session was duly held at Baden-Baden in October 1963, but Kenya was not expelled from the movement.[14] To expel a state that had so recently emerged from its status as a British colony was probably more than even Brundage felt he could risk.

Pressure continued at Baden Baden, where the Soviet Union's IOC members, Andrianov and Romanov, proposed that South Africa should be suspended. SANOC's representatives, Braun, with his colleagues J. R. Rathobo and Mr Kaplan, appeared before the IOC and argued that apartheid was an internal matter, and not the concern of the IOC. Non-white athletes chosen for the Olympics could train

among themselves and compete against white athletes outside South
Africa; the government was committed to give them passports; the
opposition stemmed from political agitation. To this the IOC replied
that there had been some progress, but a non-white athlete still could
not measure himself against a black.

The IOC took a number of votes, in order to clarify the options.
Eventually they voted 30–20, with three spoiled papers, that SANOC
must formally submit to the Olympic Charter and by 31 December
1963 must obtain from its government a modification of its
discriminatory policy. Otherwise there would be no invitation to the
Tokyo Games in 1964.[15]

The Tokyo Games, 1964

When it met again at Innsbruck in January 1964 the IOC was not
satisfied with the report received from Braun on events since Baden
Baden. Brundage pointed out that apartheid was indeed governmental, but argued that it was still reasonable for the IOC to ask the
South African Olympic Committee to profess its allegiance to the
Olympic principle of no racial discrimination. The IOC would be glad
to keep South Africa, but it must conform to the rules. Since SANOC
had failed to 'conduct its activities in accordance with the Olympic
Regulations and high ideals of the Olympic Movement' it was
resolved unanimously, minus one (presumably Mr Honey), that
South Africa's invitation to the Tokyo Games should be withdrawn.
However, recognition of SANOC was not yet withdrawn, and there
seems to have been a glimmer of hope that South Africa might still be
able to put its house in order in time for Tokyo. This would make
sense of Braun's promise to do his best before Tokyo, and of the
Marquess of Exeter's spelling out exactly what was required of
SANOC.

The South African Olympic Committee must openly and officially declare
itself to be against apartheid in sport, and to be the champions of Olympic
ideals among its people. Even if it were not entirely successful, its effort in this
direction would be noted.[16]

In the event, no South African team went to Tokyo, nor to any
other Games until Barcelona in 1992. Yet South Africa took pains to
remind the world that it was still an Olympic nation: for example,
SANOC was the sixteenth NOC to write and endorse the choice of

Mexico City for the Games of 1968. Nevertheless, by October 1965 there were suggestions that South Africa might be expelled at the Rome Session in the following year. In South Africa itself there was guarded optimism, but Kenya and Ethiopia threatened to boycott Mexico City if South Africa were readmitted, and later in the year there was speculation that American negroes might refuse to take part. At the Executive Board's meeting in Rome before the full Session Brundage expressed a fear that 'If we expel them we shall never see them again' and hoped to put off discussion until the invitations to Mexico City had been sent out. He added that South Africa had wanted to send seven black athletes to Tokyo. The seven had now become professionals and were lost to the Olympic movement.

Braun and his colleagues were then brought into the meeting, and declared their submission to the Olympic Charter. They announced that their government would allow a fifty-fifty committee, under the presidency of SANOC, to select their Olympic team. The Executive Board 'proposed to wait for convincing results of the activity of this mixed committee'. The full IOC took a similar line: it decided to give them a last chance, and to make a final decision at Tehran. Before Tehran, and before NOCs were due to accept invitations to Mexico, an IOC commission would go to South Africa to assess the situation.[17]

In fact the Commission was not able to go to South Africa in advance of the Tehran Session, because SANOC had been slow to send the information for which the IOC had asked, and which had had to be collected from SANOC's affiliates all over the country. At Tehran R. W. J. Opperman, for Braun, who was ill, presented new proposals, and there was a feeling that SANOC had made progress since Rome, although a message was received from African NOCs that the proposed measures were still inadequate; indeed, they probably saw the offer made by Opperman of equal numbers of black and white officials, with the blacks nominating their own representatives, as an entrenchment of racial separation, rather than an alleviation. Outright criticism was also made of the IOC by the newly formed Supreme Council for Sport in Africa (SCSA). This body wished (but the request was not granted) to send two observers to South Africa with the IOC Commission, and wanted NOCs to defer their decisions about participation at Mexico City until it was known whether South Africa was to be allowed to compete.[18]

The Killanin Commission

The Comission of Enquiry, on which the IOC had decided at Rome, finally set off early in September 1967. It was headed by Lord Killanin, with one white African, Reggie Alexander (the IOC member in Kenya), and one black, Sir Adetokunbo Ademola (the member in Nigeria).[19]

The Commission, whose brief was to report, rather than to recommend,[20] took extensive evidence in South Africa, and from Brutus in London, where he was living in exile. The commissioners were all accommodated in the same hotel in South Africa, which was a breakthrough, but the good impression was marred when a plain clothes policeman had seen Killanin and Ademola having a rest together on the same bench beside the sea at Cape Town and had ordered them to separate.[21]

The Commission's report, presented to the IOC's Executive Board at Grenoble in February 1968, recalled that South Africa had exercised the IOC since the 1950s, when separate development had taken off and at the same time non-white South Africans had seemed to become more interested in sport. The report reviewed the recent history and current state of South African sports policy, culminating in Vorster's parliamentary statement (to which reference has already been made) on 11 April 1967, just before the IOC's meeting in Tehran. We have seen that he then announced a change of policy, allowing South African teams to play foreign teams of other races. Nevertheless, for the sake of his domestic constituency Vorster had had to make it clear that the principles of 'separate development' applied to sport, as to every other aspect of South African life. It was true that sport was good for relations between countries, but not if too high a price had to be paid, and he had reiterated: 'No mixed sport betwen white and non-white will be practised locally, irrespective of the standards of proficiency of the participants'. If foreigners wanted to play against South Africa only if it jettisoned its policy, 'no matter how important those sport relations are in my view, I am not prepared to pay that price.'

Vorster had emphasised that the decision to allow a mixed South African team at the Olympics was a one-off, and that the decision had been taken under his predecessor, because the government had been told that racially separate teams would not be allowed to take part. There would be one team, competing under one flag, because the IOC insisted, but the team would not be unified in the sense that it would be chosen by a single group of selectors on the basis of non-racial trials: instead, as Frank Braun had already announced, the various population groups were to appoint their own representatives:

with due regard to the fact that in accordance with overseas practice South Africans of different population groups will compete against each other over there . . . Just as there is already consultation between population groups in various fields, there will also be liaison between white and non-white sports administrators under the South African Olympic Committee in regard to the composition of the South African contingent for dealing with arrangements in connection with the Olympic Games.

Vorster had drawn a distinction between personal and state relations, and had plainly seen participation in the Olympics as an act of state. 'I could receive the Prime Minister of Lesotho, as I did, because it was not a personal relationship but an inter-state relationship . . . just as the Free State Volksraad received Moshesh in Bloemfontein.'[22]

Killanin recorded that he had met Vorster on 12 September 1967, when Vorster had confirmed the concessions announced by the SANOC representative, Opperman, at the Tehran Session of the IOC. There would in future be one South African Olympic team, whose members would be allowed to travel together, share accommodation, wear the same uniform and march under the same flag; members of different racial groups could now compete against each other, at the Olympics and at international meetings. Selection had in the past been by whites only. Now it would be by an equal number of white and non-white selectors, with the President of SANOC as chairman.

Vorster had told Killanin that Opperman had stated policy correctly, but that he preferred to refer to 'one team', rather than 'an integrated team', in view of the local connotations. He would not go further and allow mixed trials, either outside South Africa or in private at home. The IOC must trust the selection committees. 'The Prime Minister said that South Africa was very anxious to compete in the Olympic Games, but not under false colours if this meant integrated sport in South Africa.' In answer to a question from Killanin Vorster had agreed that there was no present solution to the problem of selecting, for example, a mixed football team.

The Commission seems to have been not much concerned with the composition of SANOC, since there was no discrimination in its statutes, which they had examined. The commissioners had also

examined the various federations' rules and found that, although
several had no non-white members, none had restrictive rules. The
control of South African sport appeared to be largely in white hands,
because of general, rather than specific, legislation; for example,
non-whites might not carry arms, and therefore could not compete in
shooting. Athletics, boxing, weightlifting and football had what the
report called mixed affiliations, with many non-white competitors.
Judo and hockey appeared to have non-white clubs affiliated. The
Commission had also invited the views of international federations
and had found that they had widely differing attitudes to South Africa
and to relations with affiliated National Federations.[23]

The Commission summed up surprisingly favourably to South
Africa. It had found overwhelming evidence from sports administrators and competitors of all communities inside South Africa that
the Tehran proposals were an acceptable basis for a multi-racial team
at Mexico City, despite the contentious matter of selection.
SANROC, on the other hand, was 'a cause of embarrassment to the
majority in South Africa for whom it claims to speak'. The report
quotes a former leading member of SANROC (unidentified) that
SANROC was self-exiled, and should not claim to speak for those still
in South Africa.

The Grenoble Session and SCSA

At the 67th Session, at Grenoble in February 1968, the IOC, having
thanked Killanin and heard a long statement by Braun, decided after a
long discussion that the meeting was not well enough attended to
commit the whole IOC, and that a postal ballot must be taken. The
events behind the postal vote were complicated. Since only forty-two
members had said in advance that they intended to be at Grenoble, the
Executive Board had decided in the previous December that a postal
vote should be taken. In fact fifty-five members attended, so that the
postal vote was no longer strictly necessary. Indeed, some members
saw it as a highly irregular procedure, but others thought all members
should be allowed to express a view on so important a matter, and
some felt that the original decision to vote by post might have played a
part in some members' decisions not to attend the session.

The result of the postal vote, announced later in February, was that
'an absolute majority' (numbers not stated in the minutes) voted to
admit a multi-racial South African team to the Games at Mexico City

later in the year, though the IOC was still worried about the impossibility of racially mixed trials. The members seem to have reasoned that a greater good would be achieved by allowing South Africa to participate than not, and perhaps they were persuaded by Braun's passionate assertion that 'With the exception of a few expatriate professional politicians masquerading as sports leaders, from London, the sportsmen of South Africa, White and Non-White alike, are anxious and unanimous in their desire to take part in the Olympic Games'.[24]

The Supreme Council for Sport in Africa – SCSA – had not drifted out of the picture, but was biding its time; it had decided to be patient with the IOC, and to meet again at Brazzaville after the Grenoble Session. The meeting was attended by some members of the Mexican organising committee, who were there in order to beseech SCSA not to destroy the games, as well as by representatives of SANROC, and journalists. But, surprisingly, it did not allow Brutus to address it.[25]

It will be remembered that earlier the fledgling SCSA had criticised the IOC relatively quietly. This meeting was quite different, and developed into a violent attack. SCSA's president said that against all expectations, 'the Olympic firmament has become dark; the most recent scandal of the Olympic movement has just exploded at Grenoble'. SCSA thought the Session had been a sordid farce. The postal vote had allowed people to vote who did not take the trouble to go to meetings, and who would not even know the composition of a basketball team. The IOC was a sort of shameful freemasonry which lived in the twentieth century so far as its own interests were concerned but in the nineteenth in relation to sport.

SCSA decided that the measures of reform announced by South Africa consolidated apartheid and that the IOC resolution allowed it. All African states must withdraw from Mexico. The Council denounced the IOC's irresponsible attitude: it had no representative character in its present form and SCSA had no confidence in it.[26] The last point was picked up by the Kenya Sports Council, which stated that there was only one black African among the seventy-one IOC members, and that Africans could not abide by decisions made by an exclusive group of Europeans.[27]

The Mexico Games, 1968: threatened boycott

Twenty-five countries had said, even in advance of Grenoble, that they would boycott the Mexican Games if South Africa were readmitted.[28] By early March the Soviet Union was threatening to join them, and later in the month the gathering clouds prompted one newspaper to comment that perhaps the only blacks at Mexico City would be South African.[29] At first the United States press saw the IOC's decision as an invitation to boycott, but later there seems to have been a change of heart after the *New York Times* had pointed out that the United Nations had achieved nothing in South Africa, but the IOC had got 90 per cent of what it wanted.

The boycott bandwagon quickly built up steam. Like the SCSA, the foreign ministers of the Organisation for African Unity (OAU), also meeting at Brazzaville, urged the world to boycott, and Sweden was the first European country to demand the reversal of the Grenoble decision of 15 February. There were thirty-two unanimous voices in the OAU, although only sixteen African NOCs existed at that time. They were not influenced by Mexico City's conciliatory mission, nor by a letter and telegram from Brundage. India and Indonesia had already declared for a boycott; the socialist countries and Latin America were expected to do so.[30] In the face of all this, Brundage went on saying that the Games were for individuals, not nations.

The British press was divided. Naturally, the trouble was enough to sicken some commentators. John Lovesey wrote a disrespectful article in the *Sunday Times* asking why the Games should not be called off. They were hopelessly devalued and cancellation would allow the IOC time to come to its senses over South Africa, and Mexico could spend on its own national welfare the money that it would have lavished on the Games.[31] *The Times*, after many ifs and buts, just came out for staying with South Africa, because sports pressure had achieved something and might do more.[32] In *The Observer*, Christopher Brasher said that he had been in favour of South Africa's expulsion in 1963, but was now, albeit suspiciously, in favour of reinstatement because he believed the South Africans when they said that they would send a non-racial team to Mexico City, and he was impressed by the paragraph in the Killanin Commission's report to the effect that South African administrators and athletes approved the new arrangements.[33] Christopher Booker made the important point that several withdrawals had been announced by governments, and

not by NOCs, thus breaking the Olympic rule respecting the independence of NOCs. One sportsman, Kipchoge (Kip) Keino, had said it
all: 'We Kenyan sportsmen have to obey decisions of the Government
. . . (which) knows best.'[34] In general it may be said that some papers
saw South Africa's concessions as a victory over apartheid: others as a
victory for it.

Brundage refused to call an extraordinary meeting of the IOC on
the inadequate-sounding grounds that it would not be realistic to do
so, which prompted *L'Equipe* to ask 'Que lui faut-il, donc?' and to call
for a complete reform of the IOC, with votes for the 123 NOCs. It was
a pity, the magazine said, that the planned Association of National
Olympic Committees (ANOC) did not yet exist. Meanwhile Mexico
would be within its rights not to send an invitation to South Africa.[35]
Thus one possible solution was beginning to emerge, to leave it to
Mexico to fail to send an invitation. *L'Equipe* was the only paper to
point out that the loss of African confidence in the IOC was even more
serious than the Mexico Games.

While the IOC was investigating South Africa, and of course
hoping not to be obliged to expel it from the Olympic movement, the
NOCs continued collectively to oppose the Republic. They were, it
goes without saying, genuinely concerned about the issue, but the
opportunity that South Africa gave the NOCs to act jointly carried
with it the additional long-term benefit that by legitimately flexing
their muscles they built up their position as a power bloc of which the
IOC had to take notice.

South Africa's readmission was naturally received with jubilation in
South Arica itself.[36] Elsewhere the turmoil continued. About 13 April
Brundage suddenly went on a short visit to South Africa, 'to see the
Kruger Park', as he rather whimsically put it, but of course primarily
to see Olympic officials in the hope of obtaining some further con-
cession. None was forthcoming.

Brundage returned for the meeting of the Executive Board at
Lausanne on 20 and 21 April 1968, where he was unable to avoid the
topic's being raised again, although he had successfully resisted
demands for a full Session. There was general apprehension that, if
the Games were to be saved from massive boycotts, either the IOC
would have to expel South Africa by removing its recognition of
SANOC, or, at the very least, the Mexican NOC would have to take
the responsibility for refusing to issue an invitation.

Brundage deplored the deep division in the IOC, which he said threatened to destroy the movement, and was in large part due to the actions of certain of its own members. His instinct was still to gather and weigh evidence, rather than to reverse the Grenoble decision. Exeter raised an awkward point, or perhaps he was trying to help Brundage, by reminding the Executive Board that it could not alter a decision of the full IOC: it could only recommend.

The minutes of IOC meetings are usually dour, but on this occasion they convey excitement and an atmosphere of crisis. Yet there was a curious lack of knowledge: no one knew how many NOCs had announced their intention not to participate at Mexico City if South Africa were not expelled, and Brundage could not even remember the details of the postal vote, though he thought it had been 36–26, with some abstentions and spoiled papers.

On the second day of the meeting Brundage, after talking to members individually, said that the only point on which they agreed was that either decision would leave a bitter division in the IOC and the world at large. If the Grenoble decision were maintained there would be a schism in the IOC; Mexico would be reduced to despair, and even SANOC would not be happy in the end, because the presence of its team would provoke trouble, which could lead to violence. There were also arguments the other way, and the best course would be for SANOC to retire voluntarily.

Brundage went on to develop what must be any IOC president's nightmare scenario. If the South African invitation stood, and the Mexican Government then refused their athletes visas, it would become necessary to cancel the Games; in that case some IFs might set up their own World Championships as alternatives, and some NOCs and some socialist countries might retire from the movement. He had no solution, but, as always, he saw only too clearly the broader ramifications of the South African case for the whole movement.

South Africa's expulsion

After a *débat fleuve* Brundage summed up that it seemed that SANOC must not send a team to Mexico City, despite the Grenoble decision. He persisted in his conviction that an extraordinary meeting of the IOC was not desirable, yet the Executive Board was not in a position to make a binding decision. The solution adopted was for telegrams to be sent expressing the Executive Board's unanimous view that no invitation should be sent to South Africa, and asking for immediate

approval.[37] This was forthcoming, and South Africa did not go to
Mexico City, but the final withdrawal of recognition from SANOC
did not follow until the Amsterdam Session in 1970, and might have
been yet further delayed, had Reginald Honey and Frank Braun been
less aggressive in their arguments. That withdrawal kept South Africa
out of the Olympics until 1992, but Honey was asked to drop his
intention to resign from the IOC, and remained a member until his
death at the age of ninety-five.

Le Monde summed up that the South African affair was as important in the history of the IOC for the new freedom with which it began
to be criticised, and the boost it gave to collective organisation among
NOCs and IFs, as for the South African problem itself. After all, the
latter was going to be solved eventually, but it was to be hoped that the
IOC would long outlive that particular problem. 'L'affaire Sud-
africaine a mis en lumière les contradictions du comité international'.[38]

The years in the wilderness

South Africa did not occupy much of the IOC's time from 1969 to
1989. Periodically requests to send another commission of enquiry
were refused and in general there seems to have been little formal
contact. However, in 1972, at its Sapporo Session, the IOC did receive
a multi-racial delegation from South Africa and heard its report on the
progress that had already been made towards integrated sport.
Brundage would have liked, had the rules allowed, to alter the terms
of SANOC's exclusion from the Olympic movement, so that it would
merely have been suspended, but all that could be done was for the
IOC to welcome the progress made, and express the hope that it would
continue sufficiently for SANOC to return to the movement. (In 1976
Rule 25 was altered to allow suspension of an NOC, but without
retrospective effect.)

Informal contact with South Africa continued, if only because Mr
Honey remained a member of the IOC. Nor, with the growing
involvement of the United Nations and other bodies, did the South
African issue simply disappear from the IOC's life. For example, in
February 1972 Leonid Kutahov, the United Nations' Under Secre-
tary-General for Political and Security Council Affairs, sent to the
IOC United Nations resolutions concerning apartheid in sport. This
gave Madame Berlioux the chance to score a point by replying that the

IOC had always been against discrimination: 'It would seem, therefore, that the resolution passed by the United Nations in November
1971, follows the IOC after nearly a century.'[39]

In South Africa itself the South African Games were held, master-
minded by Dr Piet Koornhof, the Minister of Sport and Recreation.
In the eyes of the South African government and some sections of the
press these games were a great break-through, since they included
black–white soccer and boxing matches, between athletes who were
photographed eating together and who stayed in the same hotel,
guarded by the Special Branch. (Nowadays it is commonplace for
Olympic gatherings to be closely guarded, but then the demands of
security were less severe.) Of course the togetherness was only temporary, and there were some marvellously patronising remarks about
how well-behaved the blacks were.

The *Sunday Times* of Johannesburg ran a front page banner
headline 'Games a Racial Triumph' and Koornhof was delighted with
their success. He emphasised that they were not designed to get South
Africa back into the Olympics, but added that the Republic had now
fulfilled most of the IOC's requirements. The paper gave full credit to
Koornhof, who it said had staked his political reputation on games
which could not possibly have been predicted five years earlier, and
added that the government must be forgiven for insisting on calling
them multi-national, rather than multi-racial, games. To hold them at
all would not have been a political starter if they had not been brought
into the ideological framework of 'separate development'. Now it
must be hoped that integrated sport would spread at least to provincial
level, and it should be possible to move on to the mixed trials asked for
by the IOC.[40] The games were naturally attacked from the right, as
being the thin end of the multi-racial wedge, and from the left because
they were artificial and made no fundamental difference to policy.
Nevertheles, although the games did not attract world-class
foreigners, they were attended by 673 competitors and officials from
thirty-three countries, and did show whites in the street that progress
was being made. The varied points of view from which antagonism to
the games was expressed was nicely summed up in a cartoon showing a
group of hippies facing a group of vortrekkers, each with a placard
saying 'Stop the SA Games'.[41]

Rebel tours

By 1970 South Africa was isolated in most sports, but some sports bodies, both at home and abroad, persisted in organising tours, and western governments refused to ban them, though they did express the wish that the organisers would see the error of their ways. The numerous tours of South Africa by foreign teams, or by South African teams abroad, produced many of the highlights of the South African sports saga, and provided an intermittent counterpoint to the diplomatic and political activity.

As long ago as 1934 the British Empire Games Federation refused to award its next games to Johannesburg because South Africa had made it known that black athletes would not be welcome.[42] In more recent times sporting relations with New Zealand were for many years bedevilled by the South African insistence that whites must not play against Maoris, and when Prime Minister Vorster dropped the requirement it was too late. The British MCC called off its tour of South Africa in 1968 when South Africa refused to accept Basil D'Oliveira, a Coloured (mixed race) South African, as a member of the British team;[43] the Springboks' rugby tour (the 'Stop the Springboks' tour) of Britain in the (European) winter of 1969–70 was the first to meet major disruption, and contributed to the cricket Springboks' cancelling their proposed tour of Britain in 1970.[44] Twenty-two African nations, and Guyana, boycotted the Montreal Olympics of 1976 in retaliation for the New Zealand All Blacks' rugby tour of South Africa earlier in the year, although strictly speaking the IOC had no responsibility or standing in the matter, since rugby was not an Olympic sport. That tour had coincided with the Soweto riots, one of the turning-points of modern South African history: five years later New Zealand was to be torn apart by the South African Springboks' rugby tour in 1981.

In 1977 the Commonwealth heads of state and government repaired to the Scottish resort of Gleneagles during their conference, and produced the Gleneagles Agreement, which committed them to do their best to minimise sporting contacts with South Africa. The declaration had to be carefully worded, so that Commonwealth governments with very various conceptions of their rights and duties vis-à-vis their citizens would be able to claim to have acted in conformity with it. There were no doubt some which would not have hesitated simply to remove recalcitrant citizens' passports, but anything of that kind would have been anathema to any British government, and to large sections of the British public.

The beginning of integration in South African sport

By the late 1970s there was evidence that some sport in South Africa had become integrated, but there was still great dissatisfaction among blacks (meaning all the non-white groups), as much on account of their inferior facilities as because they were not permitted to engage in mixed sport. A study conducted in 1977 showed that Coloured sports organisations were determinedly non-racial,[45] and in 1982 the Human Sciences Research Council (HSRC) published the results of an important investigation, which had been commissioned in 1979. It emphasised the desirability of international sport to 'create feelings of patriotism and loyalty which may even be essential for political progress' and to bind people together through common interests. The Council thought sports bodies should be autonomous, and that selection, attendance and participation should be non-racial. Discriminatory legislation, in relation to sport, should be repealed, or at least studied with repeal in view. As for the control of sport, the HSRC did considerable research, in Britain and elsewhere, and recommended that an autonomous statutory South African Sports Council be set up.[46]

Despite the reservations expressed even by so establishment a body as the HSRC, Basil D'Oliveira was amazed at the extent of the integration that he found in sport when he went to South Africa in January 1980 as a member of the (British) Sports Council's investigatory mission (although he still thought that isolation should be maintained for a few more years).[47] The significance of the mingling was reduced by the facts that it was often confined to the sports field, and that different racial groups lived in separate towns, often at considerable distances from one another, which in turn made mixed sport difficult at any level below that of the élite. In any case, the degree of integration of South African sport had in a sense become irrelevant to the protests outside the Republic, which were more and more frankly directed to achieving a much more fundamental reordering of South African political life, and not merely of sporting relations. Indeed, the realisation that improvement in sport could not be separated from change in South African society as a whole was becoming accepted by establishment whites outside South Africa, as well as by radical black politicians. Missions like the Sports Council's, therefore, carried less weight than may have been expected, because they were directed to questions that had become out of date, except in purely sporting circles.

The political problem of South African tours continued. Faced with the British rugby authorities' invitation to the South African Barbarians and with the British Lions' intention to tour South Africa in 1980, the British government reiterated its devotion to the Gleneagles Agreement, but within the British interpretation of the agreement the Minister for Sport, Hector Munro, could do no more than urge, and sometimes even plead, that the tours be reconsidered. More was at stake than the tours, for in the background there were fears that African states might boycott the Moscow Olympics in 1980, or at least that British participation in many other international events might be jeopardised, and the future of the Commonwealth Games put at risk. (Nobody could foresee that a boycott would be instigated by the United States.) Fears for Moscow were even expressed in a public statement by Killanin.[48]

The rugby authorities were under great pressure, both internationally and internally, and had correspondingly great difficulty in reaching a decision. For example, Jean-Claude Ganga, president of SCSA, protested to the British Foreign Secretary, Lord Carrington, that in his view the government should accept its responsibility and annul the tour, exactly expressing a way of thinking that the British Government would in no circumstances contemplate.[49] An example of pressure within Britain was a statement by Paul Stephenson, the only black member of the Sports Council, who said that to proceed with the Barbarians' visit would be 'a Suez for British sport. The international repercussions outweigh the value of the game of rugby itself.'[50] On the other hand, British public opinion was by no means overwhelmingly opposed to the tour, and the South African case must have been helped by the presence as South African ambassador in London of the popular former rugby player Dr Dawie De Villiers.

In the end the Barbarians' tour was not called off and the team duly arrived in England on 1 October 1979, to be met by demonstrations, pickets and opposition from trades unions and the Labour Party's annual conference. The president of the National Union of Journalists wanted his members not to cover the tour, and the Transport and General Workers' Union urged hotel workers to strike, but both calls were ignored. Paul Stephenson walked out of the Sports Council after it had voted heavily against his motion to penalise the Rugby Football Union for sticking to its invitation.[51]

There was unprecedented opposition to the tour, and even reports of nails having been scattered on rugby pitches in Wales.[52] There were numerous international protests. For example, the Supreme Council for Sport in Africa demanded that Britain should withdraw from the Olympics and regretted that the British government had 'done nothing'.[53] Denis Thatcher, husband of the Prime Minister, had issued a clarion call in favour of the Lions' going to South Africa, and had been reproached for it by the *Sunday Times*, especially as the SCSA was just about to meet.[54]

The trouble caused by the Barbarians' tour did have some peripheral result in South Africa. The Minister of Sport, Punt Janson, called three hundred sports officials together after the team's return and, with an eye to British and French sports and parliamentary visits, made some concessions. First, there would no longer would be any need for whites to get permits to go to games in black areas; secondly, there was some liberalisation of rules concerning alcohol being served to blacks in the few sports clubs that had what was called 'international status'. SACOS would not attend the meeting and, consistently with its established line, said that nothing would go right in South African sport until there was real self-determination.[55]

In Britain the Central Council of Physical Recreation had the opportunity to discuss the proposed Lions' tour, but voted against doing so.[56] The Lions went ahead, and in 1981 the Springboks toured New Zealand, causing a crisis in the Commonwealth Games Association.[57] There followed a series of 'rebel' tours of South Africa, of which the most famous was the cricket tour led by Mike Gatting in January and February 1990. It was also the most important, because, having sent Ngconde Balfour to London to argue for its cancellation, unsuccessfully as it turned out, the National Olympic and Sports Congress organised the first really serious disruption inside South Africa, as opposed to protests and demonstrations outside.

The last days of isolation

South Africa's return to world sport went hand in hand with its return to other aspects of normal international life. This process stemmed from the gradual internal normalisation that followed President F. W. De Klerk's speech on 2 February 1990, in which he announced that the African National Congress (ANC) and Pan-Africanist Congress (PAC) were to be 'unbanned' and the legal framework of apartheid removed. The announcement led to protracted negotiations in the forum that came to be known as CODESA (Convention for a Democratic South Africa) which led in turn to the Multiparty Negotiating Forum, the Transitional Executive Council and the current interim constitution.

Until the late 1980s no real progress had been made towards a resolution of the South African conundrum. Pundits had agreed for many years that eventually white South Africa would have to give way, but none could forecast with any confidence when the decisive change would come. So far as sport was concerned, the blanket ban had become ever more enveloping, but it could not of itself produce the decisive push towards the political transformatiion, which had, after all, been the purpose behind Brutus's inspired policy of instituting the ban in the first place.

In the late 1980s developments in South African sport gathered momentum, and 1988 was an eventful year. The Test and County Cricket Board cancelled a tour of India, in protest against that country's operating the United Nations blacklist; the IOC's Commission on Apartheid was set up, with Sam Ramsamy, already a rising star, as one of its advisers; the National Sports Congress (later National Olympic and Sports Congress, NOSC) was founded, effectively as the sports wing of the Mass Democratic Movement (MDM), which itself was aligned with the still-banned ANC; SANROC split, leaving Ramsamy as leader of the main, MDM-aligned, faction; SACOS – the South African Council on Sport, of which Dennis Brutus was to become patron – put an end to its increasingly unhappy relationship with SANROC in 1989. SACOS had since its foundation in 1973 been the only internal umbrella body representing black sporting aspirations, but there had for about three years before the breakaway been disagreements within it, on both the ideological and the strategic and tactical levels.

The dissension was nothing new in black South African politics, but it was doubly unfortunate so late in the freedom struggle. It had its roots in the development of two main strands of thought in the ANC, which had led to the PAC's break away in 1959. The causes of the split were complicated and wrapped in ideology, but essentially the mainstream strategists saw the struggle in terms of a mass movement rooted in the working class, an analysis which permitted alliances with sympathisers across the racial divide. By contrast, the PAC's emphasis was on 'Africa for the Africans', and the party never had more than one or two white members.

When NOSC set itself up in competition with SACOS, it did so partly because the high command of SACOS was dominated by people whose sympathies lay with the PAC, and partly because the organisation had failed to develop a mass-based non-racial sports movement. Furthermore, it had become sunk in what Cheryl Roberts called 'purist arrogance', which prevented its seeing the necessity to compromise in order to negotiate with the establishment sports bodies, and develop relations with sponsors. Instead it had passed a resolution forbidding matches against non-members of SACOS and the use of white-owned playing fields.

The acerbic flavour of the debate is well conveyed in the following extract from one of Roberts's pamphlets:

Our critics are saying that this policy of unity amounts to a sellout of non-racial sport. For them to say this with reference to the NOSC's attempts to draw in oppressed sports men and women in previously unaffiliated bodies like the National Soccer League is clearly a kind of purist arrogance that can be rejected out of hand. Any reasonable thinking person will realise that the mass of working class and unemployed South Africans do not usually have the luxury of choice given the appalling material conditions under which they live, and that it is the responsibility of the non-racial sports movement to address their needs instead of doing nothing about it and adopt a holier than thou attitude. To talk about a representative national non-racial body when the African working-class is hardly represented is a joke. The solution lies clearly in grassroots involvement and struggle, not superior attitudes. The question of unity with establishment sport is a more prickly issue. This we readily concede. But again the answer lies in engagement rather than inaction and theoretical purity.[58]

While the sports movement was in turmoil inside South Africa, activity continued unabated outside. In the final years of South Africa's isolation (which was always more seriously maintained in sport than in diplomacy or commerce) the need to avoid contact seems to have penetrated deeply into the consciousness of international sports organisations, so that no detail of relations with South Africa passed without comment. In December 1988 the International Federation of Sports Acrobatics suspended a coach who had taken two young two Portuguese acrobats to South Africa in the previous summer; in February 1989 Ramsamy wrote from SANROC to the

Secretary-General of the Hungarian NOC, protesting against the prospect of a South African being given the International Equestrian Federation's cup for show jumping during its General Assembly in Budapest; and in March USOC (which was very soon afterwards to enforce a blanket ban on athletes visiting South Africa) enquired of the IOC whether an American water skier could be allowed to go there.

The flurry of anti-South African activity in the sporting world came curiously late in the day. In July 1989 twenty-three sports ministers of member countries of the Council of Europe unanimously condemned continued links with the Republic; the IOC's Executive Board decided at Puerto Rico that tennis players who played in South Africa would be banned from the Olympics, and the full IOC extended the penalty to *all* athletes. Tennis, which had been a demonstration sport at Seoul in 1988, therefore had to drop its recognition of the South African tennis federation in order to be admitted to the Olympic programme proper.[59] Ramsamy identified the first target as about six tennis players who had gone to South Africa since Seoul.[60] In the United States USOC decreed that no athlete in any sport who competed in South Africa would be allowed to compete in any Olympic sport.[61]

At the the IOC things were moving fast. Johan Du Plessis, President of SANOC, saw Samaranch in Lausanne in September 1989 (the meeting had been arranged no less than six months in advance) and had a more substantial meeting the next day with Judge Keba Mbaye, president of the IOC's Commission on Apartheid and Olympism. Mbaye arranged for him to meet Ramsamy and others, and just before Christmas 1989 it became known that the Association of National Olympic Committees of Africa (ANOCA) was to have a meeting with Ramsamy (in his capacity as an adviser to the IOC, rather than as Chairman of SANROC) in Paris on 9 January 1990. Although Samaranch was ultimately responsible for the secret arrangements that led to the meeting, it seems also to have carried with it another move in the perpetual manoeuvrings within the Olympic movement, for ANOCA insisted that the IOC could not move towards approval of South Africa without its approval. It is true that the IOC had itself always insisted that no solution should be adopted for South Africa without African approval, but that only makes ANOCA's emphasis on the point less necessary, and therefore more surprising.

Ramsamy said in advance of the meeting (taking the line worked out by NOSC) that the political changes taking place in South Africa made necessary a fresh approach to sports links, which would allow some contact even before the disappearance of apartheid. 'We have also to consider our tactics. If a little relaxation in the sporting boycott helps to accelerate the downfall of apartheid we shall have to consider it.'[62] The talks, the first formal contact for many years, broke new ground. Du Plessis said that he had not expected anything so positive, and even Ramsamy said they had been unexpectedly good. Nevertheless, there was some scepticism in South Africa about the call to the South African Cricket Union (SACU) to cancel the rebel tour by Gatting and his team, which was due to start on 26 January 1990. There was no evidence, the *Cape Times* said, that South Africa would now be nearer to readmission to world sport if earlier rebel tours had not taken place. In any case, readmission was not an immediate prospect: Ramsamy and his colleague Fékrou Kidane (an Ethiopian refugee then living in Paris, now a senior official of the IOC) reaffirmed: 'the Olympic movement cannot even consider reviewing South Africa's position until there is a single genuine non-racial unitary sports federation in all the Olympic disciplines'.[63]

Black South African sports politicians had, as we have seen, split. SACOS lost many of its members to the newly-formed NOSC, and NOSC went through many internal debates before it could bring itself to enunciate the reformist message uttered by Ramsamy in advance of the epoch-making meeting in Paris with the representatives of the old National Olympic Committee. SACOS had no intention of abandoning its insistence on 'no normal sport in an abnormal society' which, if taken literally, meant that the whole of South African society had to change fundamentally before SACOS would change its policy of isolating establishment sport, and maintaining separation from the world. NOSC, on the other hand, came painfully to the realisation that it might have to wait a lifetime for society to be sufficiently changed to satisfy SACOS, and decided to work for progress in the limited field of sport.

The return to the Olympics

The time was right for the IOC to take matters in hand. Many 'players' were involved, including ANOCA, with its unfortunate tendency to think that any IOC decision must be subject to its approval, the OAU, Ramsamy, and the various factions within South

Africa. As well as promoting a solution, the IOC needed to safeguard its own position as the lead body in world sport. Participation in the Barcelona Olympics was the goal, though at first there were many objections, notably, but not solely, from SACOS.

There was also a fascinating sub-plot, in the shape of the IAAF's attempt to get South Africa back into athletics in time for the World Cup at Tokyo in August 1991. South African athletics, which was still deeply divided on racial lines, refused the invitation to take part, whereupon the IAAF promptly reversed itself and said that South Africa was not eligible after all, because of the divided control of athletics within the country, between establishment and non-establishment bodies. The whole saga, too involved for this chapter, was widely seen as a power-play by Nebiolo to suck South Africa into athletics before the Olympics, and so to upstage the IOC, which had always said that it had been the first sports body to exclude South Africa and hoped to be the first to welcome it back. The manoeuvres may also have have been intended, as some commentators suggested, as a demonstration of Nebiolo's power, which would assist the nomination to the IOC for which he was hoping, and which Samaranch duly made soon afterwards.

Suddenly in September 1990, at the Stockholm International Conference against Apartheid in Sport, Samaranch cut through the meanderings of bureaucracy and dramatically offered South Africa a place at Barcelona, provided a political settlement could be reached. The IOC would use emergency procedures, even a month or two before the Games, to make it possible for South Africa to attend. Samaranch got support from a surprising quarter, Mluleki George, President of NOSC, who thought 1996 more likely, but 1992 by no means impossible. Everything would depend on an historic meeting, which was to be held in Harare on 3–4 November, between representatives of ANOCA (Association of NOCs of Africa), SCSA and the various factions in South African sport.[64] Even at this late hour the Stockholm conference showed no disposition to lift sports sanctions until apartheid had been abolished. To relax the bans would, it was said, prejudice political development: if anything they should be tightened. On the other hand, the conference declaration did allow coaches, funds, equipment and help in developing facilities for disadvantaged sports bodies in South Africa. [65]

Thereafter there were meetings between NOSC and sports administrators and even with potential sponsors. At last, as the *Cape Times* observed, there was some creative interaction, instead of the sterile deadlock with SACOS. Tennis and rugby agreed to join a moratorium on international tours, but NOSC was to give Sun International the green light to invite foreign players to two major golf tournaments in December.[66]

The next step in South Africa's long road back was the summit at Harare in November 1990, attended by forty-three representatives, many of whom had never met before. They came from all the factions: the NOC; NOSC; SACOS; SANROC; and COSAS – the Confederation of South African Sport, a white group which had significance at the time but has now faded away. Meanwhile Ramsamy, as executive chairman of SANROC, was to pay his first visit to South Africa for eighteen years. He had been asked by ANOCA to study the changes that had taken place, and report back to Ganga. The *Cape Times* thought that his report would be decisive.[67] The report, produced after nine days, was favourable, and at the end of his visit he left open (not surprisingly, in view of the readiness for compromise that he had already shown) the possibility of South Africa's readmission to world sport before a political settlement had been achieved.

The Harare conference did, as had been universally hoped, mark a great step forward. It is true that Ganga said – it was by now almost a ritual – that South Africa should remain isolated until apartheid had been 'utterly abolished', but then he was able to announce the formation of an eight-man committee from the disparate sports bodies – two NOSC; two SACOS; two SANOC; one COSAS; one SANROC – to be nominated by the end of November. (It became a committee of ten, with two members from each organisation.) A monitoring group, to be appointed by Ganga, was to meet the new committee to review progress by the end of March 1991, and meanwhile the South African representatives had given their word not to make any further attempt to break the UN sports embargo.[68]

The major upshot of the Harare conference, as Michael Owen-Smith said in the *Cape Times*, was that the NSC and SACOS, the latter of which had not yet committed itself to being on the committee of eight, were simply going to have to sort out their differences. The virulent disputes were not confined to representative bodies: similar difficulties were present at the level of individual sports, such as football.[69]

After Harare the IOC's Apartheid Commission made five recom-

mendations to the Executive Board. They were: (1) There should be
no change in the IOC's policy of no sporting contact with South
Africa. (2) Each South African sport must create a united governing
body. (3) Such bodies would then be able to apply for observer status
at the relevant African confederations. (4) ANOCA must do nothing
unilaterally, and all IFs should act in accordance with the IOC's
decisions. (5) The Commission could visit South Africa as early as
1991. The Commission's report was well received, and on 9
December 1990 the IOC announced its intention to send a delegation
to South Africa, the first formal contact for twenty years. Its members
were to be very senior: Judge Mbaye; Kevan Gosper, a Vice-President
of the IOC, Ganga, and Major-General Henry Adefope, with Francois
Carrard, Director-General of the IOC, in attendance.[70]

The announcement came as a bombshell to some South African
organisations. From Mluleki George, head of NOSC, it drew a rather
sour response: 'There seems to be a perception that the international
community will decide South Africa's return to world sport. But the
people of South Africa will decide this in consultation with the international community. Our destiny is in our hands.' SACOS was not
enthusiastic, but said that it would talk to the IOC visitors.[71]

Those were extraordinary times. Rugby had made little progress
towards unification of Board and Union, yet early in 1991 the Board
was pushing South Africa's candidacy, successfully as it turned out, to
host the 1995 World Cup.[72] Less surprisingly, the General Assembly
of SCSA, meeting at Tunis in February 1991, supported the view of
the IOC's Apartheid Commission that relations should be established
between sport in South Africa and in the rest of Africa; it therefore
wanted South African federations, if racially unified and integrated,
to affiliate to African sports confederations, which would sponsor
them with IFs. SCSA recommended that the Secretary-General of the
OAU should endorse the decision. Yet FIFA, which, like every other
IF, was aware that South African sport was on the move, did not rush
to readmit football. Its reinstatement would depend on unification of
its three governing bodies and approval by the African Football
Association.[73]

Early in March 1991 ANOCA gave the go-ahead to an early end to
the moratorium, a step which, it was reported, owed much to Ganga's
enthusiasm. It appears that the moratorium was to end with the
planned removal from the statute book in June of the last vestiges of
apartheid. Again, the speed of events provoked a stunned reaction.[74]

These dramatic developments followed South Africa's five major umbrella sports bodies' agreeing to form a new interim NOC, with Ramsamy, who had long been an obvious candidate (the other was Mluleki George) as its intended head. SACOS and COSAS would stay alive for the time being but, Ramsamy said, 'They will eventually disappear by natural process as their affiliates unify and apply for affiliation to the new body.'[75] Since SACOS was to participate in the interim NOC (INOCSA), the new body would not suffer the dis-advantage of being linked with only one party, the ANC.[76]

The IOC mission duly visited South Africa in March 1991, the arrangements again having apparently been handled with great secrecy in Lausanne. Mbaye and his colleagues met President F. W. De Klerk on 25 March, and after the meeting there were very up-beat comments by Carrard, and Mbaye was 'reasonably optimistic' that South Africa would be able to go to the Barcelona Games.[77] Only a day later the IOC gave conditional recognition to INOCSA, and it seemed likely that, if the government scrapped the remaining apartheid laws in June, an invitation to the Olympics would follow in July. At this stage there was still some doubt at Lausanne about who was running INOCSA, but in other respects there was no doubt that the South Africans were progressing along the right lines, and to encourage them a programme of sports aid was approved.

The conditions of recognition were:

1 The abolition of apartheid. (This of course referred to legislation. The IOC must have understood that the social and geographical separation of the races would be little altered for many years.)
2 INOCSA must comply with the Olympic Charter.
3 There must be movement towards the establishment of a final (as opposed to an interim) NOC.
4 Ruling bodies must be set up on a non-racial basis.
5 Relations with sports organisations in Africa must be normalised.[78]

According to one report, the overwhelming response from sporting and political bodies was that going to Barcelona would be premature, a point of view that the PAC, ANC and AZAPO (Azanian People's Organisation) had stressed to the IOC delegation. Furthermore, they all thought it up to the South Africans themselves to decide when they rejoined the Olympic movement.[79] Meanwhile it was clear that all was not well within INOCSA. While waiting at the airport for the IOC mission it had, according to one report, expelled COSAS, and SACOS had not even been present in the receiving line because, it said, it had

not yet finalised its delegation. Mbaye made it clear that the IOC did
not want to interfere – 'In Senegal we say you shouldn't release goats
on another man's land' – yet the IOC could not simply abdicate its
responsibility, nor be seen to give up its prerogatives, and to a report
that Mluleki George had said that the oppressed masses would make
the decision there came a swift answer: the IOC had imposed the
moratorium at Puerto Rico in 1989, and the IOC would decide when
to lift it.[80]

In the USA, which had never signed the International Convention
Against Apartheid in Sport, the State Department came out against
mandatory sports sanctions. In a statement, whose tone suggests that
it had learned something about sports administration since the
boycott of the Moscow Games, the State Department said that sports
policies were made by IFs and other sports bodies and 'US athletes are
private citizens and are free to pursue their activities when and where
they please, subject only to the restrictions of the sports organisations
which govern their sports'. The statement was seen as a counter to the
influential *New York Times*'s attempt to head off South Africa's
return, which apparently was a result of a long conversation with Joe
Ebrahim, the president of SACOS. Ebrahim was upset by the IOC
decision which, he said, meant that after the Population Registration
Act has been scrapped 'I am an equal citizen – which is totally untrue
. . . The IOC are out of touch, and undermining the fight of people in
South Africa involved in the struggle for democratic rights.'[81]

But now that Barcelona was a serious possibility both the old and
the new sports establishment embraced it. The official announcement
by the IOC, welcoming South Africa back into the fold, came on 9
July 1991, in time for an invitation to Barcelona to be issued.[82]
Chinese approval was signified by Zheu Liang He, Vice-President of
the Chinese Olympic Committee, who hoped to to give South Africa
substantial sports aid.[83]

The invitation was not universally popular, inside South Africa or
internationally. Namibia and Zimbabwe said they would be guided by
the OAU in the longer term, and for the moment would keep the ban
on sporting links. The PAC accused Ramsamy of having sold out. Dr
Andries Treurnicht, of the the far-right Conservative Party, thought
the government's tolerating multi-racial sport equivalent to an admission that it was prepared to subject whites to a future black majority
government.[84] The Council of NOSC voted unanimously for 'controlled phased entry' (into world sport) for such sports as were united

on a non-racial basis, a major departure from the blanket moratorium that it had favoured. But NOSC was not in a hurry: it disliked the 'manner and haste' of the IAAF's insistence that South African athletes should go to Tokyo, and did not wish to renew any international links in 1991, even selectively.[85]

Dennis Brutus, aged 66, came back to South Africa on a short visit, his first in twenty-five years, in July 1991. He was completely outside the new sports establishment, because of his identification with SACOS, and never had any official contact with the IOC and its staff during the period of South Africa's readmission to the Olympic movement. By now he was Patron of SACOS, which was leading the fight against South Africa's readmission to world sport with his full approval. He was stateless, had nearly been forced out of the United States in the early 1980s and had achieved permanent residence only with great difficulty, and was still travelling on a United Nations travel document. He thought President Bush was wrong to lift sanctions against South Africa. 'The pressures of apartheid are more extreme and cruel even while people are being told apartheid has been abolished'.[86] Meanwhile there were also those within the ANC who thought the concentration on the Olympics unfortunate. They cared as much about development programmes, unity and equal training facilities.[87]

During the summer of 1991 Samaranch, using the mandate that he had obtained from the Birmingham Session in June, recognised the INOCSA, which thereupon became NOCSA. The Secretary-General of the OAU thought the IOC had acted a touch hastily, but was forbearing enough to refrain from formal criticism. NOCSA did not last long in its original form (which it will be remembered consisted of representatives from SACOS, NOSC, COSAS, SANOC and SANROC) because SACOS walked out towards the end of July, stating that it would remain only if the full moratorium on foreign sport were maintained until a one-person-one-vote constitution was in place.[88] ANOCA tried to persuade SACOS back into the NOC, but without success: in the light of hindsight it was never a plausible member, but had been dragged into INOCSA by the African group and the IOC's Commission on Apartheid.

There seems to have been doubt about what organisation had the right to lift the sports ban, despite Mbaye's earlier insistence that the IOC had imposed it, and that therefore only the IOC could remove it. The African sports ministers, meeting in Cairo in September 1991, wanted the OAU foreign ministers to make the decision. Sports federations disagreed, but representatives of Zambia, Zimbabwe, Uganda and others argued that to impose the ban had been a political decision and that the SCSA lacked the authority to rescind it.[89] However, the General Assembly of SCSA, meeting at Tunis on 20–1 February 1992, cut through the demarcation dispute. It favoured relations between South African sport and the rest of Africa and gave the OAU its due by recommending that its Secretary-General should endorse the decision.

Barcelona and after

Once it had been agreed that South Africa would take part in the Olympic Games at Barcelona, there was passionate debate about its flag and anthem. Ramsamy, who seems, on this and on some other occasions, to have been rather tactless, announced formally that the team would march to the 'Ode to Joy' and have an interim flag of blue, red and green, with a grey background. This naturally drew a rebuke from President De Klerk, who said that it was not for Ramsamy and NOCSA to take decisions about national symbols.

South Africa's reacceptance did not proceed at the same pace on all fronts, for after the IOC had agreed that it should go to Barcelona there was still debate about how and when sports links should be renewed. The uneven pace of developments was not so much a consequence of any uncertainty about South Africa's being welcomed back into international sport as of the great complexity of the sporting world, and the desire of so many bodies to get in on the historic act of readmission. A further source of complication was the inexperience of the new NOC in dealing with arcane Olympic matters.

South Africa's new relationship with the Olympic movement was symbolically confirmed when Nelson Mandela, who by then was seen as certain to become President of the new South Africa once a new constitution was in place, visited the IOC's headquarters in Lausanne on 25 March 1992. Samaranch, who has a gift for the pleasantly understated felicitous phrase, greeted him with the words: 'We've been waiting for you a long time.' The visit was not just a formality, because Mandela took the opportunity to argue that a larger South African team than had been agreed by the Executive Board at Seville in May 1991 should be allowed to go to the Barcelona Games. Sam Ramsamy, who was also on the visit, had hoped to send 182 athletes and officials, but it seems that a figure of about a hundred was agreed.[90]

It was still not all plain sailing. Even a short time before the Olympics there was opposition to South Africa's return. After the 'Boipatong Massacre' during riots at Boipatong, an African township in the southern Transvaal, in June 1992, which led to forty-eight deaths, there were widespread suspicions that the South African police had been involved, and not solely the rampaging inhabitants of the hostel in which ISCOR housed some of its migrant workers. The ANC suspended its participation in the constitutional negotiations, and the greatly respected Archbishop Desmond Tutu called for South Africa to be suspended or to withdraw voluntarily from the Olympics. He was, perhaps understandably, strongly rebuked by NOSC and by Steve Tshwete, the ANC's Sports Minister-in-waiting, for not having consulted them before making his statement.[91]

Although it did not like Tutu's rocking the boat, the ANC did order teams touring South Africa to visit Boipatong and all South African competitors to wear 'peace and democracy' armbands as the condition of South Africa's participation in the Olympics. These actions drew the acid remark from the *Cape Times*, in a leading article, that the ANC was continuing the National Party's custom of laying down the law to sports administrators. François Carrard, the Director-General of the IOC, also issued a rebuke, reminding South Africans that political gestures are banned at the Olympics, and saying that the armbands would not be allowed.[92]

In the end South Africa did compete at Barcelona. NOCSA's administration of the Republic's participation was generally seen as very poor, no doubt because energy had been dissipated in political manoeuvring, and most of Ramsamy's experience had been gained in the years of struggle, which can hardly have prepared him for 'normal' Olympic life. There were calls for Ramsamy's head, but they soon evaporated, and before long he was elected President of NOCSA, putting the seal on Dennis Brutus's eclipse and on his own rise to power.

Now South Africa is moving forward as a possible host to the Olympics of 2004. Cape Town emerged the winner from a demanding internal competition for the nomination with Johannesburg and Durban, neither of which took defeat especially well. Cape Town has some advantages in the international campaign to host the Games, which will end with the IOC's making its decision at its Monte Carlo

Session in September 1997. For one thing, in the process of preparing plans with which to convince NOCSA and its international advisers to choose it as the South African candidate in preference to Johannesburg and Durban, it did a great deal of the preparatory work on its bid at an earlier stage than is usual for bidding cities. There is also a feeling at the IOC that the Games ought to go to Africa, as the continent has still never hosted them.

It is too soon to assess Cape Town's chances. There have been unfortunate differences, chronicled in great detail in the South African newspapers, between NOCSA, the Cape Town City Council and the bidding committee. Such troubles are not unusual, as readers of this book will have noticed, and the IOC is used to them at the early stages of a bid. Provided that all parties are pulling together by January 1996, when candidatures for 2004 are officially presented at Lausanne, no harm will have been done. At that point the IOC will minutely assess the degree of support enjoyed by the bid from the central, regional and local tiers of government and the warmth of interest among the public at large. It must also weigh up South Africa's ability, from both administrative and financial points of view, to lay on so huge an event. Above all it will have to make a political forecast of whether South Africa will enjoy stability in 2004, bearing in mind that the interim constitution which came into force in 1994 must be replaced with a final constitution within two years of the Constitutional Assembly's first sitting.[93]

Indubitably there would be benefits for South Africa in hosting the Games, if they can be afforded, and the central government has already promised considerable sums for improvements to the city's infrastructure. In the years before the Games the government would be restrained from authoritarian excesses, should it be tempted to them, and at least part of the country would get a kick-start into development. The difficulty is that, in emphasising, for internal purposes, the benefits of economic development and national unity which may be expected to flow from the Olympics, the bidding committee may not sufficiently persuade IOC members of the benefits that would accrue to the Olympic movement itself. Naturally, the IOC would be pleased to promote an African Games, and it welcomes any economic and social benefits to the host city and country that the Games bring with them. But in the end its duty is to itself and the movement generally, and in these times of change, when many of its members are probably perplexed about the Olympic movement's direction, it is exceptionally difficult to foresee what line it will take over South Africa.

Conclusion

Just as rejection in sport had symbolised the rejection of South Africa in many other fields, so its reacceptance in sport symbolised acceptance in the wider political field, and perhaps made the process of political reacceptance more interesting and comprehensible to a wider audience than would otherwise have been the case.

As for the frequently-asked question about the efficacy of the sports boycott, it is impossible to give an acceptably definite answer. On the one hand, it was a success in its own terms, in that it gradually took hold in the minds of sporting organisations and individuals, and led to South Africa's being deprived of much of the international sport in which it would normally have engaged. The boycott also kept the South African issue alive outside South Africa among people who might otherwise not have been especially interested. Internally, it seems likely that it played a part in De Klerk's victory in the referendum of 17 March 1992, in which the President sought approval from white South Africans to persist with the constitutional negotiations.[94] The fact of participation in world sport must also be a consolation to those South Africans who did not welcome the recent political changes.

Such arguments support the view that sport has an importance beyond sport. On the other hand, most historians of modern South Africa say very little about the sports boycott, and instead concentrate on broader issues of economics and international politics when trying to explain the extraordinary changes that have taken place. Perhaps the main legacy of the South African sports saga will have been to convince a wider public that sport and politics are inseparable.

Notes

There are a number of books on South Africa and international sport, which are not referred to in the following notes. They include: R. Archer and A. Bouillon, *The South African Game*, London, 1982; J. Brickhill, *Race against Race*, London, 1976; P. Hain, *Don't Play with Apartheid*, London, 1971; R. Lapchick, *The Politics of Race and International Sport*, Westport, Connecticut, 1975; S. Ramsamy, *Apartheid: the Racial Hurdle*, London, 1982; M. Horrell, *South Africa and the Olympic Games*, Johannesburg, 1968.

1   Memorandum by Dennis Brutus to the IOC, dated 4 May 1959.

2   Vorster had some interest in sport as a keen golfer. I once interviewed him at his golf club, a much less luxurious one than those frequented by English-speaking whites, and was disconcerted by the enthusiasm with which he was greeted by a black caddie.

3   For an early account of the policy of territorial apartheid see my *Bantustans–the Fragmentation of South Africa*, Oxford, 1968.

4   The policy did not, however, extend as far as admitting Basil D'Oliveira as a member of the MCC's cricket team in 1968.

5   58th Session, Rome, 1960, *Minutes*, p. 11; according to an undated paper prepared by the IOC's documentation service the 'gentleman of South Africa' was Nana Mahomo. He was a representative in London of the Pan-Africanist Congress, which had formally broken away from the African National Congress in April 1959.

6   60th Session, Moscow, 6 June 1962, *Minutes*, p. 4.

7   Mayer to SANOC after the 60th Session, Moscow, 1962. (It seems that officials in Lausanne generally referred to SANOC, while in South Africa the NOC was often called SAONGA.) See also D. Macintosh , Hart Cantelon and Lisa McDermott, 'The IOC and South Africa: a lesson in Transnational Relations', *International Review for the Sociology of Sport*, 28, 4, 1993, pp. 373–95.

8   *The Argus*, Cape Town, 8 June 1962.

9   *Ibid.*, 14 and 15 June 1962.

10   Brutus to Mayer, 12 October 1962.

11   Mayer to Mrs L. M. Francey, General-Secretary of SAONGA, 12 November 1962. Her letter, to which Meyer's is a reply, is not on the Lausanne file.

12   Report presented to the International Olympic Committee with the compliments of the South African Olympic Games Association, Baden Baden, October 1962.

13   *Der Neue Tip*, Basle, 24 September 1963. The point about Field Marshall Jan Smuts is that he had been a United Party prime minister, and his son-in-law was assumed by Balsiger to be a member of the same party. Balsiger was seeing the son-in-law's membership of the National Olympic Committee under a National Party government as evidence of the NOC's freedom from political influence.

14   *The Argus*, 9 August 1963; *A Survey of Race Relations in South Africa, 1963*, p. 329.

15   61st Session, Baden-Baden, August 1963, *Minutes*, Annexe 5.

16   62nd Session, Innsbruck, 1964, *Minutes*, p. 5.

17   Executive Board and 65th Session, Rome 1966, *Minutes*.

18   Annexe 8 to the Tehran minutes is a resolution of the SCSA, Bamaha, December 1966, implicitly criticising the IOC.

19   For Killanin's account of the mission see his *My Olympic Years*, Chapter V. At p. 37 he describes Ademola as one of the most cultured Africans he had ever met!

20   Brundage to Killanin, 8 August 1967.

21   Killanin, p. 40.

22   The quotations from Vorster's speech are as recorded in Killanin's report to the IOC.

23   The International Federations' views on South Africa are at Appendix Q of the Killanin report.

24   66th Session, Grenoble, 1–5 February 1968, *Minutes*. The motion to readmit South Africa is at Annexe VI, and Braun's statement at Annexe V.

25   *New York Herald Tribune*, 26 February 1968.

26   SCSA, Executive Bureau, extraordinary meeting, Brazzaville, 25 February 1968.

27   *The Times*, 21 February 1968.

28   *The Daily Telegraph*, 16 February 1968.

29   *Luzerne Neueste Nachrichten*, 8 March 1968.

30   *Le Monde*, 27 February 1968.

31   *The Sunday Times*, 25 February 1968.

32   *The Times*, 17 February 1968.

33   *The Observer*, 25 February 1968.

34   *Daily Mail*, 21 February 1968.

35   *L'Equipe*, 28 February 1968.

36   For example, almost the whole front page of the *Rand Daily Mail*, 16 February 1968, announced South Africa's readmission.

37   Executive Board, Lausanne, 20 and 21 April 1968, *Minutes*.

38   *Le Monde*, 24 April 1968.

39   Kutahov to IOC, 24 February 1972 and Berlioux to Kutahov, 8 March 1972.

40   *The Sunday Times*, 31 March 1973.

41   *The Star*, Johannesburg, 26 March 1973.

42   Bruce Kidd, 'From Quarantine to Cure: the New Phase of the Struggle Against Apartheid', *Sociology of Sport Journal*, 8, 1991, p. 38.

43   Basil D'Oliveira, *Time to Declare*, Chapter 6.

44   Adrian Guelke, 'The Politicisation of South African Sport', in Lincoln Allison (ed.), *The Politics of Sport*, Manchester, pp. 131–5.

45   Clare Digby, *A Focus on the Extent of Organised Sporting Activities Amongst the 'Coloured' People of the Cape Peninsula*, University of Cape Town, Urban Problems Research Unit, working paper, 27 June 1977.

46   Human Sciences Research Council, Sports Investigation, Main Committee Report 1982, *Sport in the Republic of South Africa*, commissioned by the Ministry of National Education, 27 October 1979.

47   D'Oliveira, *Time to Declare*, chapter 14.

48   See e.g. *L'Equipe*, 20 November 1979; *Sunday Times*, 18 November 1979.

49   *AFP* 10 September 1979.

50   *Sunday Times*, 25 November 1979.

51   *The Guardian*, 2 October 1979.

52   *Ibid.*, 13 October 1979.

53   *AFP*, 23 October 1979, Yaoundé.

54   *Sunday Times*, 9 December 1979.

55   *AFP*, 29 October 1979.

56   *The Guardian*, 16 November 1979.

57 Neil Macfarlane, *Sport and Politics*, pp. 115–17.
58 Cheryl Roberts, *South Africa's Struggle for Olympic Legitimacy*, Cape Town, 1991, pp. 13–14.
59 *Olympic Review*, 263–4, September/October 1989, p. 439.
60 *Cape Times*, 28 and 31 August 1989.
61 *Business Day* (Johannesburg), 24 October 1989.
62 *The Argus*, Stop Press, 4 January 1990.
63 *Cape Times*, 12 January 1990.
64 *Ibid.*, 5 September 1990.
65 *The Argus*, Stop Press, 7 September 1990.
66 *Cape Times*, leading article, 15 October 1990.
67 *Ibid.*, 21 July 1990; 'In Harare, South African Sport Looks to Unity', *Olympic Review*, 278, December 1990, pp. 560–2.
68 *Cape Times*, 5 November 1990.
69 *Ibid.*, 6 November 1990.
70 *Ibid.*, 10 December 1990; *Olympic Review*, 279, January 1991, p. 7.
71 *The Argus*, Dennis Cruywagen, 10 December 1990.
72 *The Argus*, Stop Press, 6 February 1991.
73 *Cape Times*, 7 February 1991.
74 *The Argus*, Stop Press, 11 March 1991, reporting from Gaborone. According to Rod McGeoch, the Chief Executive who led Sydney to victory, Ganga was not interested in sport in its wider social context in Australia. He asked to see representatives of aboriginal groups who were hoping to publicise their grievances through the Olympics, but as soon as he had satisfied himself that they were not complaining about any discrimination *in sport* he dropped the whole question. McGeoch quotes him as saying: 'I'm sorry. That's all I'm interested in. I'm a member of the International Olympic Committee, and there's clearly no discrimination against blacks in the Olympic movement of this country.' *The Bid*, Melbourne, 1994, p. 147.
75 *Ibid.*, 9 March 1991.
76 *Ibid.*, Stop Press, 14 March 1991.
77 *Cape Times*, 26 March 1991.
78 *Ibid.*, 28 March 1991; *Olympic Review*, 283, May 1991, pp. 184–6.
79 *South*, 28 March 1991.
80 *Sunday Times*, Johannesburg, 31 March 1991.
81 *The Argus*, Stop Press, 25 April 1991; *Cape Times*, 14 June 1991.
82 *Cape Times*, 10 July 1991.
83 *Ibid.*, 11 July 1991.
84 *The Argus*, Stop Press, 7 July 1991.
85 *Cape Times*, 15 July 1991.
86 *Weekend Argus*, Sport Final, 13 July 1991, Frans Esterhuyse.
87 *Business Day*, 12 July 1991.
88 *The Argus*, Stop Press, 26 July 1991.
89 *Cape Times*, 20 September 1991.
90 *Olympic Review*, 296, June 1992, p. 288.
91 *Race Relations Survey 1992/93*, pp. 461–3; *Cape Times*, 23 June 1992.
92 *Cape Times*, 2, 3 and 18 July 1992.
93 Details of the procedure for passing a new constitution are in the

Constitution of the Republic of South Africa Act, No. 200 of 1993, Section 73. If the Constitutional Assembly (both Houses of Parliament sitting together) is not able to pass the new constitution within two years an election must be held, after which the new Constitutional Assembly has a further year.

94   Adrian Guelke, 'Sport and the End of Apartheid', in Lincoln Allison (ed.), *The Changing Politics of Sport*, Manchester, 1993, p. 151.

XI

Atlanta 1996

For a long time Atlanta's relations with the IOC did not run smoothly. Even the figure of $7m that it claimed to have spent on its bid seems to have been received with some scepticism, because it was so surprisingly low.

Once the Games were awarded to Atlanta there were many causes of anxiety. For example, soon after the choice of Atlanta was made the IOC began to exhort the city's organising committee (ACOG) to improve its relations with the United States Olympic Committee (USOC). Atlanta of course protested that relations were excellent, but the IOC had good reasons for its strictures.

All Games cause the IOC anxiety, but these seem to have been worse than most. Even in public there have been suggestions that Atlanta had unduly altered the plans on the basis of which the Games were awarded in the first place, bringing into prominence once more a perennial difficulty facing the IOC. Under its post-Seoul policy of ensuring that there is a good field of candidates, one function of which is to emphasise that it alone has the power to decide where the Games are to be held, the IOC has had little difficulty in gaining the respect of candidate cities in the years preceding the decision.

Once a city has been chosen the story can become very different, for however much the IOC emphasises in its dealings with the host city that it is the supreme authority of the Olympic Games, and not merely a guiding hand, in fact a good deal of power passes to the host city as soon as the decision in its favour is made. That power grows with the passage of time, because the IOC becomes increasingly reluctant to contemplate (in the very worst scenario) taking the Games elsewhere in the event of really fundamental disagreement.

The IOC's anxiety and frustration over Atlanta became well known in the Olympic family and even found their way into print. For example, the normally emollient Raymond Gafner refers with a rare tartness, in his 'Hello from Vidy' column in an official publication, the *Olympic Review*, to 'Atlanta, discovering like so many others before it, that the candidature phase is perhaps the easiest stage of all'.[1] In the habitually coded language of the Olympic high command this amounts to a rebuke.

All kinds of difficulty have faced Atlanta. At first ACOG was so much preoccupied with political and financial troubles that it hardly had time to establish relations with the international federations and to make sure that the facilities on offer were acceptable to them. Gradually this defect was corrected, but much later than the IOC would have liked. Atlanta paid a price for its late perception of the need to form alliances with the IFs. For example, John Lucas has a marvellous story of the demands made by Primo Nebiolo, President of the International Amateur Athletic Federation. Lucas went to an meeting of the Association of Summer Olympic Federations (ASOIF) in Paris in June 1994, to which Billy Payne, the president of ACOG, was reporting. Nebiolo, ASOIF's President, said: 'Mr Billy Payne, once your Olympic stadium is completed, I would be pleased if you would reserve, free of charge, one per cent of all the seats, in prime location, for myself and international delegates and their families from the IAAF . . . the most powerful federation in the world.' Payne refused.[2]

The difficulties with USOC turned on the joint marketing agreement into which it and ACOG had entered, at the IOC's insistence. Understandably, USOC, a rich but expensive organisa-tion, wanted to share in the benefits of the Olympic Games, but the joint marketing agreement became a source of endless trouble. There was also trouble between USOC and the IOC over the extent to which the United States' Amateur Sports Act overrode the Olympic Charter in respect of licensing and the right to use the Olympic symbols. Both bodies were determined to protect what they saw as their pre-rogatives: the IOC naturally held that it was the ultimate authority; equally naturally USOC insisted that under United States law the IOC could not act without its concurrence.

Atlanta has also been disconcerted by the apparent determination of the IOC to increase the size of the Games, however much it may deplore 'gigantism'. Fears arise for two main reasons: first, because the IOC constantly recognises new NOCs (there were 169 at

Barcelona, 194 in 1994 and there could be as many as 200 in time for Atlanta). All these NOCs will insist on sending officials to the Games, even if they have hardly any athletes, or none at all (only thirty of the sixty-seven NOCs listed as participating in the 1994 winter Games at Lillehammer sent more than ten athletes).[3] Secondly, the IOC seemingly cannot resist adding new sports, and events within sports, to the programme.

The IOC has not been happy about the rises in Atlanta's estimated expenditure, caused partly by the fact that the original estimates had been made in 1988 dollars, with no allowance for inflation. Furthermore, Atlanta was obliged to borrow from the bank, to tide it over in the period when it was necessary to undertake construction, without waiting for money from television and sponsors. (TOP III is expected to yield over $300m, covering Lillehammer and Atlanta, and NBC paid a record $456m for the United States television rights.) As a result of these embarrassments and uncertainties it has been widely surmised that the IOC will in future think twice about awarding the Games to a city which will be relying, as Atlanta very largely is, on funding from the private sector, without any alternative source of essential funds as a cushion.

By mid-1992 Atlanta was estimating outgoings at $1,400m (later the estimate rose to $1,500m) and income at $1,515m, giving a comfortable surplus. But awkward questions remained about venues for various sports, relations with the city of Atlanta, and social unrest there. There were also worries about the city's reported intention to develop its own sponsorship programme, which would have been very damaging for ACOG. Even charges of 'excessive' commercialisation had to be answered, although, of course, many members of the IOC do not regard commercialisation as a fault. The charges were answered effectively in the eyes of Atlanta and the IOC, if not of the general public, by Andrew Young, former Congressman (the first black one from Georgia in 101 years, as he proudly records in *Who's Who*), United States Ambassador to the United Nations and Mayor of Atlanta, and now a member of the Atlanta Olympic team, who coined the slogan, now much used by the IOC's marketing department: 'the commercialisation of sport is the democratisation of sport'.

As the *Olympic Review* has revealed on a number of occasions, the Olympic stadium has been another major source of worry. Billy Payne had said at an Executive Board meeting, held in Atlanta in March 1993, that Atlanta would very soon be starting to build the Olympic stadium. The *Olympic Review* commented, in unusually straight-forward language (for its locutions are often diplomatic to the point of opacity): 'This announcement was a welcome surprise for the Executive Board, which had been starting to air some concern on the subject.'

The city of Atlanta has no use for an Olympic-sized stadium, whose maintenance would be an unjustifiable financial drain. The main venue will be a 'kit' stadium, much of which will be turned into a green area after the Games, and the stadium will then go down to a capacity of 45,000 from the 80,000 needed for the Games. 'This realistic project has not aroused great enthusiasm for its architectural qualities, but it has the tremendous merit of taking into account local and future sports requirements.' The reduced stadium will replace the Fulton County Stadium, where a professional baseball team, the Atlanta Braves, now plays. Sensible though this plan is, it will not be cheap. The stadium is expected to cost $209m, including the land, compared with an average $120m. All this is to be paid by the organising committee out of television rights, so that it is handed over to the city free of charge.[4] Contrary to original expectations the stadium will not be suitable for the football final, which will instead be held 113 km away at Athens, Georgia.

The addition of new events to the programme has also been a source of contention. At first the proposals for women's football and a beach volleyball tournament to be included were shelved at the request of the IFs concerned, and with ACOG's agreement, because of the additional athletes who would be involved and the extra facilities that would be needed. Yet in the end women's football was added, without age limit, no doubt as a reassertion of the IOC's intention to retrieve the sacrifice of sovereignty that it had made in allowing the international football federation – FIFA – to limit men's Olympic football to players aged 23 and under.

Beach volleyball was also admitted to the programme, though the Executive Board seems not to have been overwhelmingly enthusiastic for it. Once beach volleyball had been approved, major controversies erupted about which players would be eligible to take part. The trouble was essentially a conflict between rival beers, Miller for the Association of Volleyball Professionals (AVP) and Budweiser for the world governing body, the Federation Internationale de Volleyball (FIVP). In the words of the *ISOH Journal*:

AVP members are banned by Miller from competing in any events sponsored by rival beer companies. However, the FIVB is requiring that beach volleyball players compete in a multi-country FIVB tournament in Brazil in early 1966 in order to be eligible for the Olympics. This is further complicated by the fact that NBC, the American television network for the 1996 Olympics, pushed hard for beach volleyball's inclusion in the Olympics, and wants the best players in the world, i.e., the AVP players, to compete. Should they be banned by the FIVB, there are rumors that NBC would not telecast that sport.

Conventional volleyball has also suffered major controversy. A preliminary was to have been held in Cobb County, which was then found recently to have passed an anti-homosexual law. This had naturally caused protests, and ACOG tentatively changed the venue.[5]

After the Executive Board's meeting at Atlanta in March 1993 Samaranch had expected to meet President Clinton, but had instead to see the Vice-President, Al Gore, as Clinton had been called to his father-in-law's bedside. This visit was important, because the organisation of the Atlanta Games requires the Federal Government's support in many areas, and subsequently Gore set up a taskforce to co-ordinate the government's involvement.

The IOC understandably sets considerable store by the legal control over chosen sports sites being established as early as possible, but at Atlanta there were, in a few cases, difficult negotiations before this could be done. For various reasons, it proved necessary to move a number of sports from the sites originally proposed: a continuing bone of contention was the use to be made of Stone Mountain Park, a natural park 30 km from Atlanta, which had figured prominently in Atlanta's original bid. ACOG had intended to place a number of sports there, including rowing and canoeing, but the park authorities demanded an unreasonable rent, and it was then found that an island would have had to be moved, which was not thought worthwhile for a temporary facility. After much negotiation, rowing and canoeing were shifted, with shooting and the equestrian events, to Rockdale. Thereafter rowing was moved yet again, this time to Lake Lanier. All this left only archery, cycling and tennis at Stone Mountain, and cycling's velodrome is to be only a temporary structure, since neither government nor park authority is interested in retaining it after the Games.

So protracted and complicated did the rowing saga become that Denis Oswald, president of the international rowing federation (FISA), published an outline of what had happened.

1 In its candidature document, the bid file, Atlanta had proposed Stone Mountain, with assurances that it would become a permanent facility. FISA had liked this proposal, and had never asked for rowing to be moved.
2 For various reasons, ACOG could not deliver the file promises, and had asked FISA to abandon Stone Mountain, and choose between Rockdale and Lake Lanier.
3 With the IOC's support, FISA had done everything it could to 'save' Stone Mountain. Its efforts had not been successful, and eventually it had had to relinquish the site against its will.
4 It had chosen Lake Lanier, on conditions which ACOG has promised to fulfil, and with the Executive Board's approval.
5 Unfortunately the new site was an hour away from Atlanta, but FISA was convinced that it would be a great success.[6]

The Atlanta Games have had their teething troubles, but there is no reason to suppose that they will not be a tremendous spectacle, earning record sums and giving pleasure to millions. But the IOC will also have learned, or re-learned, some lessons, especially that it is impossible to pay too much attention to the detail of such matters as funding and legal title to sports venues, and that bidding cities are very liable to take their promises lightly, once the bidding phase is over and the contest has been won.

Notes

1 *Olympic Review*, 284, June 1991, p. 243.
2 'A Reflection: Madame Monique Berlioux Revisited', by John A. Lucas, *Olympika*, vol. III, p. 153.
3 *Olympic Review*, 317/318, May 1994, pp. 188–9.
4 *Olympic Review*, 306, April 1993, p. 125, and *Olympic Review*, 323, November 1994, pp. 455–6.
5 *ISOH Journal*, 2, 3, autumn 1994, p. 56.
6 *Olympic Review*, 316, March/April 1994, pp. 94–5.

XII

The Olympics in the third millennium

Over the past century the Olympic movement has built up extra-ordinary power, prestige and goodwill, yet it is beset with problems. Some of these are internal. In this category there are some questions which, though time-comsuming, are unlikely to go to the heart of the movement. For example, it is not surprising to find that the United States Olympic Committee is dissatisfied with its share of the money raised from the sale of North American television rights, or that some Third World countries are disappointed with their shares of the funds distributed by Olympic Solidarity. These are the types of domestic trouble which any worldwide movement must expect to suffer.

However there are also internal questions which could tear the movement apart at the roots if not dealt with. A further brand of question is linked to national and international politics, and often, as we have seen throughout this book, the domestically and the publicly political interlock.

Olympic dominance

If the Olympic Games are not at the top of the world sporting tree they are nothing, so that one constant preoccupation of the International Olympic Committee is to ensure that the Olympics retain their domi-nant place. Currently there is no worldwide organisation capable of challenging the Olympic movement's dominance of international sport. Since the IOC headed off UNESCO in the 1970s the only source of danger, short of world catastrophe, is internal dissension which could lead to fragmentation of the movement.

As we saw in an earlier chapter, the effort to maintain unity requires delicate balancing between the various powerful bodies in the movement, especially between the IOC, the IFs and the NOCs and, once a host city has been chosen, between the IOC and that city's organising committee.[1] It also requires a balance between two incompatible objectives of the Olympic movement: on the one hand to ensure that the Games obtain the best athletes in the world, while, on the other, giving an opportunity to compete to territories which may have little chance of producing the best and which, even with the help of Olympic Solidarity, have great difficulty in sending a team to the Games at all.

Other problems are those of 'gigantism', as the Games' permanent tendency to grow is inelegantly known. With gigantism must be linked the growing commercialisation of the Games, which still disquiets some of the more traditionally-minded sports people. There remain, too, vestiges of the old question of amateurism versus professionalism, although it must be said that this is a problem which lingers on more in the public mind than in that of athletes or sports administrators. By contrast, doping on its current large scale is a relatively modern problem, which the movement is tackling to the best of its ability.

While giving a say to all sections of the movement, it is also essential for the IOC to preserve its internal dominance. Samaranch has regularly reminded audiences of this, for example, in the following extract from a speech to a meeting of ANOC (a body prone to over-mightiness) at Barcelona in 1990: 'Let us not forget that at the head of this Olympic Movement there is its creator, the International Olympic Committee, whose strength is automatically channelled to each of the members of the Movement.'

In the same speech he returned to another preoccupation, the need for sport to be master in its own house: 'in short, what we must succeed in doing is achieving complete control over our spectacular development. The leadership of Olympism and sport must always remain in the hands of sports leaders, and likewise all the financial resources we may obtain must return to the world of sport.' These were brave words in the context of the frequent complaints that are made about the ruthlessness of sponsors, who are prone to treat sport as a commodity like any other, and who have already had some success in arranging the timing of events to suit television, and in changing some games' rules to make them more attractive spectacles for the mass audience.

Amateurism and nationalism

Within sport amateurism is more or less a dead issue, though it lingers on in the public mind, and perhaps in the minds of some athletes and administrators in countries which cannot expect to attract great notice from sponsors, and which hark back to old ideals. But with the general acceptance of the view that the Olympic Games' reason for existence is to promote the best in human achievement, the movement has abandoned much that was for many years thought essential to the Olympic ideal. This was in part expressed in Coubertin's very un-Greek idea that the ancient Games were strictly for amateurs and that it was more important to take part than to win, though he did not, of course, go as far as his snobbish Victorian contemporaries, who saw sport as a pastime of the leisured class, for which it was inappropriate to train. His original motive, as was shown in Chapter I, was to promote physical education in schools, and he originally promoted the Games as a means to that end, though as his life went on they seem to have become an end in themselves.

It was only in 1981 that the IOC formally abandoned the commit-ment to amateurism, by saying that eligibility to take part in the Games must be determined by individual international federations. It is true that some federations still have great difficulty in defining the exact conditions of eligibility, but from the point of view of the IOC the problem is dead.

So, in one sense, is that of nationalism. It has always been said that the Olympics are contests between individuals, but in fact they are contests between national teams, chosen by their federations and sent to the Games by their NOCs. Indeed, the NOCs insist on their athletes identifying in the most ostentatious way with their nations, by marching behind their national flags. Any suggestion that national flags be abandoned and replaced with the Olympic flag would be universally rejected by the NOCs, which have no time for the well-meant supra-nationalism of the European Community. It is only traditionalists, like Madame Monique Berlioux, who still wish that individuals could present themselves as candidates for the Games, and this preoccupation with a dead past was very possibly one of the many factors which led to her breach with Samaranch, and to her abrupt retirement.

Gigantism

Gigantism is a problem of a different kind, which has been discussed for many years, since long before the number of athletes, journalists, officials and hangers-on reached its present grotesque size. For example, at the IOC's Session at Helsinki in 1952 various methods of reducing the number of athletes were discussed and J. Sigfrid Edstrom, the outgoing President, said that the number of officials who accompanied the teams and could well be described as tourists was growing alarmingly.[2]

There is constant pressure on the Programme Commission of the IOC to admit new sports, or to enlarge the number of events within a sport. At the same time there is widespread understanding that the Olympic circus has got out of hand. So large are the Games that in practice only the richest of candidate cities, or those under the control of effective authoritarian governments, are plausible candidates to host them. Furthermore, the increasing number of journalists covering them, not to mention the proliferating Olympic family, means that accommodation for ordinary members of the public who would like to attend the Games becomes increasingly difficult to find. Indeed, COOB, Barcelona's organising committee, seemed almost to think of ordinary spectators as a nuisance, to be accommodated outside Barcelona in the already crowded coastal resorts.

Some progress has been made, though it is countered by the IOC's perpetual yielding to the temptation to admit new events to the programme. One important decision was that after 1992 'Demonstration Sports' would no longer be included. On the other hand, the IOC continues to grant recognition to new sports, which is an essential step on the way to inclusion in the programme. In April 1995 ballroom dancing and surfing were granted provisional recognition. If they achieve full recognition after two years' probation, they will join seventeen other sports in waiting.

Some of the steps taken towards limitation have been ham-handed. For example, in 1991 the Programme Commission reduced the number of medal-winning events in equestrianism, without even consulting the Princess Royal, who as well as being a member of the IOC was President of the International Equestrian Federation. Rather less attention seems to be paid to the excessive numbers of officials accompanying the teams and journalists covering the Games, though of course it might be difficult to limit the latter now that the

Olympics live to so large an extent off television, though it must be remembered that the percentage of total income produced by television is declining.

Doping

This is one of the overwhelming problems facing the Olympic movement. Unfortunately it is a vast subject, which lies outside the scope of this book: another book would be needed to do it justice.

Doping came up from time to time at the Centennial Congress of the Olympic movement (which will be discussed more fully below). As so often at the Congress, a representative of the media was forthright, though only about the past. 'Look at the past example of East Germany, which synthesised its sporting prowess in the laboratory. There, the unbridled use of pharmacological supplements was a deliberate instrument of policy, used by administrators, technical specialists and doctors to achieve a clearly defined political aim.'[3]

On the whole the attitude on doping was optimistic. No one was in favour of legalising it; all applauded the IOC for its efforts so far, and some speakers (notably the great runner Edwin Moses) saw the next step as the establishemt of a common list of prohibited substances, which all international federations would adopt.

However, it is worth observing that common sense suggests that doping's dramatic growth must be at least in part a by-product of professionalism, so that it may be fairly said that in embracing money the world of sport has invited the growth of drug taking. But that once said, the Olympic movement has taken the lead in measures, both at the Games and between them, to stamp the problem out. Yet, all good intentions notwithstanding, and despite the fact that no case of drug abuse was detected at the winter Games at Lillehammer in 1992, it seems unlikely that it ever will be stamped out, for it appears that many athletes take drugs for granted, and would continue to take them, even in the knowledge that they were thereby inviting early death.

The Olympic movement is thus somewhat in the position of an industrialist who, having made a great fortune, spends some of it in his old age on charitable works. Having grown rich by selling the movement, the IOC can now afford to spend a great deal on counteracting one of the unfortunate by-products of riches. The comparison is not entirely just, since the effort to eradicate drug taking is not solely a matter of charity. If unchecked it reduces the value of the product that is for sale. No one wants to know, as they watch their favourite athletes, that they are drugged automata, testing the latest concoction of some pharmaceutical company, and setting up records which are nonsensical.

Choosing the host city

Much has been written since the IOC chose Atlanta, Georgia, in hot competition with Athens, to host the Games of 1996, about the need for some change in the voting procedure. Now that the Games have for good or ill become as much desired as an engine for growth as for any sporting reason, and the potential for wealth creation has become so enormous, it is widely felt that the IOC's methods of making a choice on which billions of dollars hang should in some way or another be made more rational and open. It is true that important changes have been made since Atlanta was chosen, as we saw in Chapter III, but they do not so much promote openness as discourage some kinds of tactical voting, and reduce the possibility of corruption among IOC members.

Changes in procedure are for the IOC to decide, but it cannot be denied that the choice of city not only has developmental and financial effects, but also sends out powerful political signals. To revert to an earlier example, if the IOC had chosen Beijing for the year 2000, as it very nearly did, it might on the one hand have been argued that that it was playing into the hand of a coldly authoritarian regime, or on the other that it was seeking to bring the world's most populous country into the comity of nations. Nor is the political aspect of the choice confined to signals. The IOC has also to make a judgement about a country's stability and international acceptability.

Political acceptability includes the question of human rights, which the IOC has in the past often managed to ignore when making friends: one has only to think of Nicolae Ceausescu; but if it again allowed the Games to be master-minded by a government which ignored human rights, it might well find itself suffering the disapproval of governments and public opinion, at least in the West. In an age when the provision of aid to poor countries is beginning to be linked with those countries' records in the matter of how they treat their populations, it would be odd if the IOC, which in its role as an engineer of development can in a sense be seen as an aid-giver on a vast scale, were allowed to feel comfortable if it gave the Games to a country whose government displayed indifference to human rights. Although not responsible to any higher authority, even the Olympic movement cannot afford to create a mood among governments or the public that it needs to be cut down to size.

Yet it can be argued that the IOC's mission is universality, not uniformity. It does not wish to be seen as an agent of cultural imperialism – rather as a bridge between different social and political systems – and it is true that western concern about human rights can sometimes seem unpleasantly holier than thou to politicians who have somehow to govern disastrously poor countries. Nor can the IOC afford endlessly to grant the Games to conventionally democratic countries. To argue that there is only one worthwhile kind of democracy may itself be seen as a facet of cultural imperialism.

On the other hand, it must never be thought that abuses of human rights are peculiar to developing countries. Georgia has become famous in England, not because it is the host state for the next Olympics but because in April 1995 it sent to the electric chair an English-born murderer, Nick Ingram, after grimly farcical last-minute efforts to obtain a new trial. Disgust at Ingram's treatment was not confined to opponents of the death penalty, but was shared by others, who saw twelve years on death row as an extreme of cruelty which would disgrace any country, and electrocution as an especially disgusting method of execution. However, such reactions are not widespread in the state of Georgia itself, where the death penalty is enthusiastically supported, and another 112 condemned men were waiting in the euphemistically named Diagnostic and Classification Center. Nevertheless, might it not be possible for the IOC's Evaluation Commission to look into, and record a view on, such humanitarian questions, as well as paying attention, as it properly does, to political systems?

Now that the IOC has become so unequivocally linked to world capitalism it may become hard for it to continue to ignore the humanitarian demands of capitalist governments. To have given the Games to China would in some quarters have been seen as the prelude to opening up new markets for the developed nations of the West, but at the same time there would have been widespread revulsion, had so valuable a gift been given to a regime about whose credentials there are so many, and justifiable, doubts. Perhaps the time is coming when the IOC will also have to take an interest in human rights in the developed world.

The Centennial Congress, Paris 1994

The Centennial Congress of the Olympic movement, later named the Congress of Unity, was held in Paris in August 1994 to commemorate Coubertin's inaugural Paris Congress of 1894, and to celebrate the movement's first hundred years. It gave athletes, administrators, journalists, academics and a great variety of other observers a magnificent opportunity to discuss the movement's many problems, and to reinforce the sense of global solidarity, without which it could so easily fall apart.

A number of the main themes were marked out in an opening speech by Kevan Gosper, a Vice-President of the IOC and one of the leading contenders for the succession to Samaranch. He pointed to the need to restructure the programme of the Games, and somehow to combine the movement's constantly reiterated aspiration to universality with the perceived need to ensure that the very best athletes in the world take part. 'How', he asked, 'can Olympism truly sustain its universal appeal to all peoples over the world if we ultimately confine the Olympic Games only to the top athletes from the top nations?' Nor should so much space in the stadium be given to sponsors and officials that there was no room for lesser mortals: there was a danger that the Olympic finals would be 'closed off with the weight of VIP and corporate presence'.

Anwar Chowdry (President of the International Amateur Boxing Association) raised another of the main themes of the Congress, namely the extent to which the Olympic movement remained true to its original ideals. There was, he said, 'a heated dispute going on as to whether the Olympic Movement has remained faithful to its original idea . . . our critics reproach us for allegedly having sacrificed the ethical substance for an ostentatious striving for spectacular Olympic performances, and pompously organized Summer and Winter Olympic Games'.[4]

Sometimes the shadow of *Lords of the Rings* (to which no one was so tactless as to refer outright) hung heavily on the proceedings, especially in periodic references to doping, and to the extent to which the movement's credibility would be tested by its success in fighting against it. *Lords of the Rings* may also have influenced the one speaker who referred to the huge cost of the Congress, $16m, and another who suggested that half the cost of opening ceremonies at the Games might be donated to Olympic Solidarity, and simpler ceremonies put in hand.

The question of the programme was necessarily linked with that of 'gigantism'. It is almost universally agreed in Olympic circles that the Games have grown to the maximum acceptable size (a common reason is that so few cities can possibly offer to host them), though an exception is the respected modern pentathlete Dominic Mahony, who said at the Congress that in his view the Games could perfectly well become even bigger, and so give athletes from a wider range of sports the chance to take part. This view was corroborated by the President of the Lillehammer Organising Committee, who did not think there would be any organisational problem if more sports than at present were included in the winter programme.[5] Mahony's remark, though echoed by no one else, has much to be said for it, when one recalls, as none of the speakers at the Congress did, that at Barcelona no fewer than 129,000 individuals were accredited. Surely, it might be asked, so huge a number could be reduced to make room for more athletes.

Some effort is being made to reduce the number of accredited journalists, but otherwise it seems that for the time being the programme must be kept in hand by limiting the number of athletes to about the current ten thousand. This can be done variously by ejecting whole sports from the programme; by forcing the established sports to limit their numbers of individual disciplines or by establishing quotas which no country would be allowed to exceed, either for its total team or for individual sports. The difficulty about quotas is that they may look like an invitation to NOCs to fill their quotas, even if they have no athletes of truly Olympic quality. It follows that quotas must be linked with a system of heats and qualifying events and/or qualifying standards, to eliminate the less good: what kind of system is not relevant in the narrow context of the need to cut the Games down to size.

Third World problems

The tendency to introduce more preliminaries than exist already is naturally deplored by small countries in which sport is not well developed, and which fear that they could be excluded from participation in the Games. It is these countries that set most store by the universal character of the Games, and point out that if the emphasis is solely on quality the less tangible advantages of international friendship and understanding will be jeopardised. Their protests are signs of a broader nationalism than that of sport, for they need the Games, just as they need the United Nations, as a showcase in which they may briefly appear on the world's stage, and where they can gain the international respect which is normally reserved for rich countries.

Many speakers backed universality in this sense. For example the powerful Jean-Claude Ganga, who made his name in the context of the Supreme Council for Sport in Africa, and especially of its efforts to deal with the South African question, said that all countries with NOCs recognised by the IOC had 'A sacred right to take part . . . we reject the entrenched elitism which would turn the Olympic Games into a world championship'. The Secretary-General of the NOC of Tonga praised the principle of universality, without which Tonga would have no prospect of taking part in the Olympics, but Donato Martucci of the IOC's Cultural Commission introduced a *caveat*. It was important, he said, 'to ensure that the participation of less privileged countries in the Olympic Games was not tantamount to inviting poor relations for Christmas dinner'.[6]

Although the Third World countries were grateful for the aid given by Olympic Solidarity, not many were especially enthusiastic. As another great runner, 'Kip' Keino put it, the aid was significant, but not sufficient. The IOC member and security expert Ashwini Kumar thought Olympic Solidarity was hamstrung by insufficient funds and lacked a clear vision; he feared that the North/South imbalance 'may soon enlarge itself to such proportions that it may impair the global aspects of the Olympic Movement'.[7] Another IOC member thought Olympic Solidarity grants tended to be weighted in favour of the developed countries.

Indeed, one of the principal impressions made by speakers from developing countries was of disillusion, even bitterness. In a very cogent contribution, Dr Robin Mitchell, a newly-elected member of the IOC, pointed out that the governments of poor countries could not adequately fund sport, and that the shortfall was not made good from private sources. Other needs 'are so overwhelming that the development of a sporting infrastructure becomes an illogical and insensitive development'. 'Luxuries' like sports education were simply not priorities for such governments. Alpha Diallo, of the Guinean NOC, thought the Olympics, with their increasing gigantism, were straying ever further from their early ideals.

The athlete has become a pawn in a fantastic media show, a robot manufactured for the purpose of smashing records, promoting a particular brand of product or flattering the pride of a particular nation. Since this tendency seems to be irreversible in spite of all the IOC's efforts, we might ask ourselves what the place of the third-world athlete is in this setting. Is he a supernumerary, a curiosity, or simply an added recruit for the opening parade of the Games?[8]

A Mauritanian delegate referred to athletes as increasingly being seen as sandwich board men in the service of a particular product. 'Athletes have become performance-oriented machines, have impersonal relations with each other or even detest each other to the point of conducting hostilities through the intermediary of the press.'[9] His remarks suggest that it would be worth the IOC's while to stimulate research into athletes' loves and hates. Some say that participation in the Olympics is the high point of their lives, partly because of the international camaraderie of the Olympic village, while others are so seriously engaged in professional sport that they have no emotional energy for interaction with other athletes, and there are some who even prefer to stay in a luxurious hotel than in the village.

A recurring theme among Third World delegates at the Congress was the decay of their societies, and their vision of the athlete as the last respectable role model for the young, one of the few avenues of hope for the preservation of traditional values in countries where the proportion of young people in the population is much higher than in the developed world. As Fidèle Waura, President of the NOC of Gabon, said: 'Top athletes have nowadays become the last personalities in whom all the hopes of our young people are centred. Their victories give motivation to the young and show them the right path to follow.'[10] Other speakers saw youth as bewildered, prone to idleness and deliquency, and several referred to the 'muscle drain' of young athletes to richer countries.

Lost ideals

Worries about gigantism link naturally with fears that the Olympics may lose, if they have not already lost, their indefinable magic, which stems from the ideals of their founder, Pierre de Coubertin. For example, David Miller, the noted sports journalist, said: 'The perception of the virtues of the Olympic Games is abstract, intangible, and therefore especially difficult to preserve. It cannot be put in a bottle and corked.'[11] (Reference was constantly made to Coubertin throughout the Congress, yet his great-nephew had to point out that de Coubertin's name had been dropped in 1992 from the honorific words pronounced by the President at the beginning of the Games, and pleaded for its reinstatement.)[12]

The very understandable preoccupation with lost innocence led to analyses of the value and virtue of the Olympic movement which sometimes verged on the bizarre. For example, a senior IOC member, Mohammed Mzali, said: 'The Olympic ethic is essentially a mode of conduct in which the athlete, through his body, enters into communion with the whole of humanity'; another IOC member saw sport as the most significant social phenonemon of the twentieth century, and some speakers (for example the Director-General of the Olympic Council for Asia) called the Olympic movement the strongest cultural and social movement ever witnessed by humankind.[13]

As we have seen in a number of contexts, there is a very great temptation to expect too much from the Olympic movement. One participant thought that its historic commitment to international peace and understanding must be preserved, because without it 'it would cease to be a movement in the proper sense of the term', a remark which does of course provoke the response that the movement might be better advised to confine itself to sport. The same speaker hoped to 'find the common denominator in mankind', begging the question of whether such a common denominator exists, or whether people in all their variety are the product of, in the broadest sense, their environment.[14]

Some of the academics saw the Olympic ideal as relating to something much broader than sport. For example Conrado Durántez said, as he has written elsewhere, that 'Olympism is a philosophy of life which uses sport as a conveyor belt for its ideas', and Bruce Kidd, one of those who believed the Olympic movement to be at a crossroads, saw the solution in broadening its mission. The Games owed their universal appeal to the link that they created between sport and culture on the one hand and human rights and humanitarian development for all peoples of the world on the other.[15] A representative of UNESCO introduced a welcome counterweight when she pointed out that 'we must be vigilant to ensure that sport does not become a kind of myth of reconciliation which lulls us into a false sense of security, and provides backing to societies whose objectives have nothing to do with the ideals of sport'.[16]

One impression conveyed by the discussion of Third World problems was that the Olympic movement's salvation may come from the less developed countries, in which it is a far more important body than in developed countries, where it is only one among many rich organisations. Because the developing world is so poor it cannot possibly see sport as a significant contributor to the gross national product; yet it needs to attach some meaning to sport, over and above the enjoyment that it brings. Hence the nostalgia hinted at by speakers from the Third World for a pre-commercial, even pre-professional age, a nostalgia which may do something to keep the torch of old values burning and to hold in check the less sensitive excesses of commercialism.

The programme

The debate about gigantism is only one facet of the continuing debate about the programme, much of which is bound up with the contentions of established sports that they should be undisturbed because they are traditional or powerful or both. Peter Tallberg, an IOC member, made no bones about the vigorous nature of discussion of modifications to the programme:

All those taking part in the modifications foreseen on the occasion of the new millennium were aware of the financial risks involved and were playing a ruthless game in which the objective was to consolidate their position and broaden their sphere of personal influence in the context of the power struggle surrounding the programme.[17]

Various ways forward were suggested at the Congress. It was clear that two principles were involved: first, the movement's aspiration to universality, which can be interpreted in a number of ways. Three of them are that the Olympic Games should be open to all people, all over the world. Another, less common, is that they should be open to all sports, and not just to those which originated in Europe. The third, more abstract and difficult, is that sport in general, and the Olympics in particular, relates to some universal essence of humankind.

The other principle is that of popularity. It has always been a criterion for inclusion in the Games that a sport must be widely practised. Unfortunately the extent of a sport's popularity may be exaggerated, because it is most easily measured by the number of national federations affiliated to the relevant international federation. Sometimes, however (though no one made the point at the Congress), the affiliations mean little, since there may be little real infrastructure underlying them.

The principles are not easy to reconcile, and in appealing to them some speakers seem to have felt that they were making progress in the argument when all they were really doing was to restate the problem. For example Edwin Moses said: 'Olympic competition should remain an elite event but consideration must also be given to smaller countries with less competitive athletes, so that we remain a truly international and non-biased Family.'[18]

Specific examples of sports that might be dropped were given as long ago as 1990 by Richard Pound, a member of the IOC's Executive Board who is thought to be in the running for the succession to Samaranch; some of his possible casualties were football, boxing and weightlifting: the first because the upper age limit of 23 imposed by FIFA means that the best players do not take part; the second because of 'continually repeated scandalous decisions' and the third because of the misuse of steroids.[19] A suggestion made at the Congress, well worn, like all the others, for years beforehand, was that team games might be dropped. What, however, would be the reaction of João Havelange and his powerful Football Federation to any projected removal of football? Would other federations' leaders rejoice at his exclusion, or would they join forces with him, and threaten to do without the Olympic Games altogether? If Primo Nebiolo and his International Amateur Athletic Federation went that way, the Olympics would be finished.

Other candidates for exclusion are those sports where the winning score is determined by subjective judgement, rather than by reference to the stop-watch. Yet another possible solution is, as we have seen, to set quotas for sports. These, however, might lead one country to include inferior representatives, just to fill its quota, and another to exclude some of the best performers in the world because too many of them lived in the same country.

In this connection, Dominic Mahony was one of the very few speakers to introduce some hard facts. He quoted a survey of athletes, of whom 57 per cent, across all age groups, wanted objective judging; 52 per cent had seen the traditional amateur status as important; 85 per cent in the 15–24 age-group had reacted against over-professionalism.[20] A further suggestion, reflecting what seems to have been a fairly general dislike and distrust of the media, was that sports should be suppressed which have an ephemeral appeal based solely on popularity with the media. Some speakers thought very expensive sports should be excluded, or those which required lavish facilities, which would be little used after the Olympics; one thought less important sports should be allowed on to the programme in rotation, which would at least keep them intermittently in the public eye, and so increase their popularity and therefore their commercial drawing power. Dr Jacques Rogge, the Belgian IOC member, proposed that the movement should go back to the recently abandoned system of demonstration sports, and include four temporary sports in each Games. He added that IFs needed to adapt voluntarily to modern conditions, as some already had, probably to counter the threat that they might otherwise be dropped.[21]

The athletes

A great many preoccupations were aired at the Congress. One of the most important was the place of the athletes themselves in the whole Olympic structure. The athletes played a leading part at the Congress, both as speakers and as subjects of discussion. On the whole they were idealistic, although one was disillusioned, and said that she no longer believed that the important thing is to take part. 'The greatest message currently given out by the media gives importance only to victory.'[22] There seems to have been some temptation in the past to think of the athletes rather as the horses are thought of in racing – essential to the process and worthy of welfare, but not able to contribute to deliberations. The tendency was decisively scotched by the Baden Baden Congress of 1981, after which the IOC set up its Athletes Commission, but there is clearly much to be done. As one athlete put it, they should have a fuller say in the administration of sport, so that they become the fourth pillar of the Olympic movement, alongside the IOC, the NOCs and the IFs.[23]

The resettlement of athletes after their short careers was a recurring theme. This concern with the athletes is not purely disinterested. It stems also from an awareness that with increasing professionalism come higher expectations, and that athletes are increasingly being organised by other agencies than the IFs, notably their managers, who are becoming the new leaders of sport. The influential Rogge developed this point and questioned the adequacy of present structures to retain control over the athlete. The answer must be to integrate the athletes, and all those who surround them, into NOCs and IFs: 'Managers, suppliers, sponsors, even organizers should be closely integrated into our own structures otherwise they will become a counter-power.'[24]

Very few speakers had anything to say about the relations betwen Olympic institutions and their national governments. Some emphasised the need for autonomy, but acknowledged that cities hosting the Games must expect to make some sacrifice of independence, because of the need to enlist governmental support. One Nigerian representative did refer explicitly to interference with NOCs by African governments, especially those run by the military. He believed that the IOC should discourage the appointment of NOC officials by governments.[25]

The proponents of unrelieved commercialism did not have things all their own way at the Congress, but they were not silenced. For example, Dr Harvey Schiller, of the United States Olympic Committee, pointed out that in the year 2000 there would be a Gross National Sports Product in the USA of $121bn, and that the population of the United States spent more on sport than on air transport, education or clothes. His colleague, John Krimsky, said that USOC's budget for the four years leading up to the Atlanta Olympics was nearly $400m. He drew attention to the protection of the Olympic symbols conferred on USOC by the Amateur Sports Act of 1978, perhaps intending publicly to warn the IOC's marketing department that USOC did not intend to relinquish any of its prerogatives in face of the IOC's pretensions to total ownership of the Games. Yet commerce was not unbridled. One representative of the media made a plea for a stop to be put to 'the continuing escalation of television rights fees. If not we risk seeing a situation where, as is already the case in certain other sports competitions, the different disciplines of the Games will be sold off à la carte' and, in a very interesting development, Richard Pound stated his conviction that the time had come to revise the formulae for sharing revenue within the Olympic movement.[26]

A gigantism of the spirit

There is one quality above all of the Olympic movement which makes it reasonable to return to the unthinkable question 'Are the Olympic

Games really necessary?' which was posed in the Introduction, and that is the movement's overweening sense of its own importance.

In many senses it indubitably is important, as is any organisation whose decisions can affect the social, economic and diplomatic fates of whole countries. It is important, too, to sports people, particularly in poor countries, who would not without its help be able to practise and promote the sports they love.

But in the richer countries there is room for ambiguity and paradox. On the one hand it is they who are responsible for the Games' commercialisation, but on the other they can afford the luxurious feeling 'It's only a game'. But if it is only a game, there is something both ludicrous and offensive about seeing the best hotel in whatever city is holding an Olympic meeting reserved entirely for sports administrators, with all the apparatus of sniffer dogs and diverted traffic which nowadays is unhappily necessary for meetings of heads of state and government. It is important to remember that there is a difference between an IOC Session and a G7 summit meeting.

There is, too, a feeling that the endless lobbying to be host city is not merely distastefully extravagant, but rather absurd. Nor have the opening and closing ceremonies of the Games much to do with sport – though it must be admitted that they are popular spectacles for which the tickets sell out and which attract enormous television audiences.

Even those students of sport (nowadays no doubt the majority) who admit that there is nothing wrong with being a professional athlete, and that there was much wrong with some versions of the cult of amateurism, must be a little disgusted by the extremes of commercial activity into which the Olympic movement has fallen. The money, of course, is recycled for the good of sport, but one cannot help wondering if there are any limits to commercialism.

The official answer to that question is that there certainly are. As Samaranch repeatedly says, the sticking point is that the control of sport must remain in the hands of sports people. But his is a cry from the last ditch, and there must be many who wonder whether it is not already too late.

The future

It is, in short, reasonable to feel that the whole thing has got out of hand. It does not, however, seem likely that the Olympic movement will reform itself to any significant degree, and there is no external authority that can force it to do so, although, as has been suggested, governments may show disapproval if 'bad' choices of host cities are made. Internally the forces making for conflict and division are immense, but it is probable that self-interest, diplomatic skill, wealth and ideals will continue to hold the movement together.

So long as it does hold together, there will still be a market for the Games: that is, there is no reason to suppose that they will not continue to hold the attention of millions worldwide. The world needs the Games, because it needs to be reminded of what human beings can do. But the world also needs to be reminded, as does the Olympic movement, that in a sense sport is a triviality. It is foolish to try to put back the clock, but it is still worth saying that the world may need the Games, not as they are, but as they might have been.

Notes

1 In an important contribution at the Centennial Congress, John Coates, President of the Australian NOC, floated the idea that in future the IOC ought to pay far more attention to the composition and operation of Organising Committees (OCOGs). *Congress Proceedings*, vol. I, pp. 89–90.

2 47th Session, Helsinki, 16–27 July 1952, *Minutes*.

3 *Proceedings*, vol. II, p. 130.

4 *Ibid.*, vol. I, pp. 75, 76 and 78.

5 *Ibid.*, vol. I, pp. 124 and 125.

6 *Ibid.*, vol. I, pp. 82 and 125.

7 *Ibid.*, vol. I, p. 299 and vol. II, p. 187.

8 *Ibid.*, vol. I, p. 179 and II, p. 82.

9 *Ibid.*, vol. I, p. 386 and vol. II, p. 264.

10 *Ibid.*, vol. II, p. 156.

11 *Ibid.*, vol. II, p. 12.

12 *Ibid.*, vol. I, p. 407.

13 *Ibid.*, vol. I, pp. 92, 103 and 94.

14 Ibid., vol. I, p. 148. The speaker was the highly-respected Judge Keba Mbaye.

15 *Ibid.*, vol. I, p. 317 and vol. II, p. 54.

16 *Ibid.*, vol. I, p. 239.

17 *Ibid.*, vol. I, p. 120.

18 *Ibid.*, vol. I, p. 155.

19 *Sport Intern*, 11, 16, 25 August 1990, p. 4.

20 *Proceedings*, vol. II, p. 52.

21 *Ibid.*, vol. I, p. 147.

22 *Ibid.*, vol. II, p. 231.

23 *Ibid.*, vol. I, p. 90. Ken Read, a Canadian skier.

24 *Ibid.*, vol. I, p. 165.

25 *Ibid.*, vol. I, p. 264, and vol. II, p. 147.

26 *Ibid.*, vol. II, pp. 155, 159 and 165.

Select bibliography

Alkemeyer, Thomas and Alfred Richartz, 'The Olympic Games: from Ceremony to Show', *Olympika*, II, 1993, pp. 79–89.

ANOC Commission on the Olympic Games, *Review of the Preparation of the Olympic Games of Barcelona '92*, presented to the ANOC conference in Barcelona, June 1990.

Aris, Stephen, *Sportsbiz: Inside the Sports Business*, London, Hutchinson, 1990.

Barcelona '92 Olympic Organising Committee (COOB '92) *Press Dossier.*

——*Report to the ANOC General Assembly*, Barcelona, June 1990.

Bridges, Brian, *Korea and the West*, London, Royal Institute of International Affairs, 1986.

——'East Asia in Transition: South Korea in the Limelight', *International Affairs*, 64, 3, summer 1988, 381–92.

Brunet, Ferran, *Economy of the 1992 Barcelona Olympic Games*, Barcelona, Centre de Estudis Olimpics, 1993.

Carter, Jimmy, *Keeping Faith: Memoirs of a President*, New York, Bantam House, 1982.

Coubertin, Baron Pierre de, *L'Education en Angleterre. Collèges et Universités*, Paris, Librairie Hachette, 1888, reprinted in Norbert Mueller (ed.), *Pierre de Coubertin: Textes Choisies*, Zurich, Weidmann, 1986, vol. I, pp. 39–56.

——'A Typical Englishman: Dr. W. P. Brookes of Wenlock in Shropshire', *American Monthly Review of Reviews*, 15, 1897, pp. 62–5.

——'Une Compagne de Vingt-et-un Ans (1887–1908)', 1909, *Textes Choisies*, vol. II.

——'Pédagogie Sportive', Paris, 1922, reprinted in *Textes Choisies*, vol. II.

——*Mémoires Olympiques*, Bureau Internationale de Pédagogie Sportive, Lausanne, n.d., but 1931.

——New Year message, repudiating the proposed boycott of the 1936 Games, *La Revue Sportive Illustré*, 32nd year, numéro spécial, 1936, pp. 38, reprinted in *Textes Choisies*, pp. 440–1.

Coubertin, Baron Pierre de, and others, *The Olympic Games in 776 BC to 1896 AD. The Olympic Games of 1896*, Athens and Paris, 1896. Facsimile edition (with English translation), 1966.

Czula, R., 'Sport as an Agent of Social Change', *Quest*, 31, 1979.

Diem, Carl, *Pierre de Coubertin* (speech on the fiftieth anniversary celebration of the IOC), 17 and 18 June 1944.

Digby, Clare, *A Focus on the Extent of Organised Sporting Activities Amongst the 'Coloured' People of the Cape Peninsula*, University of Cape Town, Urban Problems Research Unit, working paper, 27 June 1977.

D'Oliveira, B., with Patrick Murphy, *Time to Declare: an Autobiography*, London, J. M. Dent & Sons, 1980.

Eede, A. van den, 'The National Olympic Committees and Marketing', *Olympic Message-Marketing and Olympism*, International Olympic Committee, 24 July 1989.

Edwards, H. 'Sportpolitics: Los Angeles 1984 – the Olympic Tradition Continues', *Sociology of Sport Journal*, 1, 1984, pp. 172–83.

——'The Free Enterprise Olympics', *Journal of Sport and Social Issues*, 8, 2, summer/fall 1984, i–iv.

Espy, R. *The Politics of the Olympic Games*, Berkeley, University of California Press, 1979 (new edition, 1984).

Finley M. I. and H. W. Pleket, *The Olympic Games: the First Thousand Years*, London, Chatto and Windus, 1986.

Games of the XXIVth Olympiad Seoul 1988, *Official Report*, vol. 1, 'Organization and Planning'.

Guelke, Adrian, 'The Politicisation of South African Sport', in Lincoln Allison (ed.), *The Politics of Sport*, Manchester, Manchester University Press, 1986, pp. 118–48.

——'Sport and the End of Apartheid', in Lincoln Allison (ed.), *The Changing Politics of Sport*, Manchester, Manchester University Press, 1993, pp. 151–70.

Guttman, Allen, *The Games Must Go On: Avery Brundage and the Olympic Movement*, New York, Columbia University Press, 1984.

Hazan, Baruch A., *Olympic Sports and Propaganda Games, Moscow 1980*, London, Transaction Books, 1982.

Henderson, Nicholas, *Mandarin: the Diaries of an Ambassador 1969–1982*, London, Weidenfeld and Nicolson, 1994.

Hill, C. R. *Bantustans – the Fragmentation of South Africa*, Oxford, Oxford University Press, 1968.

——'The Politics of Manchester's Olympic Bid', *Parliamentary Affairs*, 47, 3, July 1994, pp. 338–54.

Holmes, William Burton, *The Olympian Games in Athens, 1896: the First Modern Olympics*, New York, Grove Press, 1984.

Horne J., and others, *The 1988 Seoul Olympics*, North Staffordshire Polytechnic, Occasional Paper no. 5, June 1988.

Howell, Denis, *Made in Birmingham: the Memoirs of Denis Howell*, London, Macdonald, Queen Anne Press, 1990.

Human Sciences Research Council, Sports Investigation, 1982, Main Committee Report, *Sport in the RSA*, commissioned by the Ministry of National Education, 27 October 1979.

International Olympic Committee, *Bulletin*, nos. 1, 2, 3, Jan. 1894, July 1894, Jan. 1895.

——*11th Olympic Congress in Baden-Baden, 1981*, 3 vols, 1982.

——*TOP – The Olympic Programme: The National Olympic Committees' Manual of the Olympic Marketing Programme*, 1988.

——*Olympic Charter*, 1989, 1990, 1992, 1994.

——*Report for Olympic Year*, 1992.

——*1994 Olympic Marketing Fact File*, Lillehammer, February 1994.

——*Marketing Matters*, 5, summer 1994.

——Centennial Olympic Congress (Congress of Unity) *Report*, 1994, 2 vols: I, *Main Report*; II, *Texts, Summaries or Plans of Papers*.

——*Host City Contract for the XIX Olympic Winter Games in the Year 2002*.

——*Manual for Cities Bidding to Host the XIX Olympic Winter Games – 2002*.

——*Olympic Biographies*, 1989, 1991, 1995.

——*Olympic Movement Directory*, annual.

——*Olympic Review*, monthly.

Kanin, David B., 'The Olympic Boycott in Diplomatic Context', in *Journal of Sport and Social Issues*, 4, 1, spring/summer 1980.

Kidd, Bruce, 'From Quarantine to Cure: the New Phase of the Struggle Against Apartheid', *Sociology of Sport Journal*, 1991, 8, p. 38.

Killanin, Lord, *My Olympic Years*, Secker and Warburg, 1983.

Killanin, Lord, and John Rodda (eds), *The Olympic Games 1984*, London, Willow Books, 1983.

Kim, Un-yong, *The Greatest Olympics: From Baden-Baden to Seoul*, Seoul, Si-sa-yong-o-sa, 1990.

Klatell, David A. and Norman Marcus, *Sports for Sale: Television, Money and the Fans*, New York, Oxford University Press, 1988.

Lovesey, Peter, *The Official Centenary History of the Amateur Athletic Association*, London, Guinness Superlatives, 1979.

Lucas, John A., *Future of the Olympic Games*, Champaign, Human Kinetics Books, 1992.

——'Madame Berlioux Revisited', *Olympika*, III, 1994, pp. 153–5.

MacAloon, John J., *This Great Symbol: Pierre de Coubertin and the Origins of the Modern Olympic Games*, Chicago, University of Chicago Press, 1981.

——*Five Rings Over Korea*, by Richard W. Pound, 'Review Essay', *Olympika*, III, 1994, pp. 117–23.

Macfarlane, Neil, *Sport and Politics*, Collins (Willow Books), 1986.

McGeoch, Rod with Glenda Korporaal, *The Bid: How Australia won the 2000 Olympics*, Melbourne, William Heinemann Australia, 1994.

Macintosh, Donald, Hart Cantelon and Lisa McDermott, 'The IOC and South Africa: a Lesson in Transnational Relations', *International Review for the Sociology of Sport*, 28, 4, 1993, pp. 373–95.

Manchester Olympic Bid Committee, *Manchester 1996: the British Olympic Bid*, n.d., but 1990.

Martin, Paul, 'South African Sport: Apartheid's Achilles Heel', *The World Today*, 40, June 1984, pp. 234–43.

Miller, Geoffrey, *Behind the Olympic Rings*, Lynn, Massachusetts, H. O. Zimman, Inc, 1979.

Mullins, Sam, *British Olympians: William Penny Brookes and the Wenlock Games*, London, Birmingham Olympic Council in Association with the

British Olympic Association, 1986.

O'Neill, Tip, with William Novak, *Man of the House: the Life and Political Memoirs of Speaker Tip O'Neill*, London, Bodley Head, 1987.

Park Seh-jik, *The Seoul Olympics: the Inside Story*, London, Bellew Publishing, 1991.

Payne, M., 'Sport and Industry', *Olympic Message-Marketing and Olympism*, International Olympic Committee, 24 July 1989, pp. 37–43.

Poliakoff, Michael B., 'Stadium and Arena: Reflections on Greek, Roman, and Contemporary Social History', in *Olympika*, II, 1993, pp. 67–78.

Polignac, Marquis Melchior de, *Baron Pierre de Coubertin, 2 Septembre 1937 – 2 Septembre 1947* (speech on the tenth anniversary of Coubertin's death), *Bulletin du Comité Olympique*, new series, col. 6, September 1947, pp. 12–15.

Pound, Richard W., *Five Rings over Korea: the Secret Negotiations behind the Olympic Games in Seoul*, Boston, Little Brown, 1994.

Pujol, Jordi, *Afirmacio catalana d'europeisme: Paraules del President de la Generalitat a Aquisgra i Estraburg*, Barcelona, Generalitat de Catalunya, 1985.

——*The political and economic importance of the north-western Mediterranean: Statement by the President of the Generalitat in Stockholm*, Generalitat de Catalunya, Barcelona 1988.

Quantz, Dietrich R., 'Civic Pacifism and Sports-Based Internationalism: Framework for the Founding of the International Olympic Committee', *Olympika*, II, 1993, pp. 1–23.

Rees, C. Roger, 'The Olympic Dilemma: Applying the Contact Theory and Beyond', *Quest*, 37, 1985.

Reich, Kenneth, *Making it Happen: Peter Ueberroth and the 1984 Olympics*, Santa Barbara, Capra Press, 1986.

Riordan, James, *Sport in Soviet Society*, Cambridge, Cambridge University Press, 1977.

——'Elite sport policy in East and West', in Lincoln Allison (ed.), *The Politics of Sport*, Manchester, Manchester University Press, 1986.

——*Sport, Politics and Communism*, Manchester, Manchester University Press, 1991.

——'The Rise and Fall of Soviet Olympic Champions', *Olympika*, II, 1993, pp. 25–44.

Roberts, Cheryl, *South Africa's Struggle for Olympic Legitimacy: From Apartheid Sport to International Recognition*, Cape Town, Township Publishing Co-operative, 1991.

Roukhadze, Marie-Hélène, 'Great Voices in Sport: Vitaly Smirnov', interview, *Olympic Review*, 281–2, March/April 1991.

Seoul Olympic Organising Committee, *Official Report* of the 1988 Games.

Simson, Vyv and Andrew Jennings, *The Lords of the Rings: Power, Money and Drugs in the Modern Olympics*, London, Simon and Schuster, 1992.

Sipes, Richard G., 'War, Sports and Aggression: an Empirical Test of Two Rival Theories', in D. Stanley Eitzen (ed.), *Sport in Contemporary Society: an Anthology*, New York, St. Martin's Press, 1984 (first published 1979).

South African Institute of Race Relations, *Race Relations Survey 1992/93*.

Stump, Al, '1932, the "Hopeless" Dream of William May Garland', *Olympic Review*, 274, August 1990, pp. 381–7.

Tyler, Martin and Phil Soar (eds.), *The History of the Olympic Games*, London, Marshall Cavendish, revised ed. 1980 (first published 1969).

Ueberroth, Peter, *Made in America* (with Richard Levin and Amy Quinn), London, Kingswood Press, 1986.

Usher, Harry L., 'The Games in Los Angeles: a New Approach to the Organisational Tasks', *Olympic Review*, 175, May 1982, pp. 257–60.

Welch, Paula, 'Admission to the Programme: a Privilege Earned, not Given', *Olympic Review*, 273, July 1990, pp. 332–7.

Wenn, Stephen R., 'An Olympian Squabble: the Distribution of Olympic Television Revenue, 1960–1966', *Olympika*, III, 1994, pp. 27–47.

Wenn, Stephen R. and Jeffrey P., 'Muhammad Ali and the Convergence of Olympic Sport and U.S. Diplomacy in 1980: a Reassessment from Behind the Scenes at the U.S. State Department', *Olympika*, II, 1993, pp. 45–66.

Wilson, Harold E. Jr, 'The Golden Opportunity: Romania's Political Manipulation of the 1984 Los Angeles Olympic Games', *Olympika*, III, 1994, pp. 83–97.

Wilson, Neil, *The Sports Business: the Men and the Money*, London, Mandarin, 1990. (First published 1989).

Wooldridge, Ian, *Sport in the 80's: a Personal View*, London, Centurion, 1989.

Young, David C., *The Olympic Myth of Greek Amateur Athletics*, Chicago, Ares Publishers Inc, 1984.

——'The Origins of the Modern Olympics: a New Version', *International Journal of the History of Sport*, 1987, pp. 271–300.

——'Demetrios Vikelas: First President of the IOC', *International Journal of the History of Sport*, 1988, pp. 85–102.

——'How Times Have Changed', *Proceedings of the United States Olympic Academy*, XIII, 21–24 June 1989.

——'Myths and Mist Surrounding the Revival of the Olympic Games: the Hidden Story', in Fernand Landry, Marc Landry and Magdeleine Yerles (eds), *Sport: the Third Millenium*, Sainte-Foy, Les Presses de L'Université Laval, 1991.

——'A New History of the Modern Olympic Movement: Soutsos, Zappas, Brookes, Vikelas, and Coubertin', International Olympic Academy, *Proceedings*, May 1992.

Index